U.S. STAMP YEARBOOK 1989

A comprehensive record of technical data, design development and stories behind all of the stamps, stamped envelopes, postal cards and souvenir cards issued by the United States Postal Service in 1989.

By
George Amick

Published by *Linn's Stamp News,* the largest and most informative stamp newspaper in the world. *Linn's* is owned by Amos Press, 911 Vandemark Road, Sidney, Ohio 45365. Amos Press also publishes *Scott Stamp Monthly* and the Scott line of catalogs.
Copyright 1990 by Linn's Stamp News.

033016

ISSN 0748-996X

With Gratitude . . .

As always, we have depended on the generous assistance of many people in assembling the facts and figures in this *Yearbook.* My colleagues at *Linn's* and I extend to them our thanks.

For the many essays developed by the U.S. Postal Service in the creation of stamp and stationery designs, and for the information relative to this fascinating process, we are indebted to Don McDowell, general manager, Stamps Division; Joe Brockert and Jack Williams, program managers, philatelic design, and Dick Sheaff, a design coordinator for the Citizens' Stamp Advisory Committee.

Invaluable help was also rendered by Pete Davidson, Linda Foster, Rita Moroney, Jim Murphy, Jeanne O'Neill, Peter Papadopoulos, Kim Parks and Frank Thomas of USPS; Richard Sennett of Sennett Enterprises, and Carl D'Alessandro, Leonard Buckley, Peter Daly and Edward Felver of the Bureau of Engraving and Printing.

Our thanks also to CSAC members Belmont Faries, Mary Ann Owens, and Jack Rosenthal; design coordinator Howard Paine; stamp designers Bart Forbes, John Gurche, Michael Hagel, Howard Rogers, M. Gregory Rudd and Richard Schlecht; Bob Armentrout of the Government Printing Office; Norma Opgrand of the U.S. Fish and Wildlife Service; George Godin of the Bureau Issues Association, and Jim Bruns of the Smithsonian's National Philatelic Collection.

Also, to the library staff of the Bismarck, North Dakota, *Tribune;* Robert Hupke of the Toscanini Association; Elaine Freeman, Denise Harper, Jean Horrigan and Ghita Levene of Johns Hopkins University and Medical Institutions; Janet Sperry of the Montana Historical Society; Dickson H. Preston of Seattle, Washington; William R. Mackay of Roscoe, Montana; James R. Ketchum, curator of the U.S. Senate; Margaret N. Burri of the Historical Society of Washington, D.C.; Jacquie Johnson and Paula Pergament of the Art Institute of Chicago; Dr. Bruce Smith of the Smithsonian Institution; Patricia L. Sharpe of the Hull House Association, and Doniece Pitts, curator of art, Ardmore, Oklahoma, Institute of Health.

Finally, a special word of thanks to Charles Yeager, *Linn's* knowledgeable and hard-working Washington correspondent.

George Amick

CONTENTS

Introduction 6

Commemoratives 7
25¢ Montana Statehood, January 15 8
25¢ A. Philip Randolph, February 3 16
25¢ North Dakota Statehood, February 21 21
25¢ Washington Statehood, February 22 28
25¢ Steamboats booklet, March 3 33
25¢ World Stamp Expo '89, March 16 42
25¢ Arturo Toscanini, March 25 47
25¢ House of Representatives, April 4 53
25¢ Senate, April 6 59
25¢ Executive Branch, April 16 65
25¢ South Dakota Statehood, May 3 70
25¢ Lou Gehrig, June 10 75
25¢ Ernest Hemingway, July 17 84
25¢ North Carolina Statehood, August 22 91
25¢ Letter Carriers, August 30 96
25¢ Bill of Rights, September 25 102
25¢ Prehistoric Animals, October 1 109
25¢ America, October 12 118
90¢ World Stamp Expo '89 souvenir sheet, November 17 125
25¢ UPU Classic Mail Transportation, November 19 131
25¢ UPU Classic Mail Transportation souvenir sheet, November 28 141

Special Stamps 145
25¢ Christmas Madonna and Child, October 19 146
25¢ Christmas Madonna and Child booklet, October 19 150
25¢ Christmas Greetings, October 19 154
25¢ Christmas Greetings booklet, October 19 158

Definitives 161
25¢ Flag Over Yosemite, phosphored paper, February 14 162
7.1¢ Tractor, new precancel, May 26 166
$1 Johns Hopkins, June 7 169
28¢ Sitting Bull, September 14 175
25¢ Eagle and Shield, November 10 180

Express Mail 192
$10.75 Express Mail, reissue, June 19 192

Priority Mail — 197
$2.40 Moon Landing, July 20 — 197

Airmails — 203
45¢ French Revolution, July 14 — 203
45¢ America, October 12 — 212
45¢ UPU Future Mail Transportation souvenir sheet, November 24 — 215
45¢ UPU Future Mail Transportation, November 27 — 220

Officials — 223
1¢ Penalty Mail, July 5 — 223

Migratory Bird Hunting — 227
$12.50 Lesser Scaups duck stamp, July 1 — 227

Stamped Envelopes — 233
25¢ Philatelic Mail, March 10 — 234
25¢ Security, July 10 — 238
25¢ Love, September 22 — 242
39¢ Montgomery Blair aerogramme, November 20 — 245
25¢ Space Station hologram, December 3 — 253

Postal Cards — 261
15¢ The Desert, January 13 — 262
15¢ Healy Hall, January 23 — 266
15¢ The Wetlands, March 17 — 270
15¢ Oklahoma Land Run, April 22 — 273
21¢ The Mountains, May 5 — 279
15¢ The Seashore, June 17 — 282
15¢ The Woodlands, August 26 — 285
15¢ Hull House, September 16 — 288
15¢ Philadelphia, September 25 — 294
15¢ Baltimore, October 7 — 299
15¢ New York City, November 8 — 302
15¢ Washington, D.C., November 26 — 305
15¢ White House, November 30 — 307
15¢ Cityscapes sheet of four, December 1 — 312
15¢ Jefferson Memorial, December 3 — 316

Souvenir Cards — 319
Philexfrance '89, July 7 — 319
World Stamp Expo '89, November 17 — 322
Stampshow '89, August 24 — 324
Migratory Bird, June 30 — 326

Appendix — 328
The Year in Review — 328
Autopost — 336

Varieties	338
Plate numbers	346
Items withdrawn from sale in 1989	349
1988 first-day cover totals	351
Errata	352

INTRODUCTION

If there had been a *Linn's U.S. Stamp Yearbook* 100 years ago, covering the issues of the year 1889, it would have been a slim volume indeed. In 1889 the U.S. Post Office Department produced no new definitive postage stamps. It also produced no new commemoratives; they hadn't been invented yet.

It issued no new special delivery stamps, or Officials, or postage dues, or newspaper stamps, or postal cards, or stamped envelopes.

A similar inertia gripped the Treasury Department. Although Treasury was a prolific producer of revenue stamps in the 19th century, in 1889 not one new documentary or proprietary tax stamp came off its presses.

Collecting new issues that year was easy on the budget. But, as Warren R. Bower observed in an article in *The Trans-Mississippian* about the non-stamps of 1889, "maybe it was a little bit dull too."

In 1989, a century later, collecting new stamps was considerably more expensive — but it wasn't dull.

1989 was a year of innovation by the U.S. Postal Service, especially in the area of postal stationery. The Postal Service backed off a little on quantity. There were 83 new collectible varieties of stamps, stamped envelopes and postal cards issued during the year (84 if you add the Fish and Wildlife Service's annual duck stamp), compared to 100 in 1988 and 110 in 1987. But among the output were some real novelties — a hologram, picture postal cards, an unfolded pane of pressure-sensitive stamps — plus the promise of another important first, plastic stamps, in the near future.

1989 was also a year when the public was unusually critical of stamp designs; at any rate, the complaints got wider publicity than usual. But, as one USPS official cheerfully told a newspaper reporter, "At least criticism proves that people are paying attention."

In this, the seventh annual *Linn's U.S. Stamp Yearbook*, we offer the full story of each of those postal issues of 1989. There's also information on souvenir cards, on the Autopost experiment and on varieties discovered, plus a review of the highlights of the year in U.S. philately.

We hope you'll find the book interesting to read. We at *Linn's* found it fascinating to put together. Frankly, we're glad it wasn't 1889!

COMMEMORATIVES

For the second consecutive year, the U.S. Postal Service displayed relative restraint in issuing commemorative stamps.

From 1973 through 1982 USPS produced an average of nearly 40 commemoratives annually. From 1983 through 1987, that annual average rose to nearly 50. But in 1988, a year when the Stamps Division was preoccupied with the need for rate-change definitives, the commemorative total was only 31. And in 1989, despite a flurry of issues late in the year for World Stamp Expo '89 and the concurrent Universal Postal Congress, the total of (non-airmail) commemoratives was a quite-manageable 37.

In all, World Stamp Expo and the Universal Postal Congress provided the subject matter for 17 commemorative stamp varieties. Otherwise, most of the year's commemoratives were extensions of familiar series.

The Constitution Bicentennial observance continued with six issues. There were single-stamp additions to the Black Heritage, Sports, Performing Arts and Literary Arts series. As usual, there were a topical booklet and a topical block of four. A long tradition of statehood anniversary stamps was continued with commemoratives for the centennials of four Western states.

One new commemorative series was launched in 1989 with two stamps, a regular and an airmail, to mark the 500th anniversary of the voyages of Christopher Columbus. This so-called "America" series will run at least through 1992, the actual anniversary year of the first voyage, as part of a collective program with other countries of the Postal Union of the Americas and Spain.

25¢ MONTANA STATEHOOD CENTENNIAL

Date of Issue: January 15, 1989

Catalog Numbers: Scott 2401   Minkus CM1335   USPS 0452

Colors: magenta, yellow, cyan, black (offset); brown, purple (intaglio)

First-Day Cancel: Helena, Montana (State Capitol)

FDCs Canceled: 353,319

Format: Panes of 50, horizontal, 5 across, 10 down. Offset printing plates of 200 subjects (10 across, 20 around); intaglio printing sleeve of 400 subjects (10 across, 40 around).

Perf: 11.1 (Eureka off-line perforator)

Selvage Markings: ©United States Postal Service 1988, Use Correct ZIP Code®

Designer, Art Director and Typographer: Bradbury Thompson (CSAC)

Project Manager: Jack Williams (USPS)

Engravers: Thomas Hipschen (BEP, vignette)
Michael Ryan (BEP, lettering and numerals)

Modeler: Peter Cocci (BEP)

Printing: 6-color offset, 3-color intaglio D press (902)

Quantity Ordered: 165,500,000
Quantity Distributed: 165,495,000

Plate/Sleeve Number Detail: Upper panes — one group of 4 offset plate numbers alongside corner stamps; one intaglio sleeve number alongside adjacent stamps. Bottom panes — offset/intaglio numbers in reverse positions.

Plate/Sleeve Number Combination: 1111-1, 1211-1, 2211-1, 2222-1, 2232-1, 3332-1, 4332-1, 4352-1, 5352-1, 5362-1, 6362-1, 6363-1, 6463-1, 6473-1, 6483-1, 6494-1

Tagging: block over vignette

The Stamp

In 1939, when four Western states celebrated their 50th anniversaries, the U.S. Post Office Department honored them in the most economical way possible. It issued a single 3¢ stamp covering all four.

The Post Office was able to get away with giving each state one-quarter of a stamp because policy in the matter of statehood commemoratives hadn't yet been firmly established. Up to that time only two states had been honored on their anniversaries, Michigan (1935) and Arkansas (1936).

The 1939 commemorative bore a map of the four states — Washington, Montana and North and South Dakota, and adjacent territory. Its design was based on a sketch by President Franklin D. Roosevelt, the stamp collector in residence in the White House, and because of its resemblance to washing hanging on a line — the Canadian border

The so-called "clothesline stamp" of 1939 (Scott 858), issued to commemorate the 50th anniversary of statehood of North and South Dakota, Montana and Washington.

— it became known as the "clothesline" stamp.

It was unique in that it had four separate official "first days" and places of issue over a span of nine days — one in each state capital. After each one, the stamp was withdrawn from sale until the next appointed date.

Fifty years went by, and in 1989 the four states marked their centennials. Now, however, state pride, precedent and the U.S. Postal Service's own predilections made a single stamp out of the question. This time each of the four got a separate issue.

Montana was the first. The 25¢ Montana stamp was issued in the state capital of Helena on January 15, 1989, even though the actual centennial of statehood wouldn't fall until November 8. The date chosen was the 100th anniversary of a long, impassioned speech in the U.S. House of Representatives by Territorial Delegate Joseph K. Toole urging that Montana be made a state.

Montana had become a territory May 26, 1864. From that day forward, some Montanans campaigned for statehood. Territorial status, they argued, implied an inferior political position, the denial of fundamental rights of Americans and the stigma of "colonialism." Admission to the Union would put an end to "carpetbag" officials imposed from Washington, allow the expansion of an inflexible judicial system, remove limitations on debt, taxation and alien land ownership and give voters a more direct voice in government.

From time to time the territorial legislature petitioned Congress for statehood, and bills were introduced, but to no avail. Montana was Democratic and would be expected to send Democrats to Congress, and through the 1880s at least one house of Congress was always Republican and in a position to block action. Attempts to pair statehood for Montana with statehood for the Republican Dakota or Washington territories also failed.

By 1888, however, popular pressures had become almost irresistible. At the national conventions that year, both parties adopted planks calling for admission of Montana, Dakota, Washington and New Mexico; for good measure, the Republicans threw in Idaho, Wyoming and Arizona.

When the Republicans won the presidency and both houses of Congress in November, the lame-duck session of the 50th Congress recognized the inevitable and approved an enabling act for Montana, Washington and two states to be created from the Dakota Territory. Delegate Toole rather extravagantly called this accomplishment "the grandest act of this administration ... (which) in the extent of constitutional government conferred is unparalleled in the history of the republic."

On November 8, 1889, President Benjamin Harrison proclaimed Montana a state, adding the 41st star to Old Glory.

Besides the 1939 statehood issue, Montana had been associated with several earlier U.S. stamps. Its Glacier National Park is shown on the 9¢ value of the 1934 National Parks series (Scott 748). The 3¢ Oregon Territory Centennial stamp of 1936 (Scott 783) depicted a map that included a portion of Montana (then a part of Oregon), including the town of Missoula. And the Lewis and Clark expedition, which traversed Montana both coming and going, was commemorated with a 3¢ stamp of 1954 (Scott 1063).

In addition, four American Indian leaders associated with Montana history have been postally depicted.

• A 10¢ Great Americans definitive of 1987 (Scott 2176) portrayed Red Cloud, the Oglala Sioux chief who led a temporarily successful fight in the 1860s to keep the whites out of Sioux territory in what is now Montana, Wyoming and South Dakota.

• On June 25, 1876, General George Custer made his last stand against the Sioux on the Little Big Horn near where the town of Hardin now stands. One of the victorious Indian leaders, Crazy Horse, was shown on a 13¢ Great Americans stamp of 1982 (Scott 1855); another, Sitting Bull, was added to the Great Americans stamp gallery in 1989 and is discussed in another chapter in this book.

• The last major campaign of U.S. troops against the Indians ended on October 5, 1877, north of the Bearpaw Mountains, when Chief Joseph of the Nez Perce surrendered to U.S. troops after a retreat of 1,600 miles in Idaho, Wyoming and Montana toward Canada. Chief Joseph was shown on a 6¢ 1968 commemorative (Scott 1364).

These sketches for a Montana stamp design were made by Bozeman, Montana, artist Howard Rogers. Later Rogers was commissioned to paint the the Mount Rainier picture used on the Washington Statehood stamp.

The Design

From the beginning, the Montana Statehood Centennial Commission had urged that a painting by famed Montana artist Charles M. Russell be adapted for the statehood stamp.

Initially, however, the Citizens' Stamp Advisory Committee had other ideas, and commissioned concept sketches from painter-illustrator Howard Rogers, a recently adopted son of Montana. Rogers produced three landscapes, two of which he then turned into finished paintings at CSAC's request. One, vertically arranged, depicted a mountain in Glacier National Park; another was of a scene in the Beartooth range, and the third was a view of mountains, pastures and cottonwood trees as seen from the artist's own home in Bozeman.

But the pro-Russell forces were formidable, and included one member of CSAC itself, Jack Rosenthal of Casper, Wyoming, who takes a special interest in Western stamp subjects, and Bradbury Thompson, CSAC design coordinator and typographer. They had been personally lobbied on Russell's behalf by an old friend and member of the Montana Centennial Commission, lawyer James Haughey of Billings.

The Commission's specific choice was a painting called *C.M. Russell and Friends*. After considering two other Russell works, CSAC agreed to use this one, and Bradbury Thompson adapted it to the dimensions of a horizontal commemorative-size stamp. Peter Cocci of the Bureau of Engraving and Printing performed design modifications on BEP's Electronic Design Center equipment, and the stamp was printed by the offset-intaglio combination on the D press.

C.M. Russell and Friends is one of the artist's largest works. It measures 43 inches by 81 inches. Russell himself described it as a "poster." He painted it in 1922, four years before his death, for Malcolm S. Mackay, a Wall Street executive who as a young man had homesteaded in Montana.

The ex-cowboy depicted himself on a horse standing on a grassy knoll. As USPS described the design, "Russell's left arm extends toward Square Butte and the inviting, spacious plains of central Montana. Five cowhands ride past Russell in the lower right." In fact, however, the original painting also showed four mounted Indians riding ahead of the cowboys, and one is waving to Russell. These were cropped out for the stamp design, and a bison skeleton in the left foreground was also deleted. In all, designer Thompson reduced the painting by about half its width to make it fit in the horizontal commemorative format.

Brian W. Dippie, in his book *Looking at Russell,* called the painting "an exercise in unabashed nostalgia." Dippie wrote:

"An aging Russell, impresario of the paintbrush, grandly gestures to the things he loved; the curtains of his memory have been drawn back to reveal the country between Great Falls and Cascade, bathed in sunlight, unfenced, populated with the hard-riding cowboys and Indians who had inspired his work. ... (He was) dreaming of a lost world."

Malcolm Mackay's son, William R. Mackay of the Lazy E.L. Ranch in Roscoe, Montana, told this writer in a letter how the painting came to be made:

C.M. Russell and Friends, *the painting on which the Montana stamp design was based. For the stamp, four Indians and a bison skeleton were cropped out. Much sky and landscape was also deleted. (Courtesy Montana Historical Society)*

The Charles M. Russell painting on which this essay is based, like the painting adapted for the finished stamp, is part of the Mackay Collection at the Montana Historical Society. It is a 1923 oil on canvas titled Men of the Open Range.

"My father ... built a home in Tenafly, New Jersey, in 1918, and in it was a large log-lined room which we called the 'Russell Room' and in which he hung his Russell paintings. He must have met Russell during one of the times that Charley and his wife Nancy were exhibiting in New York City. They became close friends who shared the love of the West and Montana in particular.

"In the Russell room my father kept the space above the fireplace for some kind of art work by Charley. Charley measured the space, 43 by 81 inches, and at Christmas time in 1922 he sent my dad the picture 'Charley and his Friends.' It came rolled up and it was a gift to Mother and Dad from Charley and Nancy."

Malcolm Mackay died in 1932 at the age of 51. Several years later his wife Helen loaned his Russell collection to the then-new Northern Hotel in Billings, Montana. In 1952 the entire collection was acquired by the State of Montana, and it now hangs in the Montana Historical Society in Helena.

This scene on the cover of the USPS Philatelic Catalog, *used as a backdrop for the Montana stamp, is actually located near the town of Mackay, Idaho.*

Friends was the third work by Russell to appear on a U.S. stamp. The 4¢ Range Conservation stamp of 1961 (Scott 1176) showed a portion of the drawing *The Trail Boss*, and the 5¢ C.M. Russell commemorative of 1964 (Scott 1243), issued on the centennial of the artist's birth, used his painting *Jerked Down*.

A full-color reproduction of the Montana stamp was featured on the cover of the January-February *Philatelic Catalog* published by USPS. It was set into a large color photograph of cowboys driving wild horses through a river with mountains in the background. But, as collector Brent Pence pointed out in a letter to stamp publications, the scene in the photo wasn't in Montana at all, but in Idaho, near a town with the same name as the Russell painting's first owner: Mackay.

Meanwhile, Montana artist Howard Rogers was philosophical about losing the stamp assignment. "I got beat out by Charley Russell, but that's a good one to get beat out by," he said. Besides, he was given another statehood stamp design to work on (see 25¢ Washington Statehood).

Charles M. Russell's painting Jerked Down *was used on this 5¢ stamp of 1964 marking the centennial of the artist's birth.*

This essay is based on a detail from Charles Russell's 1904 painting entitled The Bolter (No. 3), *original in the Woolaroc Museum, Bartlesville, Oklahoma.*

First-Day Facts

The unusual Sunday first-day ceremony was held in the rotunda of the Montana State Capitol. Newly elected Governor Stan Stephens and Lieutenant Governor Allen Kolstad were among the speakers. Kenneth J. Hunter, associate postmaster general, dedicated the stamp.

Next door on North Roberts Street, the Montana Historical Society, where the Russell painting hangs, was open to visitors.

Collectors of first-day ceremony programs discovered a few days after the ceremony that two different varieties of cancellation had been used to tie the Montana stamp to the program page.

Programs distributed at the event itself were canceled by a rubber composition imprinter at USPS' facility in Merrifield, Virginia. The imprinter made a crisp, clear impression, similar to a handstamp.

For programs prepared for subscribers to USPS' new program subscription service, the stamps were applied and canceled by an independent contractor, Minnesota Diversified Inc. of Minneapolis, using a rubber handstamp. The handstamp markings were shorter than im-

Examples of both the Merrifield imprinter and the Minnesota Diversified hand cancel have been cut to show the size difference. The imprint, above, is about six millimeters longer than the handstamp.

printer cancels — about 37 millimeters compared to 43 millimeters — because the pressure exerted on the mechanical imprinter caused the image to distort, making it longer.

The handstamp also made a thicker, fuzzier impression than that created by the Merrifield imprinter. According to information received by *Linn's Stamp News,* the cancellation ink used by Minnesota Diversified apparently reacted with the rubber of the handstamp, causing it to deteriorate as it was used.

After *Linn's* published reports of the existence of cancellation varieties on the Montana stamp and two other items issued in early 1989 — the America the Beautiful (The Desert) and Healy Hall postal cards — USPS halted the use of an independent contractor to apply cancellations for ceremony programs. Minnesota Diversified, under its contract, would still affix stamps to those programs intended for subscribers, USPS said, but all canceling would be done using the rubber composition imprinter at Merrifield.

25¢ A. PHILIP RANDOLPH
BLACK HERITAGE SERIES

Date of Issue: February 3, 1989

Catalog Numbers: Scott 2402   Minkus CM1336   USPS 0453

Colors: light blue, magenta, cyan, yellow, black

First-Day Cancel: New York City (M.B. Rosenhaus Center for Human Rights)

FDCs Canceled: 363,174

Format: Panes of 50, vertical, 10 across, 5 down. Gravure printing cylinders of 200 subjects (10 across, 20 around).

Perf: 11.1 (Eureka off-line perforator)

Selvage Markings: ©United States Postal Service 1989, Use Correct ZIP Code®

Designer: Thomas Blackshear of Novato, California

Art Director: Jerry Pinkney (CSAC)

Project Manager: Jack Williams (USPS)

Typographer: Bradbury Thompson (CSAC)

Printing: 7-color Andreotti gravure press (601).

Quantity Ordered: 151,675,000
Quantity Distributed: 151,675,000

Cylinder Number Detail: One group of 5 cylinder numbers over/under corner stamps

Cylinder Number Combination: 11111, 12111

Tagging: overall

Printing Base Impressions: Light Blue: 1(1,037,000)
Magenta: 1(302,500)
Yellow: 1(1,037,000)
Cyan: 1(1,037,000)
Black: 1(1,037,000)

The Stamp

Each year since 1978, the Black Heritage series has honored a distinguished black American. The list has included an abolitionist and an athlete, a composer and a surveyor, a historian and an educator and an author. For the 12th subject, USPS chose a man who combined powerful civil rights advocacy with pioneering leadership in organized labor: A. Philip Randolph.

The stamp was issued in the 100th anniversary year of Randolph's birth. Like its predecessors, it made its debut in early February to help launch Black History Month. But in order to achieve this double result, USPS technically had to bend its rule that says no postal item for a person other than a president "will be issued sooner than 10 years after the individual's death." Randolph died May 16, 1979, meaning that he got his stamp in 10 years minus 102 days.

The exception drew some mild criticism from collectors. "Surely the supply of suitable candidates for commemoratives has not been depleted so soon," one person wrote to *Linn's Stamp News.* However, the Citizens' Stamp Advisory Committee doesn't interpret its rule as requiring exactly 10 years to elapse before a stamp can be issued, said Frank Thomas, acting manager of the Stamp Support Branch.

"There has never been such an intention," Thomas said. "If the stamp appears within the 10th year following the individual's death, that meets the requirement." Thomas noted that the same principle had been followed with an earlier Black Heritage stamp, for Jackie Robinson, who died October 24, 1972, and whose stamp was issued August 2, 1982.

Randolph rose from a socialist and pacifist background to become a labor leader at a time when labor unions openly espoused anti-black policies and a civil rights movement scarcely existed. In later life he was called conservative by some younger, more militant blacks whose beliefs — in violence and separatism — he opposed. They may well have been ignorant of his radical past: that he had urged blacks not to fight in World War I, had criticized W.E.B. DuBois for taking the opposite position, and was once labeled the most dangerous man in America by President Woodrow Wilson.

Later, Randolph confronted two other Democratic presidents — both of whom happened to be extremely popular with blacks — to successfully demand action on behalf of black people. In 1941 he threatened a massive march on Washington to pressure Franklin D. Roosevelt into signing an executive order barring discrimination in defense plants. After World War II, he persuaded Harry Truman to ban segregation in the armed forces by warning that black citizens would refuse induction into a Jim Crow Army.

As a young man, Randolph co-founded a black protest magazine, *The Messenger,* in Harlem, and in its pages, as well as in street-corner oratory (he was a sometime Shakespearean actor), he crusaded against economic discrimination against blacks. In 1925, he launched a campaign to organize the Brotherhood of Sleeping Car Porters. This effort, strongly resisted by the Pullman Company, was aided when porters were included in the scope of the Railway Labor Act of 1934, and ended in triumph for Randolph and his union when in 1937 he put his name to the first contract signed by a white employer and black labor leader. In the next decade, the Brotherhood was America's pre-eminent black political institution, and Randolph was its spokesman.

Still, the white-dominated American Federation of Labor resisted his pleas for racial justice. When one of his few white allies, John L. Lewis, president of the United Mine Workers, walked out of the AFL and formed the Congress of Industrial Organizations, Randolph went with him. After labor reunited in 1955, Randolph became the only black representative on the AFL-CIO executive council.

Randolph's last major act on the public stage was as director of the civil rights march on Washington in 1963. "We are not a pressure group," he told that vast audience. "We are not a mob. We are the advance guard of a massive moral revolution for jobs and freedom."

In 1965 Randolph announced the establishment of the A. Philip Randolph Institute with a grant of $25,000 from the AFL-CIO and $30,000 from other sources. Under the leadership of Bayard Rustin, the Institute sought to enlist community leaders in a broad study of conditions that create continuing poverty.

Postmaster General Frank, second from left, unveils the Randolph stamp. Looking on, left to right, are Vincent Sombrotto, president, National Association of Letter Carriers; Norman Hill, director of the A. Philip Randolph Institute, and Frederick O'Neal, president of the Associated Actors and Artists of America.

Postmaster General Anthony Frank unveiled the stamp design December 12, 1988, at the Washington, D.C., headquarters of the AFL-CIO. Joining him were Norman Hill, president of the A. Philip Randolph Institute, and Frederick O'Neal, president of the Associated Actors and Artists of America and a vice president of the AFL-CIO.

Thomas Blackshear made this pencil sketch of A. Philip Randolph before beginning the finished painting.

The Design

Artist Thomas Blackshear of Novato, California, designed the Randolph stamp. He had previously designed the Jean Baptiste Pointe du Sable (1987) and James Weldon Johnson (1988) stamps in the Black Heritage series. Jerry Pinkney, design coordinator for CSAC, who had designed the first nine Black Heritage stamps, was the art director.

As with all other stamps in the series, the A. Philip Randolph stamp was a vertical commemorative, with the subject's name at the top and the words "Black Heritage USA" at the bottom, and was printed by gravure.

Because Randolph had left no living relative, the Postal Service turned to the Randolph Institute for an appropriate photograph on which to base the stamp. From it, Blackshear produced a painting in a combination of gouache and colored pencil, with a background in a striking orange-pink color.

Blackshear's initial sketch used the portrait only. CSAC asked him to add a small foreground picture symbolic of the subject's career, following the pattern of most of the other Black Heritage stamps. So Blackshear painted in a picture of a passenger train and, behind it, three Pullman porters, basing these images on his own research in the library.

"When the painting came back, the artist had painted the porters in black dress uniforms and white caps," Jack Williams, project manager, recalled. "This is the reverse of the image most people have of porters, with the starched immaculate white jackets and black caps. We said, 'Tom, switch it around,' and he just repainted it, going over the figures and making the jackets white and the caps dark."

The Stamp

The second of 1989's stamps for the centennials of four Western states honored North Dakota and was issued February 21. This was one day short of the 100th anniversary of the date on which President Grover Cleveland signed the statehood bill into law.

North and South Dakota were formed from the Dakota Territory, which was named for the Dakota (Sioux) Indians. The word Dakota means "allied" or "many in one." The land was obtained by the United States in the Louisiana Purchase, and was explored by the Lewis and Clark Expedition in 1804-06. It was at a Mandan Indian village near the site of present-day Bismarck that Lewis and Clark hired the French trapper Charbonneau and his Shoshone Indian wife, Sacajawea, to guide them through the mountain passes to the West and on to the Pacific coast.

One of James Buchanan's final acts as president in 1861 was to sign the bill creating the Dakota Territory, which included those portions of Montana and Wyoming lying east of the Rocky Mountains. The creation of the Montana Territory in 1864 and Wyoming Territory in 1868 reduced Dakota to the size of the two states that now bear that name. The original vast Dakota Territory had only 2,402 white residents, but after discovery of gold in the Black Hills of South Dakota in 1874, the population of the territory grew rapidly.

Agitation for creation of two states out of the Dakota Territory began as early as 1872, but for years nothing came of it. As with the statehood campaigns for Montana and Washington, partisan politics delayed final action.

During the first term of President Cleveland (1885-1889), the Democratic administration and Congress preferred admission of the Dakota Territory, if at all, as one state, for the practical reason that the territory was Republican and the prospect of two new GOP senators was, to the Democrats, preferable to four. But every time the question came to a test vote, the people of the territory voted overwhelmingly for division.

In 1888 the Republican National Convention made the admission of two Dakotas, along with Montana and Washington, a campaign issue. The Republicans won in the fall elections and the lame-duck Congress yielded and passed the enabling act on Valentine's Day 1889. Outgoing President Cleveland signed it into law on Washington's Birthday. On November 2, 1889, President Benjamin Harrison — who as a senator had fought for statehood for the Dakotas — issued proclamations admitting North and South Dakota to the Union.

Harrison wanted to give neither state priority, but to bring them in as "sisters." Therefore the two proclamations were placed on his desk with the texts covered and only the lines for his signature showing. After he had signed them, an aide shuffled the two documents. This made it impossible to tell which state was admitted first; it can only be said that the two Dakotas are the 39th and 40th states. When the states are ranked numerically, the Dakotas are listed in alphabetical order with North Dakota first — and, as stamp collectors know, that's the way their respective stamps appear on the 50-stamp State Flags pane of 1976.

Other stamps related to North Dakota include the 3¢ Lewis and Clark commemorative of 1954 (Scott 1063), on which the Indian guide Sacajawea is shown, and the 30¢ Americana definitive of 1979 (Scott 1606), which pictures the Morris Township School No. 2 at Devil's Lake.

A 20¢ stamp of 1982 (Scott 2014) marked the 50th anniversary of the creation of the International Peace Garden, a 2,200-acre natural park lying partly in North Dakota and partly in Manitoba and dedicated to friendship between the United States and Canada.

The design of the 4¢ Homestead Act commemorative of 1962 (Scott 1198) was based on an 1880s photograph of a sod house eight miles north of Adams, North Dakota. Norway's 1975 commemorative for the sesquicentennial of Norwegian emigration to America (Scott 658) showed the same house, but added two little girls from the original photo.

An artist from neighboring Minnesota prepared this design depicting the pioneer statue in front of the office-building-like state capitol in Bismarck.

The Design

USPS had produced some controversial stamp designs before, but few had drawn as much criticism from the people most intensely interested in the subject as the North Dakota Statehood commemorative. As far as is known, never before had the governor of a state used the forum of a first-day ceremony to publicly criticize a stamp. But it happened this time.

From the beginning, the Postal Service and the North Dakota Centennial Commission were on different wavelengths. The commission, on its own initiative, sponsored a stamp design contest among residents of the state and submitted the winning entries to the Postal Service. USPS, whose policy it is to keep tight control over design matters, thanked the commission and looked at the offerings, but found nothing it could use.

Officials did see some promise, however, in a design the state commission had rejected because the artist lived in neighboring Minnesota rather than North Dakota. The artist had then sent his idea directly to USPS, which decided to give him a "concept" contract. His vertical design depicted North Dakota's capitol, a 19-story office building built in 1934. In the foreground he placed the bronze statue of a pioneer family that stands in front of the capitol — a statue which, in fact, was a prominent element of the state's official centennial logo.

Consistent with its practice of commissioning designs from at least two artists, the Citizens' Stamp Advisory Committee also assigned a North Dakota artist to prepare a concept sketch. What they received was another vertically arranged design, this one showing a grain elevator with a field of flowers in the foreground.

The committee was dissatisfied with both design ideas. With time getting short, Jack Williams, art director and project manager for the stamp, called Wendell Minor of New York City, a Western landscape artist whose work he had seen and liked, and asked him to try his hand at a concept sketch.

Working from photos provided by the North Dakota Historical Society, Minor prepared a colorful horizontal painting of a red grain elevator standing on a golden prairie under a blue sky with billowing white clouds. It seemed to CSAC to be an appropriate image. *The National Geographic Magazine* had once described such buildings, with their arrowhead cupolas, as "North Dakota's trademark," adding: "virtually every town and hamlet boasts a row of brightly painted wooden storehouses standing beside the railroad tracks."

CSAC was pleased with the design, and was assured by its production experts that it would print well on a Fergusson and Sons' gravure press. At the committee's request, Minor added an empty buckboard to the picture and deleted some flying birds that wouldn't have survived the reduction of the picture to stamp size. He also altered the cloud formation after Jack Williams professed to see a resemblance between one of the clouds and "Binkley," a character in Berke Breathed's then-current comic strip "Bloom County."

This essay, by a North Dakota artist, showed grain elevators with a field of daisies in the foreground. Besides containing too much empty sky, it was executed in pastel colors that were judged unsuitable for gravure reproduction.

On January 19, USPS made public the design. It noted in the accompanying news release that the vignette "suggests the strength and sustenance early settlers drew from the land," in keeping with North Dakota's motto, "Strength from the Soil."

The motto notwithstanding, several prominent North Dakotans decided they didn't like what they saw. "No stamp of approval!" *The Bismarck Tribune* headlined its story of January 28. It quoted Governor George Sinner thus:

"I wonder if the image ... is really what the rest of the country thinks of North Dakota. Neighboring states were given a more positive image in their stamps. I talked to (U.S. Senator Quentin) Burdick and found out that it would be practically impossible to get a design changed now."

Former Governor Arthur A. Link, Centennial Commission chairman, said he too was disappointed. "In 1889 there would have been lots of activity, not an abandoned building," he said. "Maybe if in addition to the abandoned elevator there could have been a modern combine in the background it would have told more of the story."

Marvis Weiser of the Hazen Art and Crafts Association told *The Tribune:* "We're writing a letter of protest to the Postal Service. ... Montana will have a Charles M. Russell design, and he lived in Montana. Washington has Mount Rainier as a symbol of its state. What do we get? An abandoned elevator in the middle of nothing."

"Long and expensive efforts by the tourism department to depict North Dakota as the interesting and people-oriented place that it is have been wiped out at one stroke," said Francie Berg, author of *North Dakota: Land of Changing Seasons.*

Artist Sharon Haag of Center, North Dakota, said: "I feel there were plenty of qualified and good artists in North Dakota who could have done the design."

It may have been USPS' misfortune that the design was unveiled just at a time when North Dakotans were debating whether there was a need to improve their state's image — and specifically whether they should drop the word "North" from the state name to avoid the connotation of coldness and bleakness. The proposal was eventually turned down, but the discussion no doubt left some residents sensitive to the way their state was interpreted to the outside.

Replying to the criticism, Frank Thomas, acting manager of USPS' Stamp Support Branch, told the *Tribune:*

"We hear complaints all the time, especially about state stamps. It's impossible to make everyone happy with one design because it is supposed to represent the entire state. At least criticism proves that people are paying attention."

Thomas denied that the Postal Service had ignored the Centennial Commission's contest entries. "Perfectly good paintings are often rejected because they don't reduce well to the size of a stamp," he explained. He added that too much was being made of the fact that designer Wendell Minor lived in New York. "He came from Illinois originally," Thomas said. "He's just living in New York because it's easier to sell paintings there."

The passage of time didn't change Governor Sinner's original opinion. When he addressed postal officials and some 300 other persons at the first-day ceremony February 21, he was blunt. Wendell Minor's painting was beautiful, he said, but "the stamp does not represent the North Dakota of today. Nor does it suggest a positive image for our future." And former Governor Link told the audience he wished the artist had visited the state "prior to taking pen in hand."

USPS had its defenders, however — even in the heart of North Dakota. Said *The Bismarck Tribune* editorially:

"Frankly, we like the stamp. It emphasizes the pastoral calm of North Dakota, the clear, sunny skies and, of course, our agricultural heritage. The design is bold, the colors rich and vibrant.

"What instead of a grain elevator would we have wanted on the stamp? Certainly not the capitol building, which looks like most any other office building to people from metropolitan areas. And for heaven's sake, not Custer — Montana can have him. ... Most of the other stamp designs we saw were far too busy, reminiscent of that weird license plate of a few years back. Stamp designs must be simple to be effective. Our new stamp is both, and attractive to boot."

Ex-Governor Link had also complained about the use of the single date "1889" in the design, but USPS considered this a plus. It signaled a new intention by CSAC to drop the current year from statehood anniversary stamps.

Artist Wendell Minor was asked to repaint the sky after a USPS official noticed a resemblance between the cloud outline in the upper left and a comic-strip character. Changes were also made in the typography.

Actually, this had already been done with the series then under way to mark the bicentennial of the original 13 states. The common format used for those 13 stamps incorporated the complete date on which statehood was achieved: month, day and year. The North Dakota stamp was the first statehood commemorative to bear only a single year as a date reference, and it followed a trend in recent years of reducing postage-stamp typography to a minimum.

"I don't know why we didn't think of it sooner," Belmont Faries, CSAC chairman, told *The Washington Post,* referring to the date simplification. "They're perfectly sensible without it (the current year). Sometimes you can have a good design, but when you add all that extraneous lettering, you end up with a mishmash.

"As far as I'm concerned, the less lettering, the better."

First-day Facts

As noted previously, Governor Sinner was a featured speaker at the first-day ceremony. Former Governor Link, chairman of the Centennial Commission, gave the welcome, and Peter K. Eichorn, senior assistant postmaster general, delivered the address and presented the souvenir albums. The invocation was offered by Bobette Wildcat, Miss Indian America XXXIII.

25¢ WASHINGTON STATEHOOD CENTENNIAL

Date of Issue: February 22, 1989

Catalog Numbers: Scott 2404   Minkus CM1338   USPS 0454

Colors: magenta, yellow, cyan, black

First-Day Cancel: Olympia, Washington (Legislative Hall)

FDCs Canceled: 445,174

Format: Panes of 50, vertical, 10 across, 5 down. Gravure printing cylinders of 200 subjects (10 across, 20 around) manufactured by Roto Cylinder, Palmyra, New Jersey.

Perf: 10.9 (L perforator)

Selvage Markings: ©United States Postal Service 1989, Use Correct ZIP Code®

Designer: Howard Rogers of Bozeman, Montana

Art Director and Project Manager: Jack Williams (USPS)

Typographer: Bradbury Thompson (CSAC)

Modeler: Richard Sennett (Sennett Enterprises) for American Bank Note Company.

Printing: Stamps printed and sheeted out by American Bank Note Company on a leased Champlain gravure press (J.W. Fergusson and Sons, Richmond, Virginia). Perforated, processed and shipped by ABNC (Chicago, Illinois).

Quantity Ordered: 264,625,000
Quantity Distributed: 264,625,000

Cylinder Number Detail: One group of 4 cylinder numbers preceded by the letter "A" over/under corner stamps

Cylinder Number Combination: A1111

Tagging: block over vignette

Printing Base Impressions: A1111 (1,300,133)

The Stamp

The third of four stamps marking the centennial of statehood of four Western states honored Washington, the only state named for a president. It made its debut on February 22, which was the 100th anniversary of the day the statehood bill was signed into law — and also George Washington's birthday.

The stamp's vertical design featured a moonlit Mount Rainier, the centerpiece of Mount Rainier National Park in west central Washington and the state's best-known physical feature. The mountain was making its second philatelic appearance; it had previously been featured on a 3¢ purple horizontal commemorative in the National Parks series of 1934 (Scott 742).

Washington, located at the far northwest corner of the "Lower 48," was originally part of the Oregon Territory. A map of the territory provided the design for a 1936 3¢ commemorative (Scott 783) noting the 100th anniversary of the arrival of the first settlers. In 1948 another 3¢ stamp (Scott 964) marked the centennial of the formal establishment of Oregon's territorial government. In 1853, a separate Washington territory was created, including parts of Idaho and Montana, and this event, too, was commemorated with a 3¢ stamp on its 100th anniversary (Scott 1019).

The campaign for statehood for Washington began in 1861. A constitutional convention was held in 1878, but Congress took no action until early 1889, when it passed an omnibus bill creating the states of Washington, Montana and the two Dakotas. On November 11, 1889, President Benjamin Harrison proclaimed Washington the 42nd state in the Union.

The 50th anniversary of the statehood of the four western states was marked in 1939 by a single stamp (see Montana Statehood). Several other stamps have had Washington connections.

The sesquicentennial of the expedition of Meriwether Lewis and William Clark to the Pacific Northwest was marked with a 3¢ stamp issued by the United States in 1954 (Scott 1063). One of the early

This 1934 stamp from the National Parks series (Scott 742) showed Mount Rainier with Mirror Lake in the foreground.

settlements in Washington, Fort Nisqually, was shown on the 28¢ Americana definitive of 1978 (Scott 1604).

Two expositions in Seattle and a third in Spokane were all marked with single commemoratives: the Alaska-Yukon-Pacific Exposition of 1909 (Scott 370), the Seattle World's Fair of 1962 (Scott 1196) and Spokane's Expo '74 in 1974 (Scott 1527). A 4¢ commemorative in 1960 noted the fifth World Forestry Congress, held in Seattle (Scott 1156). The Grand Coulee Dam, built between 1933 and 1942, was depicted on a 3¢ stamp of 1952 (Scott 1009).

The first non-stop transpacific flight, from Japan to Wenatchee, Washington, in 1931, was commemorated with a 28¢ airmail postal card in 1981 (Scott UXC19). The Indian Masks set in the Folk Art series, issued during the 1980 American Philatelic Society Stampshow in Spokane, celebrated the heritage of the Northwest Indians (Scott 1834-37).

Mount Rainier, in the Cascade range, is a long-quiet volcano — but nearby Mount St. Helens had also been considered dormant before it erupted in 1980. The first European to sight Mount Rainier was the English explorer George Vancouver, who observed it May 8, 1792, during his survey of the coast and Puget Sound. Vancouver named the mountain for a friend.

The Design

The Washington stamp was the first design project for Howard Rogers, a gallery painter who had moved to Bozeman, Montana, a few years earlier after 17 years as a magazine and book illustrator in Connecticut. Rogers has a growing reputation as an artist and sculptor in bronze whose favorite subjects, as the title of a 1989 magazine article about him put it, are "Cowboys and Pretty Women."

Rogers had originally been signed to develop concept sketches for the Montana commemorative. The Citizens' Stamp Advisory Committtee liked his work, and after the committee decided to use a Charles Russell painting for Montana (see 25¢ Montana Statehood) it decided to try Rogers on the Washington stamp. The members particularly liked a sketch of Glacier National Park in which mountain scenery was reflected in a lake, and asked him if he could in effect "move" it two states to the west by using Mount Rainier in it.

Rogers had never seen Mount Rainier, but he had pictures in his files, and CSAC furnished several other views from various angles, some of them showing reflecting lakes in the foreground. Working with oil, and using a gesso-coated illustration board rather than his customary canvas because of the small size required for the artwork, he produced a moonlit scene in cool blues, violets and greens.

USPS' Stamp Support Branch took Rogers' artwork more literally than he had intended. The USPS news release said of the design:

"In the foreground, a lone fisherman is shown drifting in a small

This 1930s-era picture postcard shows the same view of Mount Rainier as is shown on the stamp, with a lake identified as Tipsoe (Tipsoo) in the foreground.

canoe across placid Reflection Lake, its shoreline fringed with trees and grasses."

But, Dickson Preston of Seattle pointed out in a letter to *Linn's Stamp News*, "The view is from a different lake, Tipsoo Lake."

"Three alpine lakes have now become prominent in Mount Rainier philately," Preston continued. "The first of these, Mirror Lake, is on the 1934 National Park stamp. This lake is on the west side of Mount Rainier. The second lake, Reflection Lake, is to the south. This one is the lake mentioned (in the press release).

"The third lake, Tipsoo Lake, on the east side of Mount Rainier, is the one shown on the 1989 stamp. The name of this lake has been spelled several ways. 'Tipsoo' is the currently accepted spelling."

Preston enclosed a 1930s picture postcard of the mountain fronted by lake Tipsoo (spelled 'Tipsoe' on the card) in which Rainier's double-peaked profile and the prominent ridge behind the lake closely match the features shown on the stamp.

"Since the view is toward the west, what of the full moon?" Preston added. "It must be a setting one, seen shortly before sunrise. And why would anyone canoe at this strange hour? Presumably to avoid being caught by the National Park Service rangers. Boating or canoeing on any of Mount Rainier's pristine alpine lakes is, of course, strictly illegal."

Rogers laughed when he was asked about these points. "Frankly, I kind of made the lake up," he said. "I knew there was a lake there, and I figured, you know, I can take artist's license with the way the shoreline runs, and I put in some little peninsulas that went out into it just to make it more interesting. But if somebody thinks that's just what

Tipsoo Lake looks like, that's fine." He made the scene a moonlit one, he added, because "it just sort of fit with the color scheme."

Like the North Dakota stamp issued one day earlier, the Washington stamp bears only the year of statehood, 1889.

First Day Facts

Governor Booth Gardner was a featured speaker at the first-day ceremony, held in the rotunda of the Legislative Hall in the capitol building in Olympia. Also speaking were the co-chairmen of the Washington Centennial Commission, Ralph Munro and Jean Gardner, and the commission's executive secretary, Putnam Barber. John G. Mulligan, senior assistant postmaster general, delivered the address and presented the souvenir albums.

As part of Washington's centennial celebration, USPS authorized a pictorial cancellation depicting a map, Mount Rainier, a pine tree and a shock of wheat. The cancellation was used February 23 — the date on which the stamp was placed on sale nationally — at 39 Washington post offices.

$5 STEAMBOATS BOOKLET

Date of Issue: March 3, 1989

Catalog Numbers: Scott 2405-9 (stamps)   USPS 6622 (booklet)
Scott 2409a (pane of 5)   USPS 6642 (unfolded pane)
Minkus CM1339-43

Colors: magenta, yellow, cyan, black (offset); green, orange, black (intaglio)

First-Day Cancel: New Orleans, Louisiana (Delta Queen Terminal)

FDCs Canceled: 981,674

Format: Four panes of 5 different horizontal stamps. Offset printing plates of 240 subjects (20 across, 12 around); intaglio printing sleeve of 480 subjects (20 across, 24 around).

Perf: 10 by imperforate (Goebel booklet machine stroke perforator)

Selvage Markings: One sleeve number and registered markings on each pane binding stub. ©United States Postal Service 1989 inside front cover. Universal Product Code (UPC) on outside of back cover.

Stamp/Booklet Cover Designer and Typographer: Richard Schlecht of Arlington, Virginia

Art Director: Howard Paine (CSAC)

Project Manager: Jack Williams (USPS)

Engravers: Thomas Hipschen (BEP, vignettes)
Michael Ryan (BEP, lettering and numerals)

Printing: Stamps printed on the 6-color offset, 3-color intaglio D press (902). Covers printed and booklets formed on Goebel booklet forming machine.

Quantity Ordered: 37,000,000 (booklets)
1,701,000 (unfolded panes)

Quantity Distributed: 39,295,800 (booklets)
1,701,000 (unfolded panes)

Plate/Sleeve Number Detail: One intaglio sleeve number on each pane binding stub

Sleeve Numbers: 1, 2

Tagging: block over vignette

The Stamps

The U.S. Postal Service issued its third consecutive commemorative booklet featuring means of transportation when it placed on sale March 3 a $5 booklet of stamps depicting steamboats from the early days of the Republic.

The booklet followed one showing five historic American locomotives (1987) and another depicting five classic American cars (1988). Like these, it contained four panes of five varieties each.

With this booklet, USPS initiated a significant new service to philatelic customers. It made available individual booklet panes that had never been folded and with fully gummed binding stubs.

The new policy solved problems that had plagued collectors since the introduction of the Bureau of Engraving and Printing's Goebel booklet-forming equipment in the early 1970s. The Goebel equipment folded booklet panes along a horizontal row of perforations and attached them to the booklets by the adhesive on their tabs. This process weakened the pane at the fold, making it likely that eventually the stamps would separate. The intact panes were extremely difficult to remove without damage to the tabs, which contained plate numbers and other marginal markings. At best, the adhesive on the tabs had to be sacrificed in the removal operation.

The Goebel machines were designed to process booklets in one continuous process. Finally, however, BEP devised an interruption method to catch the panes before they were folded and affixed. The panes were perforated and slit from the printed web of stamp paper, collected in a box, counted, packed 50 panes to a stack and separated in a larger box with cardboard chips.

Curiously, the souvenir pages produced by USPS for the Steamboat booklet bore unfolded panes — but with the stubs torn off. After a *Linn's Stamp News* writer pointed out the anomaly to USPS, Bob Brown, manager of the Philatelic Sales Division, promised that all future souvenir pages for booklet panes would have unfolded panes with full binding stubs.

The first indication to the public that unfolded panes could be diverted from the booklet-making process had come not with the Steamboat stamps but with the Special Occasions booklet of four varieties issued in 1988 — a booklet that was produced by the American Bank Note Company, not the Bureau of Engraving and Printing.

First-day ceremony programs and USPS souvenir pages for the Special Occasions booklet bore the panes in unfolded condition, but mint panes weren't made available in that form. Postal Service officials said then that they had no plans to sell mint unfolded panes, but by the time the Steamboat booklet was produced, they had changed their minds.

USPS selected the booklet for its annual spring promotion, a sign of its confidence that the issue would be popular. It also offered use of the booklet cover to gain free admission to World Stamp Expo '89, the international stamp show that the Postal Service staged in Washington later in the year.

According to the Postal Service's original announcement — and the wording on the booklet cover — the cover could be exchanged for a single day's admission to World Stamp Expo. However, USPS later notified collectors that they could obtain a free season pass to the show, valued at $20, if they filled out the name and address blanks and mailed in the cover.

Steamboats had appeared on several previous U.S. stamps. The 2¢ Hudson-Fulton commemorative of 1909 (Scott 372-373) and the 5¢

Robert Fulton and his steamboat Clermont were shown on this 5¢ stamp of 1965 (Scott 1270) marking the 200th anniversary of the inventor's birth.

Norman Todhunter's design for the Louisiana Statehood Sesquicentennial stamp of 1962 (Scott 1197) showed a sidewheel steamboat on the Mississippi River.

Robert Fulton bicentennial stamp of 1965 (Scott 1270) each depicted Fulton's 1807 *Clermont,* the first financially successful steam vessel. The 4¢ Louisiana statehood sesquicentennial stamp of 1962 (Scott 1197) showed a 19th-century Mississippi River sidewheeler.

The idea of a series featuring a variety of steamboats had been discussed for several years, and when the decision was made to proceed, USPS gave a concept contract to veteran stamp artist Richard Schlecht of Arlington, Virginia, an authority on archaeological and historical maritime subjects.

Schlecht was originally asked to choose some steamboats on his own and prepare drawings. With the help of USPS researcher Helen Wadsworth, he selected and sketched some vessels from the middle and late 19th century. The Citizens' Stamp Advisory Committee members then decided that they wanted the series to focus instead on the earliest period of American steamboating, meaning the late 1700s and early 1800s. Mary Ann Owens and John Foxworth, who comprise CSAC's topical subcommittee, agreed to research the subject and come back with specific recommendations.

Owens headed for her favorite repository of information, the Brooklyn Public Library, where she dug into such books as *The Steamboaters* by Harry Sinclair Drago, *Steamboats — A History of the Early Adventure* by Ralph T. Ward, *Pictorial History of the Great Lakes* by Harlan Hatcher and Eric Walter, and *Sea History — The Lordly Hudson* by the National Maritime Historical Society. From these she photocopied dozens of pages of text and pictures on early vessels. She and Foxworth then presented CSAC with a list of 10 boats, each with a unique historical angle.

There was at least one notable omission: Robert Fulton's *Clermont*. "It had been done twice," Mary Ann Owens said, "and we decided, no way it was going to get into this set."

Ultimately the committee voted to use the first five on the list, in chronological order, for the booklet. "Somewhere down the way," Owens predicted, USPS would issue stamps for the five later boats — and perhaps eventually work its way to the still-later and more artistically impressive boats that were on Richard Schlecht's original list.

Steamboats answered a crying need in a land blessed with many rivers but too vast for rapid highway development. They opened up the west to expansion and helped create, for the first time, a "national" feeling, even among settlers in distant outposts.

The steamboat could negotiate the shallows and sandbars, the shifting channels and submerged snags that stood in the path of earlier river travelers. Most important, steam power enabled boats to travel against the current. For years, cargo had come down the Mississippi on large timber rafts. The rafts would then be dismantled in New Orleans, frequently leaving the crew no alternative but to walk back home to Tennessee, Kentucky or points north.

To settlers along the Ohio and Mississippi, the steamboat was a lifeline of supplies and news from the outside world, and a means of access to eastern markets for cotton, sugar cane and other goods. In the early decades of the 19th century, steamboat commerce helped turn small river towns into thriving cities.

The five boats chosen for the booklet were all from the Eastern half of the country, but as Mary Ann Owens pointed out, they covered five distinctive geographical locations.

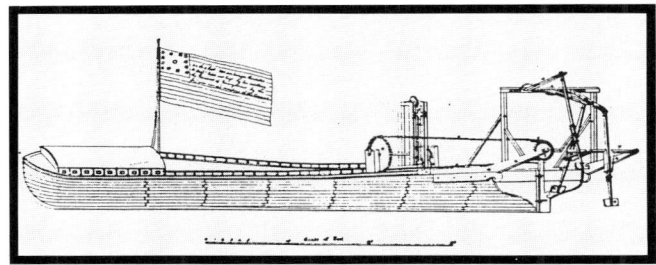

This drawing, labeled "A Draft . . . of the STEAM BOAT Experiment, now in use, 1790. Constructed by John Fitch and Henry Voight," is from the collections of the New Jersey Historical Society.

EXPERIMENT. The first stamp showed one of the steam vessels built and operated by silversmith-inventor John Fitch on the Delaware River two decades before Robert Fulton launched the Clermont. Among those who observed Fitch's experiments in the summer of

1787 were delegates to the Constitutional Convention in Philadelphia, some of whom actually ventured out onto the river in the strange-looking boat with its 12 steam-driven oars, six on each side.

Later Fitch and clockmaker Henry Voight built a vessel propelled by paddles at the stern. The boat — labeled *Experiment* in at least one contemporary drawing — made scheduled trips with passengers and freight between Philadelphia and Trenton, New Jersey, in 1790, but was a financial failure and ceased operations the next year. That ended commercial steamboating until the *Clermont* was launched on the Hudson River in 1807.

PHOENIX. Two decades after Fitch's boats crept up and down the Delaware River, John Stevens' *Phoenix* plied the same waters.

Phoenix was 100 feet long and 16 feet wide, with side wheels like Fulton's *Clermont*. Although launched from Hoboken, New Jersey, on the Hudson River, the boat was barred from operating in New York waters by a state monopoly granted to Fulton and Stevens' brother-in-law, Robert Livingston. To get to the Delaware, the *Phoenix* had to brave the open sea by sailing around New Jersey.

The 240-mile voyage, in June 1809, took 14 days, most of them stormy with heavy seas. At the helm was Captain Moses Rogers, who put the experience to good use nine years later when he guided the *Savannah* across the Atlantic in the first ocean crossing by a steam-powered vessel. (The 125th anniversary of that event was commemorated by a 3¢ U.S. stamp in 1944, Scott 923.)

NEW ORLEANS. The *New Orleans*, the first inland steamboat in history, was built at Pittsburgh for Fulton and Livingston and launched March 17, 1811. No drawings or detailed descriptions remain, but it was patterned after Fulton's Hudson River boats and apparently had two cabins, portholes and a bowsprit.

In September it embarked on a 2,000-mile journey down the Ohio and Mississippi Rivers, carrying as passengers its builder, Nicholas Roosevelt; his pregnant wife Lydia; their infant son; two servants and a Newfoundland dog, Tiger. Lydia gave birth en route, but that was a minor adventure compared to their encounter with the New Madrid, Missouri, earthquake — actually, two weeks of earthquakes — that rocked the Middle West at the end of 1811. One evening the crew tied the boat to a river island, only to find next morning that the island had vanished. Banks collapsed, currents reversed and channels shifted as the steamboat proceeded southward. Somehow the vessel and all hands survived and reached New Orleans safely January 12.

WASHINGTON. The fourth stamp featured the *Washington*, whose designer, Henry Miller Shreve, is considered the father of the Mississippi River steamboat.

Shreve, who had seen the difficulty the deep-hulled *New Orleans* encountered in shallow stretches of the Ohio River, built his side-wheel vessels with a low, almost flat-bottomed hull. He put engines and boilers on deck with a second deck built above it, a pilothouse on top of that, and two side-by-side smokestacks that rose to extraordinary height to provide a draft.

Launched at Wheeling, Virginia (now West Virginia), June 4, 1816, the vessel traveled to New Orleans, surviving a boiler explosion near Marietta, Ohio, that killed 10 passengers and crewmen and forced a layover for repairs that lasted most of the summer. After reaching New Orleans, it turned and steamed back up river to Louisville. Next spring it made another round trip, setting a record of 24 days for the return leg that drew national attention and convinced the public that the steamboat was truly master of the Mississippi.

WALK IN THE WATER. *Walk in the Water* was the third steamboat on the Great Lakes and the first on Lake Erie. Built in 1818 by Noah Brown, it was named for a friendly Wyandotte chief whose name meant "turtle," a creature the Indians described as one that walks in the water.

The 135-foot vessel had a 30-foot smokestack between two masts on which sail could be raised when the wind was favorable, and two 15-foot paddlewheels that could carry her 100 passengers (gentlemen in the forward cabin, ladies in the aft) across the lake from Buffalo to Detroit in a day and a half. As *Walk in the Water* steamed along the lake shore, wilderness residents gathered at the villages in wonderment to watch it pass by.

But Brown had constructed his steamboat too lightly, not reckoning with the sometimes-violent weather on the lakes. For three years *Walk in the Water* carried merchants, westward-moving Yankee settlers and immigrants — and the U.S. mail — across Lake Erie without mishap. Its luck ran out October 30, 1821, after it set out from Buffalo into a growing storm. Battered by waves and wind, leaking at the seams, its captain unable to find a safe haven in the darkness, the ship went aground.

All the passengers and crew were saved, but *Walk in the Water* was a total wreck. Its engine was salvaged and installed in another steamboat, *Superior*, where it served for another decade before ending its career powering a sawmill in Saginaw, Michigan.

The Designs

The stamps, like those for the locomotives and classic cars booklets, were printed on the Bureau of Engraving and Printing's combination offset-intaglio D press. But the design work and production of the printing plates took an unusual course.

Artist Richard Schlecht, working from the research material supplied by Mary Ann Owens, prepared one-to-one (actual stamp size) sketches in ink and watercolor to show USPS how the finished booklet pane might look. He had no intention of using them as final art. But when Don McDowell, general manager of the Stamps Division,

Stamp designer Richard Schlecht also designed this cachet to be used with his Steamboat booklet stamps on first-day covers.

saw the five sketches, he was enthusiastic over the spontaneity of these freely drawn images and lettering. No need for Schlecht to do finished paintings, he said; the Bureau could work with these.

"Don's a great one for enthusiasm," Schlecht recalled, "and it sounded like a good idea, but I didn't really think it would be when we got down to the actual nuts and bolts of it. Because of the amount of fussy detail that's necessary to make a ship look like a ship, the one-to-one working size wasn't ideal, and I anticipated that both I and the engraver would have problems. With the lettering, too, I wanted a little more latitude to work in. You really can't get that freehand lettering quality unless you've got more room, or at least I can't.

"So Don and Howard Paine, the art director, and I got together. Since the stamps had a lot of line work, we decided to do the art in two stages — one for the line work and another for the color. This would be pretty hard to do (registry and detail and so forth) at actual size, so Don agreed with my suggestion that I work at twice the size. This would preserve the informal character of the sketches, and would give me the latitude I needed for detail."

Accordingly, Schlecht remade the five sketches at a two-to-one size, and each in two separate parts: a line drawing in ink on a piece of Mylar plastic, and a wash painting on a piece of paper to serve as the color backdrop. By now he was working closely with Thomas Hipschen, the BEP engraver assigned to do the intaglio portions of the stamps. Using the Mylar as an overlay, Schlecht registered and "sandwiched" the two parts of the artwork for the committee's examination. Then Hipschen did his engraving from the plastic, which contained all the line work and type, and BEP's technicians made the offset plates from the other part.

The lettering, which looks at if it was done casually, required hard work. "I'll bet I did the lettering on each one 20 times," Schlecht said.

"I had to, just to loosen up and get in the flow. I'm sure people who do calligraphy all the time can do it more efficiently than that."

After Hipschen engraved the first die, a proof was made and Schlecht compared it with his drawing. That satisfied him that the process was working properly. "Tom is plenty good and has good instincts for producing the exact character of a drawing," Schlecht said. "Every little intuitive thing is there."

For some of the boats, clear and accurate period drawings weren't available. "I just had to figure how much artist's license I could take," Schlecht said, "realizing that the guy who made a boat drawing I was working from had probably (a) never had a pencil in his hand before and (b) never seen a boat before. One or two were even largely based on verbal descriptions, and I had to think, 'well, it couldn't have really been like that, but here's what this guy was probably saying, or making up, or speaking in hyperbole about.' "

Schlecht also designed the blue and black booklet cover, which featured a paddlewheel and stylized waves.

Schlecht, a native of Texas, had been a freelance illustrator since 1968. In recent years he has spent increasing time creating paintings for sale to collectors. For the Postal Service in 1988 he created the artwork for the Tugboat, Carreta, Coal Car and Conestoga Wagon stamps in the Transportation stamp series as well as the *Yorkshire* sailing ship postal card.

First-Day Facts

Postmaster General Anthony M. Frank dedicated the new booklet in a public ceremony at the Delta Queen Terminal in New Orleans. Patrick Fahey, president and CEO of the Delta Queen Steamboat Company, gave the welcome, and other speakers were W.H. LeBlanc of the Postal Rate Commission, historian J. Raymond Samuel and Colonel Barney Oldfield, USAF, Ret. Two surviving paddlewheelers, the *Delta Queen* and the *Mississippi Queen*, provided a backdrop.

For first-day covers serviced by USPS, only full panes were affixed at a cost to the customer of $1.25 per cover.

25¢ WORLD STAMP EXPO '89

Date of Issue: March 16, 1989

Catalog Numbers: Scott 2410   Minkus CM1344   USPS 4457

Colors: red, gray, black (offset); black (intaglio)

First-Day Cancel: New York City (Interpex '89 stamp show)

FDCs Canceled: 296,310

Format: Panes of 50, vertical, 10 across, 5 down. Offset printing plates of 200 subjects (10 across, 20 around); intaglio printing sleeve of 400 subjects (10 across, 40 around).

Perf: 11.1 (Eureka off-line perforator)

Selvage Markings: ©United States Postal Service 1988, Use Correct ZIP Code®

Designer, Art Director and Typographer: Richard Sheaff (CSAC)

Project Manager: Jack Williams (USPS)

Engravers: Edward Archer (BEP, vignette)
Michael Ryan (BEP, lettering and numerals)

Printing: 6-color offset, 3-color intaglio D press (902)

Quantity Ordered: 100,900,000
Quantity Distributed: 103,835,000

Plate/Sleeve Number Detail: Left-side panes — one group of 3 offset plate numbers over/under corner stamps; one intaglio sleeve number over/under adjacent stamps. Right-side panes — offset/intaglio numbers in reverse positions.

Plate/Sleeve Number Combinations: 111-1, 212-1

Tagging: overall

The Stamp

Through most of 1989, USPS was busy preparing for two major and related events which it would host in November and December at the Washington Convention Center in Washington, D.C. One was the 20th Congress of the Universal Postal Union. The other was World Stamp Expo '89, the first stamp show to be directly sponsored by the Postal Service.

Both events were years in the planning and were the subject of a long and intensive promotional campaign by USPS. Naturally, that campaign included a number of postal issues. The first of these, an advance advertisement for the show, was a 25¢ commemorative stamp that made its debut March 16, 1989, eight months before World Stamp Expo's scheduled November 17 opening.

The stamp was dedicated at another stamp show, Interpex '89, the annual spring exhibition and bourse of the American Stamp Dealers Association (ASDA) at Madison Square Garden in New York. It had been unveiled at yet another exhibition — the American Philatelic Society's Stampshow in Detroit, on August 21, 1988.

Later, on November 28 at World Stamp Expo itself, USPS issued a maximum card reproducing the stamp.

As with several earlier U.S. commemoratives having a stamp-collecting theme, this one featured a "stamp-on-stamp" design. The item it depicted was a classic of American philately — the 90¢ value of the 1869 pictorial series, a bicolor portraying Abraham Lincoln (Scott 122). The choice was influenced by the fact that Lincoln's cabinet included as postmaster general Montgomery Blair, whose call for an international postal conference in 1863 led ultimately to the organization of the Universal Postal Union.

Unlike the earlier stamp-on-stamp designs, this one reproduced the earlier stamp in full and at close to its original size. The first such issue, the Stamp Collecting commemorative of 1972, had shown a much-reduced copy of the 5¢ Franklin stamp of 1847 (Scott 1), as seen through a magnifying glass. The second, issued in 1985 as an advance promotion for the Ameripex '86 international stamp show, reproduced only the upper left portion of the 1¢ Franklin stamp of 1870 (Scott 134). And the Stamp Collecting booklet pane of 1986 depicted several U.S. stamps of various vintages, but again only partially and in miniature.

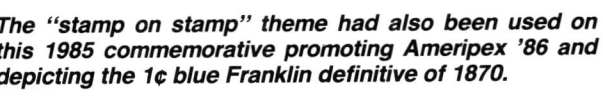

The "stamp on stamp" theme had also been used on this 1985 commemorative promoting Ameripex '86 and depicting the 1¢ blue Franklin definitive of 1870.

The 90¢ Lincoln was part of the 1869 series, a series that included the first U.S. pictorial stamps. It was the highest-denomination stamp issued up to that time, and was used on overweight mail and for international correspondence. Along with the three other high values of the set — the 15¢, 24¢ and 30¢ — it was printed in two colors, marking another first for United States postage.

The 1869s were manufactured by the National Bank Note Company of New York. In the company's original set of designs, Lincoln appeared on the 10¢ value, and the 90¢ bore a portrait of George Washington. In the set as issued, Washington was on the 6¢.

The 90¢ stamp bore a three-quarters face portrait of Lincoln taken from an 1861 photograph by C.S. German, printed in black inside an ornamental frame of carmine. It was designed by E. Pitcher, who also designed the 1¢, 6¢, 15¢ and 24¢ stamps in the series. The stamp was issued with grill, although an ungrilled variety exists (Scott 122a). In the Scott 1990 *Standard Postage Stamp Catalogue*, Volume I, the basic stamp is valued at $7,000 unused and $1,200 used, and the ungrilled variety at $13,500.

John N. Luff, in his study of 19th-century U.S. stamps, reported that at one time the 90¢ stamp was believed to exist with inverted center, like the three other bicolor stamps in the series, and in fact was listed as such in some catalogs. Later, however, experts concluded that there was no such variety.

The series didn't please the public and was criticized in the press. Luff speculated that most postal customers saw only the one-color lower denominations and not the handsome high values, or they might have rendered a different verdict. The Report of the Postmaster General, dated November 15, 1870, had this to say:

"The adhesive stamps adopted by my predecessor in 1869, having failed to give satisfaction to the public, on account of their small size, their unshapely form, the inappropriateness of their designs, the difficulty of cancelling them effectually, and the inferior quality of the gum used in their manufacture, I found it necessary, in April last, to issue new stamps, of larger size, superior quality of gum, and improved designs. ... I decided to substitute an entire new series, one-third larger in size, and to adopt for designs the heads, in profile, of distinguished deceased Americans." This was the series of 1870-71.

In 1875, the Post Office ordered reprints of a number of earlier stamp series, including the 1869s, for display at the Centennial Exposition in Philadelphia the following year. The reprints were made on hard white ungrilled paper.

The Design

Richard D. Sheaff of Needham Heights, Massachusetts, design coordinator for the Citizens' Stamp Advisory Committee, performed the triple role of art director, designer and typographer for the World Stamp Expo stamp.

Among Sheaff's previous design credits was an earlier stamp-on-stamp issue, the Ameripex '86 commemorative of 1985. This one, like the Ameripex, was printed on BEP's combination D press, with intaglio used for the black Lincoln portrait and offset for the carmine frame, background color and typography.

Sheaff tried several approaches, including a horizontal format, dark lettering, white lettering with a dropped shadow, and inclusion of the words "United States of America."

The design finally approved by CSAC was vertically arranged, with the lower half occupied by a reproduction of the Lincoln stamp that was slightly smaller than the 21¾-millimeter by 22mm original. The lettering of "World Stamp Expo '89" was white and the standard "USA" identification was employed.

There was no border, only a solid gray background that bled off all four sides. This technique had been used on only a handful of stamps in the past, such as the Father Marquette and Leif Erikson commemoratives of 1968. On those examples, the absence of a border made it difficult to determine the quality of the centering, but with the World Stamp Expo design there was no problem because the three edges of the Lincoln stamp and the block typography at the top provided visual orientation points.

As a final touch, Sheaff "tied" the replica to the larger design with a black facsimile cancellation to make it obvious that the Lincoln stamp reproduction wasn't to be detached and used to prepay 90¢ worth of postage.

The Citizens' Stamp Advisory Committee considered a horizontal as well as a vertical format and several styles and arrangements of lettering.

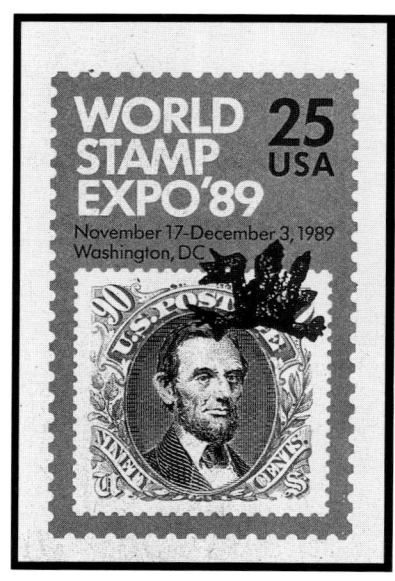

Designer Richard Sheaff suggested that the Waterbury "Running Chicken" would be an interesting simulated cancellation for the stamp-on-stamp design.

"I showed the committee a number of period cancellations that could have been correct for the 1869 issue," Sheaff said. "Most of them would actually have been of more interest to collectors, such as a flag and the Waterbury (Connecticut) running chicken. Ultimately, they picked the simpler geometric one."

The designer noted that cancellations similar to the 12-pointed specimen that was chosen appear in reference works by such authorities as E. Milliken, Tracy W. Simpson and particularly Fritz Billig, who referred to the marking as a "multiple crossroads" type. It is also akin in style to a cancellation shown in the Scott *Specialized Catalogue of United States Stamps* among examples of postal markings used in New York City on outgoing foreign mail from 1871 to 1877.

First-Day Facts

The stamp was dedicated in the lobby of the Felt Forum at Madison Square Garden in New York City, formally opening the four-day Interpex '89 show. Assistant Postmaster General Gordon C. Morison was the principal speaker. Diane K. Apfelbaum, newly elected ASDA president, also spoke. Among the honored guests was Dickey B. Rustin of USPS, director and exhibition manager of World Stamp Expo.

New York was an appropriate place to launch World Stamp Expo '89, Morison said, because of its international character as home of many ethnic groups and the site of United Nations headquarters. With more than 75 member nations and territories of the Universal Postal Union participating, World Stamp Expo would be a true international show, he said.

The new commemorative stamp was reproduced on ASDA's Interpex '89 souvenir card, which was presented to all paid showgoers.

25¢ ARTURO TOSCANINI
PERFORMING ARTS SERIES

Date of Issue: March 25, 1989

Catalog Numbers: Scott 2411   Minkus CM1345   USPS 4456

Colors: magenta, yellow, cyan, black, line red

First-Day Cancel: New York City (Carnegie Hall)

FDCs Canceled: 309,441

Format: Panes of 50, vertical, 10 across, 5 down. Gravure printing cylinders of 200 subjects (10 across, 20 around) manufactured by Roto Cylinder, Palmyra, New Jersey.

Perf: 10.9 (L perforator)

Selvage Markings: ©United States Postal Service 1989, Use Correct ZIP Code®

Designer: James Sharpe of Westport, Connecticut

Art Director and Project Manager: Jack Williams (USPS)

Typographer: Bradbury Thompson (CSAC)

Modeler: Richard Sennett (Sennett Enterprises) for American Bank Note Company.

Printing: Stamps printed and sheeted out by American Bank Note Company on a leased Champlain gravure press (J.W. Fergusson and Sons, Richmond, Virginia) under the supervision of Sennett Enterprises (Fairfax, Virginia). Perforated, processed and shipped by ABNC (Chicago, Illinois).

Quantity Ordered: 152,250,000
Quantity Distributed: 152,250,000

Cylinder Number Detail: One group of 5 cylinder numbers preceded by the letter "A" over/under corner stamps

Cylinder Number Combination: A11111

Tagging: block over vignette

Printing Base Impressions: A11111 (856,082)

The Stamp

On March 25, 1989, USPS issued a 25¢ stamp in the Performing Arts series honoring Arturo Toscanini, the Italian-born American who was the most famous orchestra conductor of his time.

The event marked the successful completion of a 22-year campaign for a Toscanini stamp by an admirer and musical scholar who had personally taken some 1,500 photographs of the maestro in action.

He was Robert Hupka of New York City, who made the pictures while working in the 1940s as a record librarian for RCA Victor. Dozens of them have since been featured on Victor's Toscanini record albums. In the end, it was was one of these Hupka photos on which the stamp's artwork was based.

Hupka's campaign began in 1967, after the Italian post office asked him for a picture to use on a stamp to mark the centennial of Toscanini's birth. He obliged, and the stamp was duly issued (Scott 948).

"I wasn't happy with it," the photographer recalled. "They used my original picture just for the face. Someone drew a hand that was unlike Toscanini's."

But the incident gave him the idea that the United States should also issue a Toscanini stamp. He wrote to the Post Office Department

This is the Robert Hupka photo of Toscanini on which artist Jim Sharpe based his painting for the stamp.

with his suggestion, enclosing the Italian commemorative and a copy of a book, *This Was Toscanini,* illustrated with 84 of his photographs. But he was politely turned down.

Next he sought help from Vice President Hubert Humphrey, whom he had met in 1965 at the New York World's Fair, where Hupka was in charge of the music in the Vatican City Pavilion. By now he had

This Italian stamp for Toscanini's centennial inspired Robert Hupka to begin his long campaign for a U.S. stamp honoring the maestro.

worked up a proposed U.S. stamp design of his own, using his favorite picture of Toscanini, and he included this in his letter. Humphrey agreed to do what he could, and contacted Postmaster General Lawrence F. O'Brien on Hupka's behalf. Still nothing happened.

Later the photographer was the subject of an article entitled "Hupka's Toscanini Mania" in the December 1968 issue of *Popular Photography.* Commenting on the one-man campaign for a Toscanini stamp, the author, David Vestal, wrote: "I don't know how long the government can hold out in the face of Hupka's determination."

It held out for many years. Then, early in 1987, Jack Williams of USPS wrote to Hupka to notify him that a Toscanini stamp had been finally approved by the Citizens' Stamp Advisory Committee. Williams asked for four or five pictures from which an artist could prepare a composite. Hupka sent a selection, and for good measure he also sent his own suggested design, now nearly two decades old.

Ultimately CSAC did opt to use only a single photograph, and chose Hupka's favorite, the one he had used in preparing his own stamp design. To his disappointment, however, the committee specified that the picture should be re-created as a painting, consistent with previous stamps in the Performing Arts series.

Toscanini was born March 25, 1867, in Parma, Italy. He entered music school at age 9, graduating at 18 with highest honors in cello, piano and composition. A year later he made a dramatic and successful conducting debut, directing Verdi's opera *Aida* as a last-minute replacement at a performance in Rio de Janeiro.

In 1898 he became music director at La Scala, Italy's leading operatic theater. He left in 1908 to become conductor of New York's Metropolitan Opera, but returned to Italy during World War I and again led La Scala.

He served as guest conductor and conductor of the New York Philharmonic from 1926 to 1936. In 1937, at age 70, he took charge of the NBC Symphony, an orchestra of specially chosen virtuoso players that was created for him by David Sarnoff, chairman of RCA. Toscanini led it for 17 years, until his retirement in 1954. On January 16, 1957, the maestro died in his home in Riverdale, New York.

The uniquely powerful style of leadership Toscanini brought to his conducting was described in detail by violinist Samuel Antek in the Hupka-illustrated book *This Was Toscanini,* (Vanguard Press, 1963). Here is Antek's account of the NBC Symphony's first rehearsal with the maestro:

"With each heart-pounding timpani stroke in the opening bars of the Brahms *First Symphony* his baton beat became more powerfully insistent, his shoulders strained and hunched as though buffeting a giant wind. His outstretched left arm spasmodically flailed the air, the cupped fingers pleading like a beseeching beggar. His face reddened, muscles tightened, eyes and eyebrows constantly moving. ...

" 'So! So! So!' he bellowed. 'Cantare! Sostenere!' His legs were bending slightly as he braced himself for his violent movements, which were becoming larger, more pile-driving, as the music reached its first

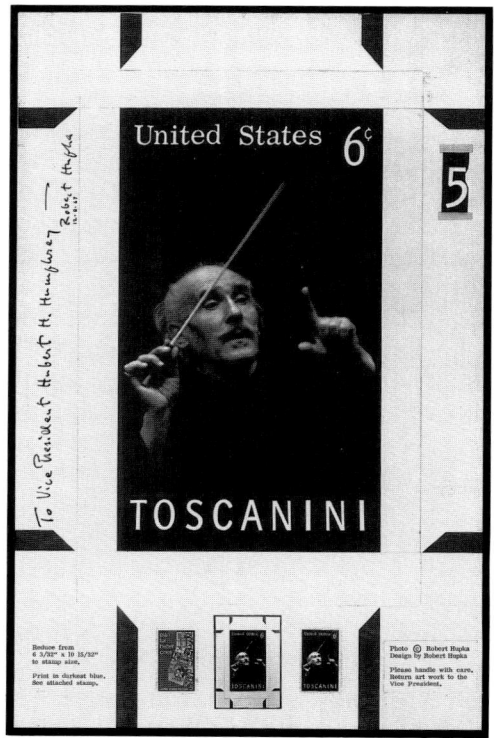

In 1967 Robert Hupka prepared this proposed stamp design, using his favorite photograph of Toscanini. Twenty-two years later the photo itself was adapted for use on the stamp that was actually issued.

great climax. 'Cantare! Sostenere!' I was to hear these words often in the years to come. 'Sing! Sustain!' Toscanini's battle cry! This was the first time they were flung at us, and for 17 years we lived by them. ...

"We played to please the Old Man, but our own taste buds of artistic awareness were sharpened and we were inspired to play and satisfy our own highest standards and instincts, in pursuit of our common goal. The terrors and abuses Toscanini hurled at us were accepted and tolerated because they sprang from his own humility, sincerity and love for the music. Every giant artist drives himself as such. We were completely won over and carried along with Toscanini's musical approach, its unerring, never exaggerated good taste. The performance was *ours*, not only Toscanini's, for he was but the voice of our own musical consciences."

The stamp was the 11th in the Performing Arts series that began in 1978 and had previously honored Jimmie Rodgers, George M. Cohan, Will Rogers, W.C. Fields, John, Lionel and Ethel Barrymore, Douglas Fairbanks, John McCormack, Jerome Kern, Duke Ellington and Enrico Caruso.

Besides Italy, other countries that have depicted Toscanini on stamps are Israel (Scott 955) and Niger (Scott 574).

The Design

Jim Sharpe of Westport, Connecticut, who had designed all 10 earlier Performing Arts stamps, designed this one also. The photograph on which he based his Toscanini portrait was one of many candid shots Robert Hupka had made of the maestro conducting the NBC Symphony at a recording session in New York City's Carnegie Hall March 4, 1947.

On that date, when Toscanini was recording Claude Debussy's *La Mer* — and at a previous session a week earlier — Hupka prowled the back of the auditorium with a borrowed Leica camera, shooting roll after roll of film as the 79-year-old conductor drew music from the virtuoso players arrayed before him.

"The existing light at Carnegie Hall was soft and beautiful against the blackness of the empty hall," Hupka recalled in his interview with magazine writer David Vestal. "Toscanini's facial expressions were so compelling, I was under the same spell as the musicians. They played their instruments, and I played my camera — my instrument. ...

"I was mesmerized. I clicked in synchronization with the music and the beauty of his face. The expressiveness and nobility of that face were absolutely unique. Even after taking 1,200 pictures of him I was still struck by expressions I had never photographed before."

The "stamp" photograph was one published on page 92 of the book *This was Toscanini*. Sharpe arranged his painting in the vertical format that has been used for all the Performing Arts commemoratives. But he elected to crop the portrait much more closely than any previous designer in the series had done, so that the Toscanini head, with its white mane and mustache, would fill the frame.

Having done that, Sharpe had to move the conductor's right hand, holding the baton, to the right in order to get it into the stamp design. On the photograph, the baton crosses Toscanini's forehead diagonally, just over the right eye; on the stamp, however, it bisects his mustache, and is only partly visible.

Sharpe made another major alteration. In Hupka's rehearsal photographs, Toscanini wears a black alpaca jacket and is portrayed against a black background, so that virtually nothing is visible except face, hands and baton. For the stamp, however, Sharpe gave him a white bow tie, formal collar and shirtfront.

In keeping with the current minimalist trend in U.S. stamp typography, the design identified the subject simply as "Toscanini." Similar last-name-only treatment had been used occasionally in the past, most recently with "Hawthorne" (Nathaniel) on a 20¢ Literary Arts stamp of 1983 and "The Barrymores" on a 20¢ Performing Arts stamp of 1982.

First-Day Facts

The dedication ceremony was held on Toscanini's 122nd birth anniversary in the place most closely associated with his career: Carnegie Hall, where he conducted.

Two national anthems opened the program in the Weill Recital Hall. "The Star Spangled Banner" was sung by long-time Metropolitan Opera baritone Robert Merrill (who invited the audience to join in), and Italy's anthem was sung by Francesca Bachi. Violinist Isaac Stern, president of Carnegie Hall, welcomed the guests, and the speakers included Rinaldo Petrignani, Italy's ambassador to the United States; Stephen Stamas, president of the New York Philharmonic, and Norma Pace, a USPS governor. The stamp was dedicated by Kenneth J. Hunter, associate postmaster general.

During her remarks, Norma Pace announced that in 1991 a Historic Preservation series postal card would be issued honoring the 100th anniversary of Carnegie Hall. Isaac Stern, who fought to save Carnegie Hall from the wrecking ball, was described as "visibly moved."

Honored guests were the maestro's daughter, Wanda Toscanini Horowitz, who was the wife of the late pianist Vladimir Horowitz, and grandson, Walfredo Toscanini, and Robert Hupka, whose long effort to have a Toscanini stamp issued had finally come to pass.

Wanda Horowitz reminded postal officials in the audience of her father's insistence on promptness, and said she expected letters with the Toscanini stamp to meet his high standards for prompt delivery. Toscanini's grandson said he was doubly pleased to be present because the occasion involved two of his interests: music and philately.

25¢ U.S. HOUSE OF REPRESENTATIVES CONSTITUTION BICENTENNIAL SERIES

Date of Issue: April 4, 1989

Catalog Numbers: Scott 2412   Minkus CM1346   USPS 4458

Colors: magenta, yellow, blue-black (offset); olive (intaglio)

First-Day Cancel: Washington, D.C. (U.S. Capitol)

FDCs Canceled: 327,755

Format: Panes of 50, vertical, 10 across, 5 down. Offset printing plates of 200 subjects (10 across, 20 around); intaglio printing sleeve of 400 subjects (10 across, 40 around).

Perf: 11.1 by 11 (Eureka off-line perforator)

Selvage Markings: ©United States Postal Service 1989, Use Correct ZIP Code®

Designer: Howard Koslow of East Norwich, New York

Art Director and Typographer: Howard Paine (CSAC)

Project Manager: Joe Brockert (USPS)

Engravers: Thomas Hipschen (BEP, vignette)
           Michael Ryan (BEP, lettering and numerals)

Modeler: Frank Waslick (BEP)

Printing: 6-color offset, 3-color intaglio D press (902)

Quantity Ordered: 138,250,000
Quantity Distributed: 138,760,000

Plate/Sleeve Number Detail: Left-side panes — one group of 3 offset plate numbers over/under corner stamps; one intaglio sleeve number over/under adjacent stamps. Right-side panes — offset/intaglio numbers in reverse positions.

Plate/Sleeve Number Combination:	111-1, 211-1, 221-1, 321-1, 422-1, 522-1, 622-1, 722-1, 723-1, 724-1, 823-1
Tagging: overall	

The Stamp

The drafters of the U.S. Constitution provided for three co-equal branches of government — executive, legislative and judicial — in order that the branches might "check and balance" one another and prevent any one from becoming dominant.

The 200th anniversaries of two of these three branches, the legislative and executive, were commemorated by stamp issues in 1989. The third, the judicial, was scheduled for a stamp in 1990.

As it turned out, the legislative branch — Congress — received two stamps, one for each of its two houses.

"We realized that for practical political considerations we couldn't do just one stamp for the two chambers of Congress," explained Joe Brockert, project manager for the series. "We knew that they started at different anniversary dates, and that we would have to do two stamps. We were then looking at a total of four: executive branch, judicial branch and two for the legislative branch."

Once before, the three branches had been postally recognized, but on that occasion each got only one stamp. That was in 1950, when a set of 3¢ commemoratives (Scott 989-992) marked the 150th anniversary of the creation of the District of Columbia. One stamp depicted the Capitol, another the White House and a third the Supreme Court building, while a fourth, showing the statue atop the Capitol dome, referred to no specific branch.

The first of the 1989 Branches of Government bicentennial stamps to appear honored the House of Representatives and was issued April 4. This was actually three days after the anniversary of the House's first formal session.

After the Constitution had been ratified by the required nine states, the Confederation Congress designated the first Wednesday in March 1789 (March 4) as the date for the House and Senate to convene. The designated place was New York City, where carpenters and other artisans were carrying out Major Pierre Charles L'Enfant's plans for remodeling the municipal building into a new Federal Hall.

When March 4 dawned, church bells throughout New York pealed and cannon boomed 11 times, one for each state that had ratified the Constitution up to then. But the celebrating was premature. Only 13 of the 59 elected representatives reported in at the ground-floor House chamber, and upstairs only eight senators from five states were on hand. Without a quorum, neither house could convene.

The members were making the trip by ship, wagon and stagecoach; some were delayed by bad roads, others by storms and shipwreck. Ironically, the absentees included all the New York representatives and senators. New York's state government was split between Federalists under Alexander Hamilton and antifederalist followers of Governor George Clinton, and this had delayed the appointment of New York's members of Congress.

Finally, on April 1, the House could count a bare quorum of 30 of its 59 members. It formally convened and elected Frederick A.C. Muhlenberg of Pennsylvania as its speaker — an office whose title derived from that of the president of the English House of Commons, who historically had served as the spokesman, or speaker, for that body when its members met with the king.

Several people who have served in the House of Representatives over the years have been pictured on U.S. stamps. They include Presidents James Madison; John Quincy Adams (who was elected to the House after his presidency ended); Andrew Jackson; William Henry Harrison; John Tyler; James K. Polk (who also served as speaker); Millard Fillmore; Franklin Pierce; James Buchanan; Abraham Lincoln; Andrew Johnson; Rutherford B. Hayes; James A. Garfield; William McKinley; John F. Kennedy and Lyndon B. Johnson.

Also, Abraham Baldwin; Albert Gallatin; John Marshall; John Sevier; Manasseh Cutler; Anthony Wayne; Henry Clay; Daniel Webster; Davy Crockett; Jefferson Davis (whose sculpted image appears on the Stone Mountain Memorial commemorative of 1970); Sam Houston; Horace Greeley; Horace Mann; Stephen A. Douglas; William Jennings Bryan; Joseph Pulitzer; George Norris; Fiorello LaGuardia; Cordell Hull; Sam Rayburn (who served as speaker almost 17 years, longer than any other person) and Everett Dirksen. Joseph C.S. Blackburn of Kentucky, who was later a senator and then member of the Isthmian Canal Commission, was shown on a Canal Zone stamp of 1929.

This early essay of a House of Representatives stamp depicted the historic mace of the House. The mace actually did appear on a $1 silver coin minted by the Treasury Department to commemorate the bicentennial of Congress.

The Design

The unified design format used for all the stamps in the Branches of Government series evolved during the planning of the individual stamps. In fact, two of artist Howard Koslow's early concept sketches for the House and Senate stamps had incorporated a similar design for those two subdivisions of the legislative branch. To the right was the

Capitol; to the left was a symbol of the chamber being honored — the historic mace of the House, and the carved gilt eagle in the old Senate chamber.

The Citizens' Stamp Advisory Committee wasn't satisfied with these designs. The members wanted to avoid the cliche of showing oft-depicted buildings, such as the Capitol, to represent the institutions that occupied them, said Howard Paine, art director for the series. So CSAC and USPS staffers went back to the drawing boards.

What they ultimately produced was a single design layout, arranged vertically, that could be adapted for each of the four stamps, using as a common theme sculptural objects representative of the institutions. Among the principal advocates of this idea, as one might expect, was committee member Douglas Lewis, who is curator of sculpture at the National Gallery of Art.

At one point, Paine said, USPS even contemplated having the Bureau of Engraving and Printing print all four stamps on a single sheet of 200, with each variety grouped in a quadrant of 50 stamps that would be cut off and issued separately. BEP had used this technique, which makes possible a single long press run rather than four individual runs, in 1984 with the National Archives, Federal Deposit Insurance Corporation, Credit Union Act, and Soil and Water Conservation stamps. But the idea was turned down in favor of conventional printing.

Artist Koslow and Brockert visited the Capitol and the Supreme Court and solicited the advice of resident historians and other experts on what sculpture would be appropriate symbols of the two legislative branches and the judicial branch.

For the House stamp, they decided to use an 1819 marble clock by Carlo Franzoni, known as the "Car of History." Koslow painted the clock, with its hands at 12, in acrylic, the same medium he would use for the Senate and Executive Branch stamp designs.

Long associated with the House, the Franzoni clock now is on display above the north entrance to Statuary Hall (the old House chamber) in the Capitol. Clio, the Muse of History, stands in the winged Chariot of Time, recording events as they occur. Beneath the chariot's wheel — which serves as the face of the clock — is the top of the globe, on which appear the signs of the Zodiac.

Carlo Franzoni, a native of Carrara, Italy, came to America in 1815 as one of a group of Italian sculptors recruited to decorate a Capitol that was being rebuilt and enlarged after the British had burned it in the War of 1812. His model for Clio was said to be his niece, the daughter of his brother Giuseppe, a man who had also produced sculptures for the Capitol. Carlo, a tall, handsome man who wore rich clothing in the latest styles, died unexpectedly of a heart attack at age 30 in 1819, the year the clock sculpture was completed. His portrait, by Pietro Bonnani, hangs in the office of the Architect of the Capitol.

The uniform design concept for the series that was developed by Paine and Koslow has some unusual features.

For one thing, the stamp surface is almost completely covered with ink. The design bleeds off the stamp on all four sides — black to the left and right, red to the top and bottom — and the yellow background color fills in the corners. This kind of four-way bleed has been used on only a relatively few stamp designs, most recently earlier in 1989 on the World Stamp Expo '89 commemorative.

On a pane or block of the Branches of Government stamps, the red stripes that line the top and bottom edges of each stamp merge into a logical pattern — what art director Paine calls a "plaid look." A single stamp on an envelope has a curiously cornerless appearance, however, because the red stripes stop short of the vertical perforations, and the

Postmaster General Frank, center, officiates at the design unveiling for the House of Representatives stamp during a joint session of House and Senate. Unveiling the stamp is Representative Lindy Boggs, D-La. House Speaker Jim Wright and Senate President Pro Tem Robert Byrd are rear.

yellow background color at the four corners tends to blend into the white paper behind it.

To provide a uniformity of execution to match the design concept, BEP assigned the same engravers to all three of the 1989 stamps of the series. Thomas Hipschen executed the vignette and Michael J. Ryan did the lettering.

Designer Koslow's previous stamp designs included the Antarctic Treaty, 1971; Wolf Trap Farm Park, 1972; Tennessee Valley Authority and Brooklyn Bridge stamps, 1983; Lawrence and Elmer Sperry airmail, 1985; Rural Electrification, 1985, and Signing of the Constitution, 1987.

First-Day Facts

Postmaster General Anthony M. Frank dedicated the stamp in a public ceremony in Statuary Hall in the Capitol. Presiding was William T. Johnstone, assistant postmaster general. Participants included the House majority and minority leaders, Representative Thomas S. Foley, D-Wash. — who later in the year would become Speaker of the House — and Representative Robert H. Michel, R-Ill., and Representative Lindy Boggs, D-La., chairman of the Commission on the Bicentenary of the U.S. House of Representatives.

The first-day cancellation consisted of a drawing of the Capitol Dome and a circular datestamp linked by the four-line inscription in upper-case letters: "Bicentennial/of Congress/U.S. House/of Representatives."

A special envelope for a combination first-day cover bearing both the House and Senate stamps was designed by Michigan's Senator Carl Levin and Representative Sander Levin, the only brother team in Congress. The cachet featured a drawing of the U.S. Capitol as it looked in 1800 when it was first occupied by Congress. The covers sold for $15 each, with proceeds going to the American Philatelic Society's youth activities fund.

25¢ U.S. SENATE
CONSTITUTION BICENTENNIAL SERIES

Date of Issue: April 6, 1989

Catalog Numbers: Scott 2413   Minkus CM1347   USPS 4459

Colors: magenta, yellow, blue-black (offset); olive (intaglio)

First-Day Cancel: Washington, D.C. (U.S. Capitol)

FDCs Canceled: 341,288

Format: Panes of 50, vertical, 10 across, 5 down. Offset printing plates of 200 subjects (10 across, 20 around); intaglio printing sleeve of 400 subjects (10 across, 40 around).

Perf: 11.1 by 11(Eureka off-line perforator)

Selvage Markings: ©United States Postal Service 1989, Use Correct ZIP Code®

Designer: Howard Koslow of East Norwich, New York

Art Director and Typographer: Howard Paine (CSAC)

Project Manager: Joe Brockert (USPS)

Engravers: Thomas Hipschen (BEP, vignette)
Michael Ryan (BEP, lettering and numerals)

Modeler: Frank Waslick (BEP)

Printing: 6-color offset, 3-color intaglio D press (902)

Quantity Ordered: 138,250,000
Quantity Distributed: 137,985,000

Plate/Sleeve Number Detail: Left-side panes — one group of 3 offset plate numbers over/under corner stamps; one intaglio sleeve number over/under adjacent stamps. Right-side panes — offset/intaglio numbers in reverse positions.

Plate/Sleeve Number Combination: 111-1, 211-1, 212-1, 213-1, 313-1, 314-1, 315-1, 414-1, 514-1, 615-1, 715-1

Tagging: overall

The Stamp

The second stamp in the Branches of Government series honored the United States Senate and was issued April 6, 1989, on the 200th anniversary of the Senate's first formal session in Federal Hall, New York City.

The Senate, like the House, was supposed to convene March 4, 1789, but neither chamber had a quorum on that date. By April 1 the House had the necessary minimum number of members on hand and was able to meet and organize. The Senate, however, still lacked the necessary 12 members.

Finally, on the evening of April 5, Senator Richard Henry Lee of Virginia appeared in the city. Lee was a pivotal figure in history; it was his resolution, introduced in the Continental Congress, that produced the Declaration of Independence. Although he later opposed — unsuccessfully — his state's ratification of the Constitution, he accepted appointment to the Senate, and now his arrival enabled that body to hold its first session.

Convening April 6, the Senate chose as its temporary president John Langdon of New Hampshire. Langdon's election filled a vital need: The Constitution required that the president of the Senate receive and open the certificates containing the votes of the states' electors for president and vice president. The vice president, when elected and inaugurated, would become the Senate president. But as yet there was no one to fill that role, and in a sense Langdon — an ardent patriot who had personally paid the expenses of the New Hampshire delegation to the Constitutional Convention — became the first, but unofficial, presiding executive of the new nation.

The Senate and House then met in joint session to observe the counting of the votes of the electors. Langdon announced at the conclusion that George Washington had recieved a vote from each of the 69 electors of the reporting states and was therefore the unanimous choice for president. John Adams, with 34 votes, was second and would become vice president.

Many people who were elected to the Senate over its 200-year history have been depicted on U.S. stamps. They include Presidents James Monroe; John Quincy Adams; Andrew Jackson; Martin Van Buren; William Henry Harrison; John Tyler; Franklin Pierce; James Buchanan; Andrew Johnson (both before and after his presidency); Benjamin Harrison; Warren G. Harding; Harry S. Truman; John F. Kennedy and Lyndon B. Johnson (who served as majority leader).

Also, Albert Gallatin (who was denied his seat because he hadn't been a citizen long enough); Abraham Baldwin; Daniel Webster; Henry Clay; Sam Houston; Jefferson Davis; John C. Fremont; William Seward; Stephen A. Douglas; Carl Schurz; Hugo L. Black; Cordell Hull; George W. Norris; Robert A. Taft (another majority leader); Walter F. George; Brien McMahon; John Foster Dulles; Everett Dirksen; Richard Russell and Robert Kennedy. John Glenn's orbiting space capsule Mercury was shown on a 1962 stamp — with the future senator inside, one presumes.

A 1929 Canal Zone stamp portrayed Joseph C.S. Blackburn of Kentucky, who served in both the House and Senate.

The Design

Howard Koslow's design is a tightly cropped close-up of a carved gilt eagle, wings outstretched, a ribbon in its beak and arrows in its talons, sitting on an ornate shield faced with stars and stripes. The device is of wood and gesso, except for the arrows, which are metal. It is suspended above the vice president's chair in the Old Senate Chamber of the U.S. Capitol.

After a long separation, the Eagle and Shield were reunited when the Old Senate Chamber was restored and opened to the public as part of the Bicentennial of Independence celebration.

This close-up photograph of the eagle and shield served as the model for the stamp design.

Capitol Architect Benjamin Henry Latrobe included the ornament in his plans for the chamber, and an eagle and shield appear in drawings dated 1809. Although the maker and the date of installation are unknown, an 1829 guidebook describes the vice president's chair as "canopied by crimson drapery, richly embossed and held by talons of an o'er hovering eagle."

The powerful but graceful artifact can be seen in important period engravings of the Senate Chamber, projecting over the presiding officer's chair on an architectural device called a baldachin. One of the best-known of these pictures is by Robert Whitechurch, titled *The United States Senate, A.D. 1850,* and shows Henry Clay presenting his program of sectional compromise, with Senators Daniel Webster and John C. Calhoun, among others, in rapt attention.

In 1859 the Senate moved out of the chamber, which was then converted for use by the Supreme Court. The eagle and shield were separated, and the eagle was remounted on a horizontal rod draped with a red metal banner and was hung on the wall above the chief justice's chair. The shield was displayed in the corridor outside.

In 1935 the Supreme Court moved into its own building on Capitol Hill, and the historic room was used sparingly thereafter. Finally, decades later, Congress decided to restore the room to its early-19th-century condition, as a way to help celebrate the bicentennial of

John Mercanti's design for the reverse of the $5 gold coin commemorating the bicentennial of Congress features the same carved eagle and shield shown on the Senate stamp.

American independence. In 1976 the refurbished Old Senate Chamber was thrown open to the public, with furnishings and decorations as they were when the Senate of Webster and Clay deliberated there — decorations that included the reunited eagle, shield and arrows in their original position over the vice president's desk.

Coincidentally, the Treasury Department, in its own commemoration of the bicentennial of Congress, also chose the eagle and shield as a design subject. Sculptor-engraver John Mercanti placed the artifact on the reverse of a $5 gold coin minted for the occasion. Two other 1989 coins also honored Congress: a $1 silver piece for the House, which depicted on the reverse that chamber's historic mace, and a half-dollar coin with a view of the capitol on the reverse.

An early design treatment proposed for the Senate stamp by artist Koslow also showed the gilt eagle — but as it had appeared in the decades before the Old Senate Chamber was restored, without the shield and arrows.

This early essay of a Senate stamp depicted the carved eagle in the old Senate chamber of the U.S. Capitol as it appeared before the chamber's restoration in 1976.

First-Day Facts

Unlike the first-day ceremony for the House stamp, the ceremony for the Senate stamp was by invitation only. It was held in the Capitol's Old Senate Chamber, where the Senate met until 1859 (and where the 1983 3¢ Henry Clay stamp of the Great Americans series had been dedicated). The room was used by the Supreme Court until 1935, and in 1976 was restored to the general appearance it presented when the Senate used it. Chosen by Senate officials for the ceremony, the chamber was too small to accommodate a public event.

Senator John Glenn, D-Ohio, presided, and speakers included Senator Robert C. Byrd, D-W.Va., chairman of the Commission on the

Bicentennial of the United States Senate; Senator George J. Mitchell, D-Maine, the majority leader, and Senator Bob Dole, R-Kans., the minority leader. Postmaster General Anthony M. Frank dedicated the stamp. Musical selections from the late 18th century were played by the U.S. Marine Band String Quartet.

The first-day cancellation consisted of two circles of equal size, linked by the four-line inscription in capitals: "Bicentennial/of Congress/United States/Senate." The left circle contained the seal of the Senate; the right contained the datestamp.

USPS prepared no official program for the ceremony, but the Senate produced 225 copies of its own program.

Postmaster General Frank, standing at left, officiates at design unveiling for Senate stamp during joint session of House and Senate. Unveiling the design is Senator Richard Lugar, R-Ind. House Speaker Jim Wright and Senate President Pro Tem Robert Byrd are at rear.

25¢ EXECUTIVE BRANCH
CONSTITUTION BICENTENNIAL SERIES

Date of Issue: April 16, 1989

Catalog Numbers: Scott 2414   Minkus CM1348   USPS 4460

Colors: magenta, yellow, blue-black (offset); olive (intaglio)

First-Day Cancel: Mt. Vernon, Virginia

FDCs Canceled: 387,644

Format: Panes of 50, vertical, 10 across, 5 down. Offset printing plates of 200 subjects (10 across, 20 around); intaglio printing sleeve of 400 subjects (10 across, 40 around).

Perf: 11.1 by 11 (Eureka off-line perforator)

Selvage Markings: ©United States Postal Service 1989, Use Correct ZIP Code®

Designer: Howard Koslow of East Norwich, New York

Art Director and Typographer: Howard Paine (CSAC)

Project Manager: Joe Brockert (USPS)

Engravers: Thomas Hipschen (BEP, vignette)
Michael Ryan (BEP, lettering and numerals)

Modeler: Frank Waslick (BEP)

Printing: 6-color offset, 3-color intaglio D press (902)

Quantity Ordered: 138,250,000
Quantity Distributed: 138,580,000

Plate/Sleeve Number Detail: Left-side panes — one group of 3 offset plate numbers over/under corner stamps; one intaglio sleeve number over/under adjacent stamps. Right-side panes — offset/intaglio numbers in reverse positions.

Plate/Sleeve Number Combination: 111-1, 211-1, 311-1, 312-1

Tagging: overall

The Stamp

The nation's first Inauguration Day, in 1789, dawned overcast, but the skies cleared as the day wore on. Thousands of citizens jammed the streets of New York, then a city of 28,000 population, to see their 57-year-old president-elect drive to the inauguration in his splendidly decorated carriage, drawn by four bays.

George Washington waved to the crowd, but as usual he was solemn and unsmiling. He wore a suit of homespun brown cloth, made in Hartford, as a token of his interest in fostering American industry. Over white stockings he wore black shoes with silver buckles.

After taking the oath of office on the balcony of Federal Hall before a cheering crowd, Washington entered the second-floor Senate chamber, where he delivered the first presidential inaugural address to a small audience. Vice President John Adams sat on his right, and Frederick Muhlenberg, the first Speaker of the House, on his left. In front of him to the right were the nation's first 22 senators, and to the left, the first 61 representatives. Behind Congress sat a handful of officials of the new administration, the representatives of France and Spain, and other dignitaries.

Two hundred years later, the entire great ritual was re-enacted, beginning with Washington's departure from Mount Vernon on April 16. Actor William Sommerfield, playing the role of the president-elect, retraced Washington's route to New York, with stops and ceremonies at key places along the way.

At Federal Hall National Memorial on April 30, before an audience that included President George Bush and 100 descendants of U.S. presidents, actor Sommerfield stood on a dais built over the steps (the current building has no balcony), repeated the presidential oath to "preserve, protect and defend the Constitution of the United States" and, as Washington did, kissed the Bible used for the swearing-in — the same Bible Washington had used two centuries earlier.

USPS originally announced that the 25¢ stamp marking the bicentennial of the inauguration and the beginning of the federal government's Executive Branch would be issued on the anniversary date, April 30. Later it changed the date and place of issue to April 16 at Mount Vernon to coincide with the re-enactment of Washington's departure. There were at least two reasons for the change, said Joe Brockert, project manager for the stamp.

For one thing, USPS officials felt the stamp would get better exposure if its issuance was separate from the elaborate program planned for New York City on April 30. In 1986 the Statue of Liberty centennial commemorative had been issued as part of the general celebra-

This 1939 commemorative (Scott 854) depicted George Washington taking the oath of office as president on the balcony at Federal Hall.

tion of the anniversary in New York, and there was a feeling at USPS that it had been somewhat lost in the shuffle. Also, an earlier issuance of the Executive Branch stamp would allow it to be used with pictorial postmarks along Washington's Mount Vernon-to-New York route.

Two previous U.S. stamps are closely related to this one. In 1939, a 3¢ commemorative (Scott 854) marked the 150th anniversary of the first president's inauguration. It depicted a painting of the ceremony on the Federal Hall balcony (with a railing, not in the original artwork, interpolated into the stamp design). And in 1988, a 25¢ stamp for the bicentennial of New York statehood (Scott 2346) pictured Federal Hall and nearby buildings as they looked during the time of Washington's presidency.

Washington has been portrayed on more U.S. stamps than any other person, beginning with one of the nation's first two stamps, the 10¢ of 1847. Until 1984, when USPS removed from sale the 5¢ Washington stamp of the Prominent Americans series (Scott 1283B), he had never been absent from at least one definitive stamp in current use.

The Design

Although the Executive Branch stamp was the third of the Branches of Government series to be issued, it was designed first and its design was the prototype for the entire series. Like the others, it featured a piece of carved artwork against a solid black background, framed at top and bottom by stripes of red and beige.

As mentioned earlier (see 25¢ House of Representatives Bicentennial), the idea of a series for the Branches of Government arose from the Citizens' Stamp Advisory Committee's discussions of a stamp to mark the anniversary of Washington's inauguration. In the early stages, CSAC looked at a pair of sketches, one using the Jean Houdon bust of Washington — a frequently used image for stamps — and the other the presidential seal.

"The committee decided it preferred the bust, and thought it might work if it was engraved in a couple of colors, but the members weren't wildly enthusiastic about it," said project manager Brockert.

The presidential seal and the Houdon bust of Washington were subjects proposed during the early planning of the Inauguration Bicentennial stamp.

Some time earlier, while working on the New York Statehood stamp, Brockert had done some research on New York's Federal Hall. Now he showed designer Howard Koslow a photocopy of a brochure from the Federal Hall National Memorial that depicted John Quincy Adams Ward's bronze statue of Washington, which stands on the approximate spot of the first inauguration. They agreed the statue, erected in 1883, was appropriate as a subject for the stamp.

Koslow used the head and shoulders of the Ward statue in the design. To make it consistent with the House and Senate stamps, he converted the dark surfaces of the sculpture into light ones. "He basically turned bronze into marble," Brockert said.

One important detail to be settled was the wording on the stamp. CSAC looked at essays bearing the words "Washington's Inauguration" and "White House" before it settled on "Executive Branch."

" 'White House' was totally inconsistent with the rest of the series," Brockert said. " 'Washington's Inauguration' was considered originally because the stamp had been announced that way, but then it became obvious that it was more than that, that it was actually for the establishment of the Executive Branch, consistent with the other branches. It was clear from the portrait who it was; we didn't really need to say it was Washington."

First-Day Facts

Postmaster General Anthony M. Frank dedicated the stamp at Mount Vernon and distributed the souvenir albums. John Sununu, White House chief of staff, was on hand to accept President Bush's album as well as his own.

Former Chief Justice Warren Burger, chairman of the Commission on the Bicentennial of the United States Constitution, was the featured speaker.

Following the first-day ceremony, the re-enactment of George Washington's 1789 ride to New York for his inauguration began. The trip got off to a bumpy start. Shortly after "Washington" had bid good-bye to his wife "Martha," the antique horse-drawn carriage in which he was riding struck a fence post, which knocked off the tongue, or pole, connecting the four horses with their passengers. A Ford van took the company the first nine miles of their journey, until they were met by a replacement carriage.

The events at Mount Vernon were open to the public, but collectors and others were required to pay the $5 admission fee to get in if they did not receive an invitation.

As part of the re-enactment of Washington's trip, USPS provided a pictorial cancel for 18 cities along the route. The cancel bore a profile portrait of Washington, a facsimile signature and the words "First Inaugural Journey Station." It was used in each city on the appropriate date between April 16 and April 23. In New York, it was used on the latter date and again on April 30, the inauguration anniversary.

The American Bank Note Company announced plans to produce the company's first-ever first-day covers for the Executive Branch stamp, using archival engravings of Federal Hall and Washington taking the oath. ABNC later canceled its plans, explaining that it had received too few advance orders.

The bronze statue of George Washington at Federal Hall on which the Executive Branch design was based.

25¢ SOUTH DAKOTA STATEHOOD CENTENNIAL

Date of Issue: May 3, 1989

Catalog Numbers: Scott 2416   Minkus CM1349   USPS 4461

Colors: red, yellow, blue, black

First-Day Cancel: Pierre, South Dakota (State Capitol)

FDCs Canceled: 348,370

Format: Panes of 50, horizontal, 5 across, 10 down. Gravure printing cylinders of 200 subjects (10 across, 20 around) manufactured by Roto Cylinder, Palmyra, New Jersey.

Perf: 10.9 (L perforator)

Selvage Markings: ©United States Postal Service 1989, Use Correct ZIP Code®

Designer: Marian Henjum of Sioux Falls, South Dakota

Art Director and Project Manager: Jack Williams (USPS)

Typographer: Bradbury Thompson (CSAC)

Modeler: Richard Sennett (Sennett Enterprises) for American Bank Note Company.

Printing: Stamps printed and sheeted out by American Bank Note Company on a leased Champlain gravure press (J.W. Fergusson and Sons, Richmond, Virginia) under the supervision of Sennett Enterprises (Fairfax, Virginia). Perforated, processed and shipped by ABNC (Chicago, Illinois).

Quantity Ordered: 164,680,000
Quantity Distributed: 164,680,000

Cylinder Number Detail: One group of 4 cylinder numbers preceded by the letter "A" alongside corner stamps

Cylinder Number Combination: A1111

Tagging: block over vignette

Printing Base Impressions: A1111 (952,111)

A sod house and its occupants were the design subject of this 4¢ 1962 stamp marking the centennial of the Homestead Act.

The Stamp

The last of the four 1989 state centennial stamps honored South Dakota and was issued May 3. Its design featured a sod house, or "soddie," a type of residence that housed thousands of prairie settlers in the 19th and early 20th centuries.

The catalyst for the populating of the Dakota Territory was the Homestead Act of 1862, which gave to every man or woman 160 acres (a quarter section) of public domain after five years of continuous residence for the price of the filing fee — $18 in parts of Dakota. Railroads reached Yankton, the territorial capital, in 1872, giving homesteaders ready access to the territory.

The soddie was often the homesteader's only option if he wanted a roof over his family's head. Typically, a man built a soddie by cutting long strips of three-inch deep sod, which the prairie grasses held together as he stripped and furrowed the soil. Then, with a spade, he cut the strips into three-foot lengths. The entire family worked together in stacking the sod like bricks into four walls with openings for a door and a window that would be put in later.

Poles made of willow from the nearest creek bottom were used to support the roof. By criss-crossing enough poles, the settler got the support needed for the roof sod with only a slight sag in the middle. Typically, two layers of sod were placed on the roof, the lower one with the grassy side down to prevent dirt from dropping into the interior, the outer one with the grassy side up.

The completed house was windproof, fireproof and sturdy, but it wouldn't keep out water during the rainy season. As historian John R. Milton puts it, this was one of the paradoxes of "sodbusting" — the

South Dakota's most famous landmark, Mount Rushmore, first appeared on this 3¢ stamp of 1952.

man "had to pray for rain for his crops while his wife felt like praying for a dry house. They could not have both."

South Dakota's best-known tourist attraction is Mount Rushmore, where sculptor Gutzon Borglum carved the massive heads of Washington, Jefferson, Theodore Roosevelt and Lincoln. The mountain has been pictured on two stamps: a 3¢ commemorative in 1952 marking the 25th anniversary of the creation of the Mount Rushmore National Memorial (Scott 1011) and a 26¢ airmail stamp of 1974 (Scott C88). It also was shown on the back of a 6¢ Tourism Year of the Americas postal card in 1972 (Scott UX61).

The Oglala Sioux chief Crazy Horse was portrayed on a 13¢ Great Americans definitive of 1982 (Scott 1855). A colossal equestrian statue of Crazy Horse, begun by the late sculptor Korczak Ziolkowski, is being carved from the granite of Thunderhead Mountain in South Dakota's Black Hills, only a few miles from Mount Rushmore.

The state bird, the ring-necked pheasant, was featured on a 25¢ booklet stamp in 1988. The stamp had its first-day sale in Rapid City (Scott 2283).

In this version, Marian Henjum added a child at the committee's request. The committee decided the proportions were wrong and asked her to take the child out again, make the woman and building larger and the pasqueflower less dominant.

The Design

In 1986 South Dakota's Centennial Commission, like North Dakota's, sponsored a stamp design competition, doing so on its own without USPS sanction. The commission selected six top entries and sent them off to Washington. The Citizens' Stamp Advisory Committee found none that it could use, but noted that some of the artists had depicted sod houses, and decided that a soddie would be an appropriate design element.

The Art Department at the University of South Dakota gave the names of two South Dakota artists to Jack Williams, the stamp's art director and project manager. The two were given pictures of sod houses obtained from the South Dakota Historical Society and asked to submit concept sketches.

Of the two sets of submissions, CSAC preferred the work of Marian Henjum of Sioux Falls. Working with colored pencils, she sketched a pitched-roof soddie with a golden-haired pioneer woman standing amid windblown prairie grass in front. At Williams' suggestion, Henjum added two large pink and lavender pasqueflowers at the lower left

A second artist prepared this design showing a peaked-roof "soddie." The artist said the two trees standing alone on the horizon symbolized pioneer perseverance.

to provide extra color. The pasqueflower ("pasque" is old French for Easter) is South Dakota's state flower.

"The committee felt something should be added. A child and a basket of clothes were mentioned," Williams recalled. "Someone said, 'Oh, no! Not laundry on the line! Not mother's-role-is-doing-the-wash!' So they settled on a little golden-haired prairie girl at the mother's side.

"But when they saw it they decided the figures were too small; they would just flat disappear in stamp size. So they said, 'Take the child out again.'"

A sod house had been postally depicted once before, on a 4¢ 1962 stamp commemorating the 100th anniversary of the Homestead Act. Designed by Charles Chickering of the Bureau of Engraving and Printing, it depicted a pioneer husband and wife, the woman standing in the open doorway, the man spading in the garden.

At an early stage, CSAC considered trying to adapt a painting by Harvey Dunn, a well-known South Dakota commercial illustrator. In 1985, USPS had used a Dunn work on its 22¢ stamp honoring World War I veterans. But after studying slides of more than a dozen Dunn paintings of prairie life, the subcommittee's printing experts said the art, with its many fine strokes, wouldn't work well when printed by gravure in stamp size.

This alternative design by the second artist showed a woman and child in front of a flat-roofed "soddie," with cottonwood trees in the river bottom in the distance.

First-Day Facts

The first-day ceremony was held on the steps of the state capitol in Pierre, where Governor George S. Mickelson, the main speaker, and Michael J. Shinay, executive assistant to the postmaster general, who dedicated the stamp, arrived in a horse-drawn carriage. Lieutenant Governor Walter Dale Miller gave the welcome.

South Dakota is described as a "relatively youthful state" on the cachet of this first-day cover.

At the ceremony's conclusion, Governor Mickelson and Shinay presented South Dakota stamps to a horseman acting as a Pony Express rider. The rider took them to the Pierre Airport, where they were transferred to a Waco biplane and flown to Elk Point, near the starting location for the Eastern Division of the Centennial Wagon Train, one of the features of the centennial celebration.

The stamps and a pictorial cancellation were available at post offices during scheduled stop points along two Wagon Train routes covering 2,600 miles within South Dakota. The Eastern Division began May 10 and the Western Division left Philip June 5.

25¢ HENRY LOUIS ("LOU") GEHRIG
AMERICAN SPORTS SERIES

Date of Issue: June 10, 1989

Catalog Numbers: Scott 2417   Minkus CM1350   USPS 4462

Colors: yellow, magenta, cyan, black, line green, line black

First-Day Cancel: Cooperstown, New York (National Baseball Hall of Fame and Museum)

FDCs Canceled: 694,227

Format: Panes of 50, vertical, 10 across, 5 down. Gravure printing cylinders of 200 subjects (10 across, 20 around) manufactured by Roto Cylinder, Palmyra, New Jersey.

Perf: 10.9 by 10.8 (L perforator)

Selvage Markings: ©United States Postal Service 1989, Use Correct ZIP Code®

Designer: Bart Forbes of Dallas, Texas

Art Director and Project Manager: Jack Williams (USPS)

Typographer: Bradbury Thompson (CSAC)

Modeler: Richard Sennett (Sennett Enterprises) for American Bank Note Company.

Printing: Stamps printed and sheeted out by American Bank Note Company on a leased Champlain gravure press (J.W. Fergusson and Sons, Richmond, Virginia) under the supervision of Sennett Enterprises (Fairfax, Virginia). Perforated, processed and shipped by ABNC (Chicago, Illinois).

Quantity Ordered: 262,755,000
Quantity Distributed: 262,755,000

Cylinder Number Detail: One group of 6 cylinder numbers preceded by the letter "A" over/under corner stamps

Cylinder Number Combination: A111111

Tagging: block over vignette

Printing Base Impressions: A111111 (1,600,288)

The Stamp

Lou Gehrig, baseball's "Iron Horse" whose record for consecutive major league games played (2,130) endures after half a century, was honored June 10, 1989, with a 25¢ stamp in the Sports series.

The stamp was issued at Cooperstown, New York, as part of ceremonies marking the 50th anniversary of the dedication of the National Baseball Hall of Fame and Museum in that city.

Gehrig played first base for the great New York Yankees teams of the 1920s and 1930s. He and Babe Ruth — who preceded him in the Yankee batting order (and also preceded him into the Sports series of stamps in 1983) — confronted enemy pitchers with a frightening one-two punch. His lifetime batting average was .340. He drove in 100 or more runs 13 seasons in a row and bettered 150 RBI seven times, setting the American League mark of 184 in 1931. The following year, he became the first 20th-century player to hit four consecutive home runs in one game. He holds the major league record for grand-slam homers at 23.

His record of consecutive games played is by far his most impressive, though. After more than a century of pro baseball, the runner-up — Everett Scott of the Boston Red Sox, with 1,307 — is some five years behind Gehrig. A potential challenger to the record was in sight at the end of the 1989 season, however. The Baltimore Orioles' Cal Ripkin Jr. had moved to third on the all-time list, with 1,250, and if both he and the game of baseball were to stay healthy, he could break Gehrig's mark in the 1995 season.

Unlike Ruth, Gehrig never performed for any other big league team save the Yankees. They signed him as a hard-hitting southpaw pitcher out of Columbia University in 1923, and he saw action intermittently, pinch-hitting and learning to play first base.

Lou Gehrig's great teammate Babe Ruth, who preceded him in the New York Yankees' batting order, also preceded him onto a stamp in the Sports series (Scott 2046).

That changed on June 2, 1925, when the Yanks' regular first baseman, Wally Pipp, decided to take the day off — and unwittingly earned a place in the future treasury of baseball trivia. Young Gehrig played in Pipp's place that day, and the next, and the next — until 14 years had gone by. Pipp never again started at first for the Yankees, and after a while it seemed that no one else but Gehrig ever would.

It took a tragic turn of events to finally remove him from the lineup. He contracted an illness that the Mayo Clinic ultimately diagnosed as amyotrophic lateral sclerosis — a progressive, incurable degeneration of the nervous system. On July 4, 1939, "Lou Gehrig Appreciation Day" was held at Yankee Stadium, and the Yankee organization, the fans, present and former teammates and opponents turned out to honor the stricken star. That was when Gehrig delivered, with the nation listening by radio, the graceful valedictory that began: "Fans, for the past two weeks you have been reading about a bad break I got. Yet today I consider myself the luckiest man on the face of the earth. ...."

Later that year, the Baseball Writers Association of America moved to place Gehrig in the Baseball Hall of Fame immediately "to commemorate the year in which he achieved his record," and the Hall of Fame Committee accepted the nomination. He was the only player to enter the Hall in 1939.

On June 2, 1941, 16 years to the day after he entered the Yankee lineup, Gehrig died at age 37. "It was his character," *The New York Times* declared in an editorial, "his patient steadiness, his keeping himself in condition for his task, that made him a hero of boyhood." The affliction that took his life is still without a cure, and is universally known as "Lou Gehrig's disease."

In recognition of the 50th anniversary of his retirement, Major League Baseball and the ALS (Amyotrophic Lateral Sclerosis) Association joined forces to dedicate the 1989 season as a tribute to Lou Gehrig. The campaign was designed to raise awareness and funds to help conquer the disease, which will take the lives of an estimated 300,000 Americans who are apparently well today.

Major League Baseball also recognized June as Lou Gehrig Month, with ceremonies and tributes held across the country. On July 4, 1989, the 50th anniversary of Gehrig's farewell, a commemorative ceremony was held in Yankee Stadium before the home team's game with the Detroit Tigers. As part of the event, a videotaped message from President George Bush was shown on the stadium message board.

Calling Gehrig one of his "childhood heroes," the president stressed the need to do more to combat ALS. "So today let's remember the man Connie Mack called the crown prince," Mr. Bush said, "as we move toward the day when Lou Gehrig's name stands only for courage, simple elegance and one of the greatest figures baseball will ever know."

This photograph of Gehrig breaking from the plate after hitting the ball was made at Cleveland's Municipal Stadium in 1939, near the end of the "Iron Horse's" career, by Cleveland Press photographer Herman Seid.

By USPS count, the Gehrig commemorative was the 74th sports-related stamp, and the sixth to recognize baseball. Besides Babe Ruth, the other stars of the game to appear on U.S. stamps have been Brooklyn Dodger Jackie Robinson, in 1982, and Pittsburgh Pirate Roberto Clemente, in 1984.

On June 12, 1939 — the same day Gehrig entered the Mayo Clinic — a 3¢ stamp (Scott 855) was issued to commemorate the centennial of the game, which according to legend was invented in Cooperstown by Abner Doubleday. The first-day ceremony was held in conjunction with the dedication of the National Baseball Hall of Fame and Museum. In 1969, a 6¢ stamp (Scott 1381) marked the centennial of professional baseball.

The Gehrig stamp created copyright problems for cachetmakers similar to those they encountered with the Girl Scouts of America commemorative of 1987 and the Olympic Games stamps of 1988. The problem was particularly acute for small-volume operators, who reportedly had to pay $45 in royalties for up to 200 covers, or about 22¢ each.

The royalties were required of anyone depicting or naming Gehrig on a cachet or other commercial item by the Curtis Management

Group of Indianapolis, which managed the copyright for the Gehrig estate. There were no surviving relatives, and all royalties went to the Columbia Presbyterian Hospital for medical research.

In an editorial, *Linn's Stamp News* called on USPS to block any such deals in the future. "The USPS should not pay licensing fees, even token fees, to the owners of images that appear on our stamps," *Linn's* said. "The publicity generated by a stamp is more than adequate payment. Much more. So much more, in fact, that USPS can insist, as a precondition of honoring anyone on a stamp, that cachetmakers be able to use the subject's image on their envelopes. Without this right, there should be no stamp."

Frank Thomas, acting manager of USPS' Stamp Support Branch, explained the USPS position in a written statement.

"There is no question that the trend of protecting the rights of publicity for individuals, especially celebrities, is swiftly expanding," he wrote. "Many athletes, entertainers and retired politicians, to name a few, have retained agents to protect them from non-remunerative commercial exploitation in the marketplace. Simply, people, and/or their heirs and estates, are seeking payment for commercial use of their names and likenesses. In our society, this is an acceptable and appropriate marketing practice. ...

"Consequently, it is becoming more frequent that the U.S. Postal Service must negotiate with heirs or an estate for the right to use a person's likeness on a postage stamp. However, in negotiations we attempt to keep in mind the interests of philatelic product vendors.

"First, we ask for non-exclusive and non-discriminating licenses to protect the interests of all manufacturers. Also, we ask agents to waive up-front financial commitments related to future royalties. As many vendors know, such non-refundable commitments, usually in the form of guarantees and/or advances, are largely a matter of guesswork regarding projected sales volumes.

"It is important to remember that with licensing on the rise, negotiating becomes a way of life. Refusing to negotiate merely limits the choice of possible subjects, leading to lower standards of selection.

"Traditionally, it has been Postal Service policy to memorialize on stamps only those people who are leading contributors or innovators.

"More and more, we anticipate that these are exactly the type of individuals for whom it may be necessary to negotiate with the heirs

The first U.S. stamp with a baseball theme was this 1939 commemorative (Scott 855) marking the centennial of the game.

Bart Forbes' poster of Lou Gehrig was the second in a series of stamp-related posters produced by USPS. The first was the Classic Cars poster of 1988.

and/or estates, or their agents, for the rights of publicity. We do not believe that lowering the caliber of stamp subjects by refusing to do so would be in the best interests of the Postal Service or philately."

As a companion piece to the Gehrig stamp, USPS commissioned a commemorative poster by the stamp's designer, watercolor artist Bart Forbes of Dallas. It depicted Gehrig standing, leaning on his bat, in front of a bank of stadium seats crowded with fans. Forbes based his painting on a photograph he had clipped from a baseball magazine showing Gehrig with Babe Ruth, taken during a trip to another team's stadium. He eliminated the Babe, painted a new face on Gehrig (the face on the original picture was in heavy shadow) and changed the uniform from the gray flannels used on the road to the famous "Yankee pinstripes" that the team wore at home.

USPS had issued an earlier stamp-related poster in 1988 in connection with the 25¢ Classic Cars booklet. The Gehrig poster, at $10, quickly sold out. USPS also offered, for $7.95, a baseball scrapbook and stamp album called *Legends*, accompanied by copies of the Gehrig, Babe Ruth, Roberto Clemente and Jackie Robinson stamps.

The Design

Bart Forbes was in Washington working with USPS officials on his designs for the 1988 Olympic Games stamps when he mentioned the fact that he was a baseball fan. Jack Williams, program manager for philatelic design, asked him if he'd like to have a try at the Gehrig stamp, and Forbes eagerly accepted the offer.

"It seemed like a natural until I got into it and found that Lou Gehrig was really hard to do," Forbes said. "And I couldn't figure why I wasn't getting a good likeness, or something I was happy with, until I realized that it was because he was such a handsome guy.

"Babe Ruth is very easy, with the round face. Ty Cobb had beady eyes. Most guys, most ballplayers or athletes, have some distinguishing feature that is fairly easy to capture. But Gehrig had almost perfect features. He had the face of a shirt model — you know, the Arrow Shirt man — and he kept just looking like a generic good-looking guy. So it took a while to get what I wanted."

Forbes sought a profile likeness of Gehrig as a model and finally found the one he liked at a baseball card collectors' convention in Dallas. It was a photograph owned by Mike Aronstein of New York, and it was on display at a dealer's booth among several photos of old-time ballplayers. "It was a really nice shot of Gehrig that I had never seen before, and the head angle on it was just right," Forbes said.

Bart Forbes based his stamp portrait of Lou Gehrig on this photograph he found at a baseball card collectors' convention in Dallas.

These are two unused essays prepared by Bart Forbes for the Lou Gehrig stamp.

Forbes offered a selection of sketches, and the Citizens' Stamp Advisory Committee chose a vertical, with the profile portrait dominating. The artist emphasized the Yankee pinstripes of Gehrig's uniform by making them stylized parallel lines. In the foreground he painted a smaller image of Gehrig at the plate, adapting it from a photograph by Herman Seid of *The Cleveland Press* that Forbes picked from a package of reference pictures from the Baseball Hall of Fame and Museum. The picture had been made in Cleveland's Municipal Stadium in 1939, the final year of Gehrig's career.

The American Bank Note Company used electronic modification to give a uniform smoothness to Forbes' green watercolor background. The artist chose green, he explained, as being "as close to a baseball color as I could get." It's identified with baseball fields and is also the color of many outfield fences, "or," he added, "at least it was back when I was growing up." That was in suburban Cincinnati, and Forbes is still a Reds fan.

The artist's previous postal design credits include the Abigail Adams stamp of 1985, the 1988 Winter and Summer Olympics stamps, and the 1988-89 America the Beautiful postal card series. He celebrated his 50th birthday July 3, 1989, which means he was born the day before Lou Gehrig's emotion-filled retirement ceremony in Yankee Stadium. "It was an interesting coincidence," he said, "that all of us were celebrating 50th anniversaries at once — the Baseball Hall of Fame, Lou Gehrig Day at the Stadium, and me."

First-Day Facts

Postmaster General Anthony M. Frank, keeping to a busy 1989 schedule of dedicating new stamps, did the honors for the Gehrig stamp at Cooperstown June 10. Also speaking were A. Bartlett Giamatti, commissioner of major league baseball, and Edward W. Stack, president of the National Baseball Hall of Fame and Museum Inc. Giamatti died of a heart attack less than three months later.

USPS produced no official program for the ceremony. However, the Utica sectional center of USPS sponsored an item called the "Iron Horse souvenir," a double folder that included the stamp with a first-day cancellation, which it sold for $5 at Cooperstown June 10. The Albany division of USPS produced a 24-page booklet entitled "Baseball on United States Stamps," bearing on the inside two Gehrig stamps, one with a first-day cancellation, the other with a Baseball Hall of Fame commemorative cancel.

25¢ ERNEST HEMINGWAY
LITERARY ARTS SERIES

Date of Issue:	July 17, 1989
Catalog Numbers:	Scott 2418 Minkus CM1351 USPS 4467
Colors:	yellow, red, blue, black, line black
First-Day Cancel:	Key West, Florida (Hemingway home)
FDCs Canceled:	345,436
Format:	Panes of 50, vertical, 10 across, 5 down. Gravure printing cylinders of 200 subjects (10 across, 20 around) manufactured by Roto Cylinder, Palmyra, New Jersey.
Perf:	10.9 (L perforator)
Selvage Markings:	©United States Postal Service 1989, Use Correct ZIP Code®
Designer:	M. Gregory Rudd of Trumbull, Connecticut
Art Director and Project Manager:	Jack Williams (USPS)
Typographer:	Bradbury Thompson (CSAC)
Modeler:	Richard Sennett (Sennett Enterprises) for American Bank Note Company.
Printing:	Stamps printed and sheeted out by American Bank Note Company on a leased Champlain gravure press (J.W. Fergusson and Sons, Richmond, Virginia) under the supervision of Sennett Enterprises (Fairfax, Virginia). Perforated, processed and shipped by ABNC (Chicago, Illinois).
Quantity Ordered: 191,755,000 **Quantity Distributed:** 191,755,000	
Cylinder Number Detail:	One group of 5 cylinder numbers preceded by the letter "A" over/under corner stamps

Cylinder Number Combination: A11111

Tagging: block over vignette

Printing Base Impressions: A11111 (1,078,457)

The Stamp

Ernest Hemingway, one of the most influential American writers of the 20th century, was honored July 17 with a 25¢ stamp in the Literary Arts series. The site of the first-day ceremony was Key West, Florida, where Hemingway had a home. A second ceremony was held July 21, the 90th anniversary of the author's birth, in his city of birth, Oak Park, Illinois.

With the issuance of the Hemingway stamp, all the American recipients of the Nobel Prize for literature who were eligible for U.S. postal recognition had received it. T.S. Eliot, William Faulkner and John Steinbeck all preceded Hemingway on Literary Arts commemoratives, Eugene O'Neill was shown on a Prominent Americans definitive, and Sinclair Lewis and Pearl Buck were honored in the Great Americans series.

The Hemingway stamp wasn't included in the Postal Service's preliminary listing of 1989 stamps and stationery. It was announced November 10, 1988, and information on date and place of issue was released three months later.

Hemingway was more than a great writer; he was an original personality. From his earliest expatriate days, when he knew James Joyce and Gertrude Stein in post-World War I Paris, he enjoyed being a celebrity among celebrities. While serving with the Italian infantry in the war, he had been badly wounded, and some believe the experience gave him a fear of his own fear and a lifelong need to assert his own manhood by associating with bullfighters and boxers, hunting big game and serving as a war correspondent in World War II.

Danger became a theme of his fiction as well, and his heroes faced it with bravery — he called it "grace under pressure" — and fatalism. "His best stories," wrote one critic, "catch people at times of great stress, balancing courage against cowardice or decency against loutishness. He wrote with genius of decisive moments."

He developed a prose style that was universally recognizable and was paid the honor of frequent parody. "He performed a major operation on the English sentence," as *Time* observed. "He cut out the adjectives and prompting words that tell a reader how to feel and replaced them with spare, brisk monosyllables that he called the 'ugly short infantry of the mind.'... Though he relied on the common speech of the commonest men — race-track touts, prizefighters, soldiers — Hemingway wrote brilliant dialogue that was highly stylized, just as an X-ray is a highly stylized picture of the body. It revealed more than it ever laconically said."

His best-known works include the novels *The Sun Also Rises* (1926), *A Farewell to Arms* (1929) and *For Whom The Bell Tolls* (1940); the short story *The Snows of Kilimanjaro;* the brief novel *The Old Man and the Sea* (1952), which won the Pulitzer Prize, and the non-fiction book about bullfighting, *Death in the Afternoon* (1932). He received his Nobel Prize in 1954 for lifetime achievement in literature. It was said that a person could learn of World War I, the postwar Lost Generation, the mystique of the bullring, the Spanish Civil War or big-game hunting in Africa without knowing Hemingway — but, once having read him, one could never see these subjects again without some angle or color of his own vision.

In July 1961, burdened by illness and depression and loss of confidence in his talent, Hemingway shot himself to death at the Idaho home he shared with his second wife, Mary. His father, similarly ill, had committed suicide in the same way in 1928.

The Karsh portrait on which Gregory Rudd based his stamp design.

In this design, Artist Gregory Rudd paired the Hemingway portrait with a bullfighting scene, evocative of the author's Death in the Afternoon.

The Design

In December 1987 the Citizens' Stamp Advisory Committee chose M. Gregory Rudd, a 36-year-old illustrator from Trumbull, Connecticut, to design the Hemingway stamp. (It was Rudd's first stamp assignment, but while he was at work on it in 1988, he got a second one on a rush basis when Jack Williams of USPS asked him to put Hemingway aside and produce a painting of golfer Francis Ouimet that could be used on an upcoming Sports Series commemorative.)

USPS officials considered several different Hemingway portraits before settling on one made in 1957 by the well-known photographer Yousuf Karsh of Ottawa, showing the bearded writer in a turtleneck sweater. Karsh had described the photo session this way:

"I expected to meet in the author a composite of the heroes of his novels. Instead, in 1957, at his home near Havana, I found a man of peculiar gentleness, the shyest man I ever photographed — a man cruely battered by life, but seemingly invincible. He was still suffering from the effects of a plane accident on his fourth safari in Africa.

"I had gone the evening before to La Floridita, Hemingway's favorite bar, to do my 'homework' and sample his favorite concoction, the daiquiri. But one can be overprepared! When, at nine the next morning, Hemingway called from the kitchen, 'What will you have to drink?' my reply was, I thought, letter-perfect: 'Daiquiri, sir.' 'Good God, Karsh,' Hemingway remonstrated, 'at *this* hour of the day!' "

Artist Rudd did some research and prepared several sketches that illustrated themes from the author's life and career. One, depicting a bullfighter, was turned down by CSAC because of concern that it would offend animal lovers. As Jack Williams observed, "Bullfighting is not exactly a revered American sport."

The cover for the first-day ceremony program for the Hemingway stamp was adapted from an unused stamp essay by Gregory Rudd showing Hemingway's portrait and a view of the author fishing for marlin.

Rudd created two other essays using the theme of deep-sea fishing. One, adapted from a magazine photo, showed Hemingway, his back to the viewer, seated at the stern of a fishing boat with a marlin on his line. For the accompanying portrait, Rudd relied on another magazine photo, of the writer in a fishing cap with his head slightly turned. He used the Karsh photo for reference in painting the eyes, which were shaded by the bill of the cap.

However, CSAC members felt that if a fisherman was to be depicted it should be "The Old Man and the Sea" — a poor Cuban alone in a small boat — rather than the author himself. Besides, the shadow of the cap bill would have obscured much of the face on the finished stamp. So the design was turned down for use on the stamp. (It didn't go to waste, however; USPS adapted it for use on the cover of its first-day ceremony program.)

Rudd then prepared another "Old Man and the Sea" color rough, based on pictures of Caribbean fishing boats from his local library. This also proved unsatisfactory, however. Committee members felt that the man standing in the vessel looked awkward, and the proportions of the sketch seemed wrong.

The committee was dissatisfied with this sketch based on Hemingway's **The Old Man and the Sea.**

Ultimately, Rudd and the committee turned to another Hemingway theme: hunting in Africa. Rudd prepared a vertical design showing a plain with running antelopes behind the portrait. The antelopes were gazelles, Rudd said, copied from a book on African wildlife. He made the sky and the plain a golden orange to suggest the heat of the tropics, then incorporated cooler tones in the portrait for contrast.

In his original painting, Rudd placed snow-capped Mount Kilimanjaro in the distance and two bull water buffalo in the foreground in front of the portrait. "The bulls, to me, represented Hemingway's strength and his courage and this power that he kind of went through life with," Rudd said. "But the committee decided, I think wisely, that there was just a little bit too much information there. They wanted to bring him to the foreground. So they had me paint out the mountain and paint out the bulls, and emphasize him as an individual."

At one point in the development of the final art for the stamp, the gazelles were higher in the picture, but the artist lowered them after "someone said that it might look as if they were running in one ear and out the other."

In this earlier version of the approved design, the portrait is smaller, two water buffalo stare out of the foreground and the snow-capped peak of Kilimanjaro rises in the distance.

Rudd paints on an illustration board onto which he has first brushed a coating of gesso. "It's a real good surface," he said. "It's not too rough, and the paint sits on the surface long enough that it's not drying too quickly, and gives me time to manipulate it at will." He draws his subject with pencil, fixes the graphite markings with a spray, then lays down washes of oil. "I start with a deep umber," he said. "I like the flesh tones that you can build up on umber. It's an old, old technique. Then I begin to build up in kind of a dry-brush fashion layer upon layer upon layer. It's fairly quick, and it gives you a realistic deep flesh tone that's believeable."

Rudd made an instantaneous choice of careers, he said, when he was about 6 years old and chanced to come upon a Norman Rockwell magazine cover. "I knew I was going to be an artist," he recalled. He excelled in art in school, developed his skills in college courses and workshops, and since 1978 has been a free-lance illustrator in the highly competitive New York market.

In preparing the lettering for the stamp design, typographer Bradbury Thompson provided only the last name of the subject, a practice USPS has used with a handful of other individuals over the years. "The committee felt that Hemingway's name was so well known that the 'Ernest' was unnecessary," Jack Williams said. "Using it alone gave it more typographical prominence. Who could mistake that face and that last name together?"

First-Day Facts

Key West, Florida, site of the July 17 first-day ceremony, is the southernmost city in the continental United States. Senior Assistant Postmaster General David H. Charters dedicated the stamp on the veranda of Hemingway's home at 907 Whitehead Street, now a museum. Speakers included Lorian Hemingway, the author's granddaughter; Dr. James Nagel, professor of English at Northeastern University, and Michael Whalton, chairman of the Hemingway Days Festival. Honored guests included two other granddaughters, Ann and Edwina Hemingway.

At the follow-up ceremony in Oak Park, marking Hemingway's 90th birthday anniversary, the presentation of the stamp was made by Jerry K. Lee Sr., regional postmaster general. Speakers included the author's son, Patrick Hemingway; A.E. Hotchner, author of the book *Papa Hemingway,* and Scott Schwar, chairman of the Ernest Hemingway Foundation of Oak Park. Another son, Jack Hemingway, was scheduled to speak but was unable to attend. USPS made available a pictorial Hemingway Birthplace cancellation.

25¢ NORTH CAROLINA STATEHOOD BICENTENNIAL
CONSTITUTION BICENTENNIAL SERIES

Date of Issue: August 22, 1989

Catalog Numbers: Scott 2347   Minkus CM1353   USPS 4464

Colors: red, green, brown, gray, black

First-Day Cancel: Fayetteville, North Carolina (First Presbyterian Church)

FDCs Canceled: 392,953

Format: Panes of 50, vertical, 10 across, 5 down. Gravure printing cylinders of 200 subjects (10 across, 20 around) manufactured by Roto Cylinder, Palmyra, New Jersey.

Perf: 10.9 (L perforator)

Selvage Markings: ©United States Postal Service 1989, Use Correct ZIP Code®

Designer: Bob Timberlake of Lexington, North Carolina

Art Director and Project Manager: Jack Williams (USPS)

Typographer: Bradbury Thompson (CSAC)

Modeler: Richard Sennett (Sennett Enterprises) for American Bank Note Company.

Printing: Stamps printed and sheeted out by American Bank Note Company on a leased Champlain gravure press (J.W. Fergusson and Sons, Richmond, Virginia) under the supervision of Sennett Enterprises (Fairfax, Virginia). Perforated, processed and shipped by ABNC (Chicago, Illinois).

Quantity Ordered: 179,800,000
Quantity Distributed: 179,800,000

Cylinder Number Detail: One group of 5 cylinder numbers preceded by the letter "A" over/under corner stamps

Cylinder Number Combination: A11111

Tagging: block over vignette

Printing Base Impressions: A11111 (1,006,160)

The Stamp

On August 22, USPS issued a 25¢ commemorative stamp for the 200th anniversary of North Carolina's ratification of the Constitution.

The stamp was the 12th in a series launched in 1987 to salute the original 13 states on the bicentennial of their entry into the union, but an interval of nearly 13 months separated it from its immediate predecessor, the New York stamp, issued July 26, 1988. The gap was the result of North Carolina's long delay, 200 years earlier, in giving its approval to the charter of the new government.

The interval between stamps would have been even longer if the North Carolina commemorative had been issued on the exact anniversary date of ratification, as most of the previous stamps in the series had been. Instead, it was issued three months early, so as not to come out at the beginning of the Christmas mailing season, when USPS prefers not to schedule new stamps if it can avoid it.

Raleigh, the capital, was originally announced as the first-day site, but later at the request of Governor James G. Martin the location was changed to Fayetteville, where the ratification had taken place. This change made the stamp the first in the series to be dedicated in a city other than the state's capital.

North Carolina's delegation to the 1787 convention that created the Constitution was not one of the high-profile groups there. It had one member, Hugh Williamson, a doctor and experimental scientist from Edenton, whom historian Clinton Rossiter classifies among the best of the delegates, "a member of five committees and a thoughtful participant in key debates." Two others, lawyer and ex-soldier William R. Davie and the wealthy young Richard Dobbs Spaight, Rossiter rates as "useful." The other two were hardly heard from.

Nevertheless, the five men fully supported the finished Constitution, sending it to Governor Richard Caswell with these words:

"When you are pleased to lay this plan before the General Assembly, we entreat that you will do us the justice to assure that honorable body that no exertions have been wanting on our part to guard and promote the particular interest of North Carolina."

The Constitution ran into a host of antifederalists, however, at the ratifying convention that met in Hillsboro July 21, 1788. By this time nine other states had ratified, putting the Union in business. Virginia had also come in, and within a few days New York would enter as the 11th member. Unimpressed, the North Carolinians voted 184-84 on August 2 to take no action until a second federal convention should have considered the bill of rights, which they considered essential.

The practical meaning of the vote was that for the time being the state would rather be out of the Union than in it.

Davie, Spaight and James Iredell, later to be a United States Supreme Court justice, argued vainly for ratification. The opposition was led by English-educated Willie Jones, who voiced the widely held belief that the people's rights were in danger from the strong new central government.

North Carolina, as historian Carl Van Doren notes, "was a large state with a population widely dispersed, often in isolated communities. Most of its people were farmers or frontiersmen who had to depend on their own resources to live, and who consequently lived as individuals, self-sufficiently. They suspected their state government, which was for the most part in the hands of men living close to the Atlantic. All the more they suspected the proposed federal government, which seemed vast, remote and not likely to be attentive to the people's interests."

Willie Jones thought North Carolina should remain out of the Union for several years, until it could enter more nearly on its own terms. But once the new government was set up, and North Carolina found itself regarded (though not altogether treated) as a foreign state like any other, there was a change of opinion. A second convention met at Fayetteville November 19, 1789, and on November 21 ratified the Constitution by a vote of 194-77.

With North Carolina's entry, only Rhode Island among the 13 original colonies remained outside the United States. It would grudgingly agree to join the following year, 1790.

A contributing factor in bringing in both North Carolina and Rhode Island was the fact that a bill of rights was in the process of being added to the Constitution; James Madison and other federalists in the First Congress had kept their pledge to submit one to the states. As Clinton Rossiter put it, North Carolina and Rhode Island "found the Bill of Rights a commodious bridge over which to march back into the arms of the Republic."

North Carolina has been well-represented on stamps and postal cards of the United States.

The 400th anniversary of the Roanoke voyages under the sponsorship of Sir Walter Raleigh was marked with a 20¢ commemorative in 1984 (Scott 2093). These voyages were followed by establishment on Roanoke Island of an English colony that produced the first child born of English parents in America, Virginia Dare. Her 350th anniversary was commemorated by a 3¢ stamp in 1937 (Scott 796) that was designed from a sketch made by President Franklin D. Roosevelt. Virginia, her parents and the other settlers vanished without a trace, and are remembered in history as the Lost Colony.

The Carolina Charter of 1663, granting to eight Englishmen lands extending coast to coast roughly from Virginia to Florida, was noted on a 5¢ stamp in 1963 (Scott 1230). A 1980 postal card (Scott UX85) commemorated the Revolutionary War battle of Kings Mountain, fought along the North and South Carolina border, and an 18¢ stamp in the 1975 Contributors to the Cause set (Scott 1562) honored Peter Francisco, who fought in the Battle of Guilford Court House near Greensboro. The first successful flight of a heavier-than-air machine, by the Wright brothers at Kitty Hawk in 1903, was celebrated by a 2¢ stamp in 1928 (Scott 649) and a 6¢ airmail stamp in 1952 (Scott C47). In addition, the Wrights and their flyer were shown on a 6¢ airmail of 1949 (Scott C45) and a pair of 31¢ airmails in 1978 (Scott C91-C 92).

One of the most significant events in human history took place in North Carolina: the 1903 flight at Kitty Hawk of the Wright brothers, shown here on this 1949 airmail stamp.

Great Smoky Mountains National Park, which straddles the North Carolina-Tennessee state line, was publicized with the 10¢ stamp of the 1934 National Parks series (Scott 749); the landmark shown, Mount Le Conte, is actually in Tennessee. The same stamp was reproduced on an imperforate souvenir sheet in 1937 to mark a convention in Asheville of the Society of Philatelic Americans. A later National Parks set, in 1972, included a se-tenant block of four 2¢ stamps showing Cape Hatteras National Seashore (Scott 1448-1451). Richard Morris Hunt's Biltmore House in Asheville was shown on an 18¢ American Architecture stamp of 1981 (Scott 1929).

Native North Carolinians to appear on stamps include two presidents, James K. Polk and Andrew Johnson; a president's wife, Dolley Madison, and Anna McNeill Whistler, the artist's mother.

The Design

The stamp's design followed the format established for the 13 original states series by Richard Sheaff, design coordinator for the Citizens' Stamp Advisory Committee. Vertically arranged, it presented a vignette appropriate to the state in a rectangular image area, with the date of ratification and name of the state underneath.

The vignette chosen for North Carolina was a twig from a dogwood, North Carolina's state flower, showing all or parts of nine white blossoms, all against a black background. Dogwood had previously been featured on the North Carolina stamp of the 1982 pane that displayed the state birds and flowers of all 50 states (Scott 1985).

The North Carolina stamp was the third in the series for the 13 original states to depict a botanical symbol. The state trees of Georgia

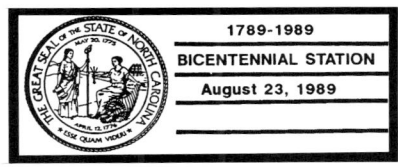

This pictorial cancellation was authorized by USPS for use in every city in North Carolina beginning August 23, 1989.

(live oak) and South Carolina (palmetto) had been shown on those states' stamps in 1988.

Bob Timberlake of Lexington, North Carolina, who had designed the South Carolina commemorative, performed the same honors for his home state. One of the South's best-known painters, Timberlake had also created the design for the 1980 Christmas contemporary stamp that featured toys in a window.

First-Day Facts

Governor Martin and Samuel Green Jr., Eastern regional postmaster general, were featured speakers at the first-day ceremony in Fayetteville's First Presbyterian Church.

USPS authorized a bicentennial pictorial cancellation for every city in North Carolina beginning August 23. On November 21, the actual ratification date, a pictorial Statehood Station cancellation was available in Raleigh, the state capital.

25¢ LETTER CARRIERS

Date of Issue: August 30, 1989

Catalog Numbers: Scott 2420   Minkus CM1354   USPS 4468

Colors: blue, yellow, magenta, cyan, black

First-Day Cancel: Milwaukee, Wisconsin (Exposition and Convention Center)

FDCs Canceled: 372,241

Format: Panes of 40, horizontal, 5 across, 8 down. Gravure printing cylinders of 160 subjects (10 across, 16 around) manufactured by Roto Cylinder, Palmyra, New Jersey.

Perf: 10.9 (L perforator)

Selvage Markings: ©United States Postal Service 1989, Use Correct ZIP Code®

Designer: Jack Davis of St. Simons Island, Georgia

Art Director and Project Manager: Jack Williams (USPS)

Typographer: Bradbury Thompson (CSAC)

Modeler: Richard Sennett (Sennett Enterprises) for American Bank Note Company.

Printing: Stamps printed and sheeted out by American Bank Note Company on a leased Champlain gravure press (J.W. Fergusson and Sons, Richmond, Virginia) under the supervision of Sennett Enterprises (Fairfax, Virginia). Perforated, processed and shipped by ABNC (Chicago, Illinois).

Quantity Ordered: 188,400,000
Quantity Distributed: 188,400,000

Cylinder Number Detail: One group of 5 cylinder numbers preceded by the letter "A" alongside corner stamps

Cylinder Number Combination: A11111

Tagging: block over vignette

Printing Base Impressions: A11111 (1,300,133)

The Stamp

From time to time the Postal Service has used postage stamps to mark significant anniversaries in its own history and to pay tribute to its employees. It did so again on August 30, 1989, with a stamp honoring letter carriers.

The place of issue was Milwaukee, Wisconsin, at the centennial celebration of the National Association of Letter Carriers (NALC). That the anniversary was considered worthy of commemoration wasn't surprising. NALC is one of the largest of the postal unions, and its goodwill is obviously a valuable asset to USPS management.

Home mail delivery is taken for granted today, but for nearly a century of the nation's existence, people had to collect their mail at post offices. It wasn't until the middle of the Civil War, after the secession of the South with its many unprofitable rural mail routes had enabled the Post Office to eliminate a chronic deficit, that Abraham Lincoln's postmaster general, Montgomery Blair, instituted free city delivery in 49 American cities. (See Montgomery Blair Aerogramme chapter.)

City delivery was launched July 1, 1863 (on the same day that the Battle of Gettysburg began). At the prodding of Congress, the Post Office gradually extended the service to smaller towns and in 1902 made the principle of "every man's mail to every man's door" universal by creating rural free delivery on a permanent basis.

For the carriers out on the streets and sidewalks of America in those days, work was demanding and low-paid. In 1889 mailmen were earning $600 a year at entrance, $800 for their second year and $1,000 a year thereafter. Thanks to laws sponsored by Representative Samuel Sullivan "Sunset" Cox, a New York Democrat whom letter carriers still revere in memory, they were granted 15 days paid vacation a year and — on paper — enjoyed the privilege of an eight-hour day. However, the law set no limits within which the eight hours had to be worked, and many carriers were forced to stay on the job as long as 18 hours, on a stop-and-go basis, to fulfill their daily obligation.

Half the letter-carrier force worked in small post offices and was unprotected by Civil Service. In these offices, postmasters often forced the carriers to falsify their timecards to meet the requirements of the eight-hour-day law. If they refused, they could be fired, and there was no appeal.

(Postal clerks, who had no congressional angel to fight for them, endured conditions that were even more Dickensian. They were paid less, averaging only $700 a year, and were given no vacations or days off. In 1889, 90 percent of the clerks worked 365 days a year at an average of 14 hours a day. The workrooms were filthy, dust from dirty mailbags filled the air, and tuberculosis was so prevalent that it was known in the service as "the clerk's sickness.")

But the labor movement had a foothold in the country and was growing. Letter carriers in many cities secretly joined the militant Knights of Labor, and some of them became leaders in its ranks. Then, in 1889, a Detroit mailman and Civil War veteran named William H. Wood and some of his friends devised a plan for organizing their co-workers. A call went out, and in Milwaukee, under the cover of the annual encampment of the Grand Army of the Republic, approximately 100 mailmen formed the NALC on August 30, 1889.

Postal management was shocked. In many cities reprisals were carried out against union members. In some, leaders of local branches were summarily fired; in others, known members were given the least desirable routes and often made to work their eight hours, on and off, over the entire 24 hours of every day. Nevertheless, membership in NALC grew swiftly and steadily.

The young union established its credentials with a major court victory in 1893. The Post Office's lawyers had declared that an eight-hour day really meant a 56-hour week and that if a carrier worked nine hours a day for six days, he still owed two hours on Sunday. After this interpretation was put into effect, the union sued the federal government for the unpaid overtime the carriers had been forced to work. The U.S. Supreme Court found for the union, and individual letter carriers were awarded a total of $3.5 million to settle the thousands of individual claims that had accumulated.

The centennial of free city delivery in 1963 was marked by a 5¢ commemorative stamp (Scott 1238) designed by popular illustrator Norman Rockwell. Other stamps that have depicted letter carriers include special delivery stamps issued from 1885 to 1944; three of the 12 parcel post stamps of 1912-1913; the 15¢ certified mail stamp of 1955, and three of the 10 8¢ "Postal People" stamps of 1973.

The Design

One magazine profile has called Jack Davis "the undisputed king of commercial caricature artists." Another article, noting the speed with which he works, termed him "the fastest draw in the East or West."

His speed, in particular, has made Davis popular with magazines, like *Time,* that deal in breaking news and sometimes need a custom-made cover in a hurry. "I work like a maniac," he told an interviewer. "If you want to make money, you've got to produce."

Until the Letter Carriers stamp, postage stamps were one of the few places Davis' distinctive drawings hadn't appeared. They could be found in books, advertisements and many other magazines, including *TV Guide,* which frequently used his covers, and *MAD,* where his funny faces and on-target celebrity likenesses had been turning up since the first issue in 1952. The memorable, crowded poster for the film *It's a Mad, Mad, Mad, Mad World* was also his.

At USPS' request, Davis, along with other artists, had submitted concept sketches for the 1988 joint-issue commemorative stamp hon-

One of several concept sketches prepared by Jack Davis for the 22¢ Australia Bicentennial stamp of 1988 but not used by the Postal Service.

oring Australia on its bicentennial. In the end, however, the Postal Service decided to use the cartoon eagle-and-koala design prepared by Australian Roland Harvey for his own country's stamp. Davis' first stamp assignment to actually bear fruit — the Letter Carriers commemorative — would come the following year, and stemmed directly from a different kind of job he had done for USPS.

Back in 1986, he had drawn a self-confident, outgoing mailman for a Postal Service promotional campaign. "Everyone on the committee thought it was a rather positive image," said Jack Williams, the stamp's art director and project manager. "So we decided to ask him to do two or three sketches for the Letter Carriers project."

CSAC specified that the stamp should show at least three letter carriers, and that one should be black. Varying seasonal attire was requested, to emphasize the official NALC motto: "Neither snow, not rain, nor heat, nor gloom of night stays these couriers from the swift completion of their appointed rounds." (That motto, a quotation from the Greek historian Herodotus describing the couriers of the ancient Persian empire, is chiseled on the stone facade of the main post office in New York City.)

Using his customary watercolor and India ink on illustration board, Davis sketched differing versions of a letter-carrying threesome. He made the black carrier a female in acknowledgment of the fact that "mailman" is an obsolete term and the 240,000-plus letter carriers now include more than 40,000 women. One of the two males was visibly older, as a nod to USPS' senior employees.

The committee chose a sketch showing the figures side by side, facing forward against a solid-color backdrop. The stamp had originally been planned as standard commemorative size, 50 to a pane, but after examining Davis' concepts the committee decided a semi-jumbo size, 40 to the pane, would allow a deeper image that would be appropriate to the subject.

Williams showed the sketches to Vincent Sombrotto, president of the National Association of Letter Carriers, to get his reaction.

"Vince liked the approaches," Williams said, "but he and I both agreed that in the one we wanted the older fellow looked a little bit smug, almost smirking. He had a kind of wiseacre look about him. We asked Jack Davis to change that in the final version, which he did, and

Jack Davis' drawing of a self-confident letter carrier used in a 1986 USPS promotional campaign led to his selection to design the 1989 commemorative stamp.

he's now more like the congenial, loving older letter carrier that you see so many good letters written about, making the rounds every day."

Davis was also asked to add touches of red wherever he could — on uniform patches, stamps, package wrappers — to offset the predominant blue and gray of the design. The uniform details, including the three different styles of headgear, were checked for accuracy with the appropriate USPS office, Williams said. "We got out actual manufacturers' manuals so we would be sure we were correct," he added.

The slogan "Letter Carriers: We Deliver!" was chosen to tie in with USPS' own "We Deliver" advertising campaign, launched earlier.

Like the Australia Bicentennial stamp before it, the cartoon-like Letter Carriers design stirred controversy. "I enjoy the artwork of Jack

These were two of Jack Davis' proposed approaches to the Letter Carriers stamp design. The mustached carrier in rain gear was later replaced by an older man wearing a fur cap.

Davis, but on a stamp? Are you kidding?" one *Linn's* reader wrote. "So it continues — United States postage stamps with designs that are fit for the pictures on cereal boxes," wrote another. "Ugh!" added a third. A Davis defender, however, labeled such critics "stodgy, ultra-conservative, no-imagination types" whose reaction was "wrong." And another offered a tongue-in-cheek concurrence:

"For once, I agree with Uncle Sam's choice of stamp designs 100 percent. Only an artist with a background in *MAD* magazine could really do justice to the U.S. Postal Service."

This was close to the finished design, but the Citizens' Stamp Advisory Committee didn't like what seemed to be a "smug" smile on the face of the older carrier.

First-Day Facts

Postmaster General Anthony M. Frank dedicated the stamp at a ceremony at the Mecca, the Milwaukee Exposition and Convention Center. NALC President Vincent Sombrotto presided, and Dennis L. Nott, Milwaukee postmaster, gave the welcoming remarks.

25¢ DRAFTING OF THE BILL OF RIGHTS
CONSTITUTION BICENTENNIAL SERIES

Date of Issue: September 25, 1989

Catalog Numbers: Scott 2421   Minkus CM1355   USPS 4465

Colors: red, blue, black (offset); black (intaglio)

First-Day Cancel: Philadelphia, Pennsylvania (Independence Hall)

FDCs Canceled: 900,384

Format: Panes of 50, vertical, 10 across, 5 down. Offset printing plates of 200 subjects (10 across, 20 around); intaglio printing sleeve of 400 subjects (10 across, 40 around).

Perf: 11.1 (Eureka off-line perforator)

Selvage Markings: ©United States Postal Service 1989, Use Correct ZIP Code®

Designer: Lou Nolan of McLean, Virginia

Art Director: Derry Noyes (CSAC)

Project Manager: Jack Williams (USPS)

Typographer: Julian Waters of Gaithersburg, Maryland

Engravers: Gary Slaght (BEP, lettering and eagle)
              Kenneth Wiram (BEP, stars and stripes)

Modeler: Peter Cocci (BEP)

Printing: 6-color offset, 3-color intaglio D press (902)

Quantity Ordered: 192,130,000
Quantity Distributed: 191,860,000

Plate/Sleeve Number Detail: Left-side panes — one group of 3 offset plate numbers over/under corner stamps; one intaglio sleeve number over/under adjacent stamps. Right-side panes — offset/intaglio numbers in reverse positions.

Plate/Sleeve Number Combination: 111-1, 112-1, 122-1, 123-1, 223-1, 234-1, 235-1, 376-1, 377-1, 446-1, 456-1, 466-1, 467-1, 477-1, 676-1

Tagging: overall

Printing Base Impressions:
Intaglio Black: 1(1,390,500)
Offset Red: 1(166,500), 2(42,000), 3(393,500), 4(653,500)
Offset Blue: 1(178,500), 2(75,000), 3(75,000), 4(165,000), 5(122,500), 6(84,500)
Offset Black: 1(178,500), 2(42,000), 3(75,000), 4(75,000), 5(75,000), 6(197,500)

The Stamp

On September 25, a 25¢ stamp was issued to commemorate the 200th anniversary of the drafting of the first 10 amendments to the U.S. Constitution, those guarantees of basic liberties that are known collectively as the Bill of Rights.

The stamp was dedicated in a joint ceremony with a new America the Beautiful postal card in Philadelphia. That city was chosen for the honor even though the First Congress, when it drew up the amendments, was meeting in Federal Hall in New York City.

USPS, in an August 11, 1989, press release giving details of the stamp, mistakenly reported that the amendments were drafted in Philadelphia's Congress Hall. Later, when the writer of this book pointed out the error, a correction was issued.

However, USPS asserted that the choice of Philadelphia for the ceremony, which had been made about a year earlier, hadn't been based on misinformation.

Frank Thomas, acting manager of the USPS Stamp Support Branch, said: "I don't remember the exact discussion, but I can't imagine that we weren't aware at that point" that the amendments were written in New York.

Philadelphia was selected because it was "tied in very closely with the Bill of Rights," he explained. For example, the subject of an explicit guarantee of rights was first brought up (and voted down) during the 1787 Constitutional Convention in Philadelphia.

Another factor, Thomas said, was that Philadelphia's Independence Hall complex "is such a natural place to hold the ceremony."

The stamp was the 24th in a series of stamps and postal cards celebrating the bicentennial of the writing and adoption of the Constitution, the organization of the new federal government and related events. The series began May 25, 1987, with a postal card for the Constitutional Convention.

Early in the planning stages, the Citizens' Stamp Advisory Committee considered and rejected the idea of celebrating the drafting of the Bill of Rights with a booklet of 10 stamps, one for each amendment.

"For one thing, they decided we didn't need that many more new issues," said Joe Brockert of USPS, the stamp's project manager. "It would have been difficult to put all that type on the stamps, or to come up with three or four buzzwords appropriate to each of the amendments, or to graphically illustrate each of them.

"So we thought that one graphic, symbolic kind of representation was the approach to take."

The great majority of the delegates who toiled through the summer of 1787 to create the Constitution didn't believe it was necessary to include in the document a guarantee of individual rights.

They wanted to keep their finished product simple. They believed they had sprinkled through the text an adequate number of securities for personal liberty. Besides, eight states already provided their own bills of rights.

Some delegates disagreed, including George Mason, author of Virginia's Declaration of Rights of 1776, and Massachusetts' Elbridge Gerry. On September 12, as the convention was reviewing a draft of its work, Mason said he wished the plan had been prefaced with a bill of rights. "It would give great quiet to the people," he said, "and with the aid of the state declarations, a bill might be prepared in a few hours." Gerry then moved to add such a bill, and Mason seconded it. But every state delegation voted no — including Virginia's.

Explains historian Clinton Rossiter: "They were in the home stretch, and whereas it would indeed have taken only 'a few hours' for any one of a dozen candidates for immortality to draw up a bill of rights, it would have taken several weeks, not to mention some hard fighting and sharp bargaining, to get one accepted on the floor. And that, the Framers thought, was an end to that irrelevant issue."

Once the Constitution was sent out to the states for ratification, however, its lack of a bill of rights drew widespread criticism. Delegate Roger Sherman, back home in Connecticut, was bucking the tide when he argued that "no Bill of Rights ever yet bound the supreme power longer than the honeymoon of a new married couple, unless the rulers were interested in preserving the rights." So was Alexander Hamilton, writing in *The Federalist* that a declaration of rights was irrelevant in a constitution of delegated powers.

Several state conventions that ratified the Constitution insisted on attaching non-binding but earnest "recommendations" that a bill of rights be added. To gain support for ratification, Federalists in Massachusetts, South Carolina, New Hampshire, Virginia and New York pledged that this would be done once the new government was in place.

When the first House of Representatives met, James Madison was there as a member from Virginia. On June 8, 1789, Madison introduced 19 amendments, which he had distilled from the dozens of proposals submitted to Congress. After extensive work in a select committee and a committee of the whole, the House on August 24 approved 17 of the amendments and sent them to the Senate.

The Senate in turn worked them over, combining some and eliminating others. Late in September, conferees of the two houses agreed on the final form of 12 amendments. The House accepted the conference report September 24, and the Senate concurred September 25, the date marked by the commemorative stamp.

The first two amendments were actually unrelated to the others. They dealt with apportionment in the House and the pay of members of Congress, and they fell by the wayside on their journey through the state legislatures. But the remaining 10, which defended the ancient rights of persons against Congress — freedom of speech, press, religion, assembly and petition, protection against unreasonable search and seizure, self-incrimination and cruel and unusual punishment, guarantees of due process and a speedy jury trial — and acknowledged the reserved powers of the states, received a much warmer reception.

New Jersey was the first state to ratify the 10 amendments, followed by Maryland, North Carolina (only newly arrived in the Union), New Hampshire, South Carolina, Delaware, Pennsylvania and New York.

In May 1790, Rhode Island became the 13th state to ratify the basic Constitution and join the Union, and the following month its General Assembly approved the 10 amendments. Vermont was admitted as a state March 4, 1791, and became the 10th state to ratify them. Finally, on December 15, 1791, a laggard Virginia accepted the Bill of Rights, completing the 11 states (three-fourths of the total number) needed to make the Bill officially part of the Constitution. The bicentennial of this event is scheduled to be marked by a postal card in 1991.

Virginia's procrastination was nothing compared to that of Connecticut, Georgia and Massachusetts. They didn't get around to ratifying the amendments until 1941, as a token gesture to commemorate the 150th anniversary of the Bill of Rights' adoption.

That 150th anniversary, incidentally, wasn't marked by a postage stamp. In 1941 the United States was on the brink of World War II,

Cartoonist Herbert Block ("Herblock") designed this dramatic 1966 stamp (Scott 1312) commemorating the 175th anniversary of the ratification of the Bill of Rights.

and issued only one lonely commemorative — for Vermont's sesquicentennial. However, in 1966 the Post Office produced a 5¢ stamp to note the 175th anniversary of the Bill of Rights (Scott 1312).

Several other stamps have also been inspired by the ideas incorporated in the first 10 amendments.

A 1¢ stamp (Scott 908) issued in 1943, in the midst of the war, saluted the "Four Freedoms" that President Franklin D. Roosevelt had identified as the basis for a secure world in the future: "Freedom of speech and religion, from want and fear." The same message was inscribed on the 5¢ FDR memorial stamp of 1945 (Scott 933).

"Religious freedom in America" was the theme of a 3¢ commemorative in 1957 (Scott 1099). "Freedom of the press" was saluted on a 4¢ stamp issued the following year (Scott 1119).

And the Americana definitive series of 1975-1981 (Scott 1581-1612) included such slogans as: "Freedom to speak out — a root of democracy"; "Right of people peaceably to assemble"; "People's right to petition for redress"; "Liberty depends on freedom of the press" and "Freedom of conscience — an American right."

Lou Nolan's concept sketch for the Bill of Rights stamp included a "cutout" in the field of stars to define the eagle's right wing. This was left solid in the finished design.

The Design

CSAC wasn't sure what it wanted for a Bill of Rights stamp, but it was sure what it didn't want: portraits. James Madison would have been an obvious candidate, but an argument also could have been made for George Mason, or for others. To select a Founding Father or two and put them on the stamp would have been to honor them rather then the Bill of Rights, the committee believed.

Still, finding a design that would appropriately represent the lofty, diverse yet related series of ideas represented in the Bill was no simple matter. "It was one of the toughest design assignments we've given to anybody," confessed Joe Brockert.

Artist Lou Nolan, tapped for the job, came back with one basic image. On a vertical layout he depicted a stylized American eagle, silhouetted in white against a solid black background, using a quill pen in its beak to write in script: "Bill of Rights." Superimposed over the right wing and body like a shield were the red, white and blue stars and stripes of the U.S. flag vertically — a dramatic splash of color.

"The artist told us he could give us the same thing in a horizontal orientation, or change the position of the script, or adjust the wings, but he just couldn't think of any other graphic device that was going to do much better than this as a symbol," said Joe Brockert. "The committee's feeling was: "It's not worth trying a whole lot of other concepts because we really like this idea. Let's make a few adjustments to it and go with it."

The adjustments, it turned out, were minor. Nolan had so defined the eagle's silhouette as to create a black gap in the field of stars where the right wing separated from the body; CSAC preferred to have no gap there. Some notches were added to the vane of the quill pen. The denomination was moved to the eagle's left wing. And a professional calligrapher, Julian Waters of Gaithersburg, Maryland, was hired to execute a fancy "Bill of Rights" inscription surrounded by loops and flourishes.

Someone on the committee pointed out that the 1987 stamp commemorating the signing of the Constitution itself had also featured a quill pen (in a human hand, shown against a background of the Constitution's opening sentences). Was the device becoming a cliche?

"Nolan's design was a much more graphic representation than the 1987 one, and not as realistic," Brockert said. "The orientation was different. The committee didn't see it as too similar to the other. At the same time, though, they saw it as being a natural tie-in to that earlier approach. It sort of carried over the Constitution theme and was very complementary to everything that had gone before."

In the end, though, he added, the deciding factor was that "No one could suggest anything better."

To prepare the stamp, the Bureau of Engraving and Printing made an engraving that was used as the basis for offset plates. The only portion of the design to be actually printed in intaglio was the inscription "USA 25." Edward R. Felver, manager of BEP's Product Design and Engraving Division, explained why the image was engraved first:

"Basically, we use three different approaches in converting artwork to offset printed stamp images. The first is the commonly used method whereby the artwork — painting, photograph, etc. — is photographed directly.

"The second approach is photographing engraved dies when we wish to emphasize or perfect details. This was the case with the Bill of Rights commemorative. When the artwork was reduced to stamp size, the fine lines in 'Bill of Rights' became so narrow that all or part would have been lost in the printing process, and those that were not would have been overpowered by the solid black background surrounding them.

"Therefore, Gary Slaght did the engraving to embolden and emphasize the lettering so that the balance between black and white would be pleasing to the eye. Ken Wiram engraved the flag — as we usually have to do. The reason is that the stars have to be 'fattened' and the points evened so that they appear on the stamp as stars rather than polka dots.

"The third method is engraving so that the offset printing will appear as line work rather than as a dot pattern. This technique was used for the Carousel Animals block of four in 1988."

Black backgrounds had previously been uncommon on U.S. stamps, but that wasn't the case in 1989. The Bill of Rights stamp was the fifth of the year to fit that description; the others commemorated the bicentennials of the House, Senate and Executive Branches, and North Carolina statehood.

Artist Nolan, of McLean, Virginia, had previously designed five Transportation series definitive stamps, the 1987 Take Pride in America postal card, and the 22¢ Certified Public Accountants commemorative of 1987 (which, coincidentally, had as its central image a steel pen point in silhouette).

Varieties

Bob Dumaine of Sam Houston Philatelics reported soon after the stamp went on sale that his firm had discovered a mint copy missing the black intaglio portion — the "US" and the denomination.

First-Day Facts

The stamp and the America the Beautiful postal card for Philadelphia were dedicated in a ceremony at Independence Hall that featured remarks by "James Madison," who in real life was actor James Gallagher. Elwood A. Mosley, assistant postmaster general, was the principal speaker. Others participating were Herbert M. Atherton, deputy director of the Commission on the Bicentennial of the United States Constitution; Thomas O. Muldoon, president of the Philadelphia Convention and Visitors Bureau, and Hobart G. Cawood, superintendent of the National Park Service's Independence National Historical Park.

25¢ PREHISTORIC ANIMALS (BLOCK OF FOUR)

Date of Issue: October 1, 1989

Catalog Numbers: Scott 2422-25 (stamps)　　Minkus CM1356-59
　　　　　　　　　　Scott 2425a (block of 4)　　USPS 4466

Colors: red, magenta, yellow, cyan, black (offset); black (intaglio)

First-Day Cancel: Lake Buena Vista, Florida (Epcot Center)

FDCs Canceled: 871,634

Format: Panes of 40, horizontal, 5 across, 8 down. Offset printing plates of 160 subjects (10 across, 16 around); intaglio printing sleeve of 320 subjects (10 across, 32 around).

Perf: 11 by 10.8 (Eureka off-line perforator)

Selvage Markings: ©United States Postal Service 1989, Use Correct ZIP Code®, USPS poster promotion and picture.

Designer: John Gurche of Alexandria, Virginia

Art Director and Typographer: Howard Paine (CSAC)

Project Manager: Joe Brockert (USPS)

Engraver: Dennis Brown (BEP, lettering and numerals)

Modeler: Peter Cocci (BEP)

Printing: 6-color offset, 3-color intaglio D press (902)

Quantity Ordered: 407,000,000
Quantity Distributed: 406,988,000

Plate/Sleeve Number Detail: Top panes — one group of 5 offset plate numbers alongside corner stamps; intaglio sleeve number adjacent to stamps below. Bottom panes — offset/intaglio numbers in reverse positions.

Plate/Sleeve Number Combination: 11111-1, 12111-1, 12121-1, 12122-1, 12232-1, 27367-1, 28367-1, 29367-1, 29368-1, 29668-1, 29669-1, 44443-1, 44444-1, 44445-1, 44455-1, 45555-1, 45556-1, 46556-1

Tagging: overall

The Stamps

For a theme for National Stamp Collecting Month and the stamps to launch it, USPS reached back millions of years to the early morning of life on earth. To promote the stamps, it turned to the most modern of multimedia marketing techniques.

The stamps, issued October 1, were a block of four topical commemoratives depicting prehistoric animals that once lived in what is now the Western United States. They were widely referred to as "dinosaur stamps," although one of the creatures — the winged pteranodon — doesn't fit in that category.

As part of a promotional campaign unprecedented for a stamp issue, USPS joined forces with MCA Home Video, which released the movie *The Land Before Time* on videocassette September 14. The film, co-produced by George Lucas and Steven Spielberg, featured a friendly dinosaur named Littlefoot. An insert was placed in the videocassette to advertise the stamps and special dinosaur T-shirts.

To dramatize this joint-venture — which USPS said was initiated by MCA — Postmaster General Anthony M. Frank flew to Universal City Studios in Los Angeles July 24 to unveil the stamp designs with MCA President Robert Blattner. Media coverage of the event included a page-one picture of the stamps in color (captioned "Fearsome Foursome") in the newspaper *USA Today* July 25.

"Some of the world's most important fossil deposits have been unearthed in the United States," Frank said at the ceremony. "Because of the richness and diversity of that prehistoric life, the Postal Service is especially pleased to unveil these four stamps."

Other methods used by USPS to promote the stamps included prime-time TV commercials, dinosaur buttons, a 1990 dinosaur calendar (produced by the American Museum of Natural History and marketed exclusively by USPS), magazine advertising, direct mail, a toll-free 800 number for ordering stamps and a "Name the Dinosaurs" contest with a grand prize of a family vacation for four at Utah's Dinosaur National Monument.

Finally, there was a dinosaur poster, similar to those prepared in connection with the Classic Cars booklet pane of 1988 and the Lou Gehrig and Priority Mail stamps of 1989. To advertise the poster, USPS took the novel step of using the selvage of the stamp pane itself for a commercial message in black and red. The inscription read: "LIKE THESE STAMPS?/GET A POSTER!!/Send check or money order/for $10.00 to:/DINOSAUR POSTER/USPS, ROOM 5610/Wash., DC 20260-6755/Offer expires 12-31-89."

The selvage also bore a picture in red of a fanciful beast USPS called the "Stamposaurus." Stamposaurus, a cartoon dinosaur with a row of stamps arranged like plates down its back and tail, also appeared on many of the pictorial cancellations used across the country in the summer and fall to carry the slogan of National Stamp Collecting Month: "Begin an Adventure of Giant Proportions — Collect Stamps."

Like the creatures it depicted, the Prehistoric Animals block of stamps followed an evolutionary course.

As originally conceived by the Citizens' Stamp Advisory Committee's Topical Subcommittee, it would have illustrated a wide variety of primitive fauna. The first proposal was for four stamps that would depict an ancestor of the horse, a woolly mammoth, a flying reptile and a dinosaur. But when the idea came to the full committee for discussion, there was dissent.

The foursome seemed unbalanced, members said. They pointed out, for instance, that early horses were midget-sized — quite out of scale with these other creatures — and suggested that a saber-tooth tiger might be more appropriate.

There was also a feeling that the variety of beasts was too broad — that "we might be trying to do too much," said Joe Brockert, project manager for the issue. "We rethought it, and the consensus was that we ought to limit the block to four from the Age of Reptiles."

Brockert later went to the Topical Subcommittee with a list of five he considered "the most popular, most widely recognized, most identifiable" examples: tyrannosaurus, pteranodon, stegosaurus, brontosaurus and triceratops. The subcommittee and full committee agreed, and they settled on the first four for stamp subjects.

"They kept triceratops in reserve, in case there were objections from our consultants that pteranodon didn't really belong with the others," Brocker said. "The committee wanted to keep pteranodon, though, because otherwise it would have been four big brutish-looking beast with no element of elegance or variety."

The issue marked the second appearance of dinosaurs on U.S. stamps. In 1970, a se-tenant block of four 6-centers commemorated the 100th anniversary of the American Museum of Natural History in New York City. One of the stamps reproduced a dinosaur mural by Rudolph Zallinger in Yale's Peabody Museum.

This 1970 stamp (Scott 1390) for the centenary of the American Museum of Natural History depicted a brontosaurus, stegosaurus and allosaurus from a mural by Rudolph Zallinger in Yale's Peabody Museum.

Dinosaurs have been described as the most successful animals that ever lived. For more than 140 million years — more than 30 times as long as man has existed — these reptiles, which ranged from creatures the size of a chicken to the largest land animals of all time, dominated the earth.

Their sudden disappearance from the geological record has baffled scientists and led to numerous theories as to what killed them off. One possibility is that massive upheavals in the earth destroyed their habitat. A popular recent theory is that a collision between the earth and a comet or meteorite threw up great quantities of debris, darkening the sky and altering the climate.

TYRANNOSAURUS. One of the most vivid memories of Americans who as children saw Walt Disney's animated cartoon film *Fantasia* was of the fearsome tyrannosaurus stalking its prey. Tyrannosaurus was as large a flesh-eater as ever walked, weighing seven tons, rising to 19 feet on its massive hind legs, with a skull more than four feet long, armed with saberlike teeth. It lived in the late Cretaceous period, the last of the three periods of the Mesozoic era, or Age of Reptiles, during which the dinosaurs flourished.

PTERANODON. With a wingspan of 25 feet, the pteranodon was by far the largest flying animal ever recorded. It belonged to a group of winged reptiles from the Cretaceous period called pterosaurs, related to the dinosaurs, and was descended from the small pterodactyl of the Jurassic (second) period. Its skull was long, narrow and covered by a horny bill. Pterosaurs probably dove for fish like ospreys or kingfishers. Like bats, they hung suspended by their hind limbs when at rest.

STEGOSAURUS. This plant-eating dinosaur of the late Jurassic-early Cretaceous period was armored for protection. It had a back that rose steeply from the small head to a considerable height above the long and powerful hind legs before sloping downward to the tail. Large vertical bony plates ran down its back, and its tail was armed with two pairs of long, pointed bony spikes. Its two-ton bulk was controlled by a brain no larger than a walnut.

BRONTOSAURUS. The herbivorous "thunder lizard" of the Jurassic period was vast in bulk, averaging 70 feet in length and weighing up to 35 tons. Some scientists believe it spent considerable time in the water, which helped to support its weight and offer protection from land-roaming carnivores. Fossil hunters found the first bones of the creature in Wyoming in the 1870s, but a brontosaurus skull wasn't positively identified until a century later.

The term "brontosaurus" is actually an obsolete one. "It seems clear," writes Donald F. Glut in *The Dinosaur Dictionary,* "that brontosaurus is the same as the earlier-named apatosaurus, which by the rules has 'priority' and should be the proper name." The decision of the Postal Service to use the old designation on the stamp drew some surprisingly sharp criticism.

Representative George E. Brown of Riverside, California, wrote to Postmaster General Frank on behalf of a constituent, Ruth Kirkby, executive director of the Jurupa Mountains Cultural Center, urging that the inscription be changed to avoid confusing "an entire generation of children" who had learned the correct name. "The stamp is simply wrong," he told *The Washington Post* after his request was turned down, "and the only reason why it hasn't been recalled is because the Postal Service has already invested a quarter of a million dollars in printing it." Jack Pierce, chairman of the Department of Paleontology at the Smithsonian Institution's Museum of Natural History, complained in a letter to USPS that use of the obsolete term "suggests that the Postal Service cares little for the accuracy of the stamps they issue and they prefer 'cartoon' nomenclature to scientific nomenclature."

Frank Thomas, acting manager of the Stamp Support Branch, told *The Post* that USPS knew the name brontosaurus was technically incorrect but the decision was made to go with it because "brontosaurus was more familiar to the general public." A random check of contemporary books on dinosaurs showed that some science writers still use the term in preference to "apatosaurus."

The Designs

For its designs, USPS turned to John Gurche of Alexandria, Virginia, a specialist in painting prehistoric animals and hominids, whose list of illustration credits includes books, magazines *(The National Geographic, Discover)* and murals and other displays for the National Museum of Natural History at the Smithsonian Institution. When Howard Paine, the stamps' art director, proposed Gurche to CSAC, he asked jokingly: "Who better to do a one-inch postage stamp than someone who does 10-foot walls?"

Gurche was well aware that as a large-scale painter he had to guard against including excess detail in a work that would be reduced to postage-stamp size. So he specified when taking the job that he would work at 1½ times stamp size rather than "five times up" as stamp artists normally do. As it turned out, he said, producing his acrylics in such small dimensions presented no problem.

The artist would have preferred to give the Postal Service some less familiar, more exotic creatures — the beaked, egg-robbing oviraptor

John Gurche made these preliminary sketches for the prehistoric animals block. In the final paintings, the picture of the pteranodons was reversed and the brontosaurus picture underwent major revision.

(an Asian dinosaur), for example, or the parasaurolophus, with its long, backward-slanting horn. However, CSAC had already decided that it wanted "the old standbys," as Gurche termed them. To compensate, the artist resolved to try to put some fresh ideas about dinosaurs into the work.

"Some of these ideas had to do with body positions, posture and locomotion," he said. "I painted them basically in more active poses, which goes along with the current idea that some dinosaurs perhaps were warm-blooded." In keeping with this concept, he depicted his subjects holding their limbs underneath their bodies rather than as "sort of sprawling, lizard-limbed" creatures.

"I showed a tyrannosaurus running, a pretty active pose," the artist noted. "The stegosaurus is climbing a rocky hillside, also an active pose. My pteranodons are sort of active, flapping flyers. That's a hot subject of debate these days — whether the big ones were really active flyers. Some think they were really gliders.

"Also, the more you find out about dinosaurs the more social some of them seem to be, and I wanted to put that in also. So except for the stegosaurus, you see a couple of them together in each one. In the brontosaurus picture, there's a juvenile — not a real baby, but a juvenile. I wanted to get across something implying parenting behavior and herd behavior.

"You'll also see some evidence of 'social coloration.' That means basically just spots and dots. One thinks of social coloration in terms of birds; there's a reason why the male cardinal is red. When you get animals that have a high degree of sociability and also have color vision, as dinosaurs probably did — all their modern relatives do — it's a fair guess that they're going to use social coloration.

"I don't know if you can see this on the stamp or not, but the pteranodons have fur. They have found skin impressions of pterosaurus in the Soviet Union, and they show that at least some of them were furred. The brontosaurus has a 'new' head on it — they identified an actual skull only a few years ago. Also, there are new ideas about the plate arrangement on stegosaurus, and that is incorporated to some degree in the stamp."

For his research, Gurche read extensively and used the facilities of the Smithsonian. He returned often to the fossilized bones of a stegosaurus that is jokingly called the "road-kill" because the bones are strewn just as they were found at the dig.

"I kept looking at the arrangement of the vertebrae to decide how much the tail should droop," he said. "The traditional view of the stegosaurus is to have a fairly drooping tail, with a big humped back. I finally decided that it really didn't droop very much." In his painting, the stegosaurus holds its tail at close to the horizontal.

As is his custom, Gurche made some clay models as a preliminary to preparing concept sketches. He and Howard Paine roughed in type and rearranged figures — reversing the direction of the pteranodon, for instance — to get the effects they wanted.

Stamp designer John Gurche also painted this dramatic scene of a death battle between a tyrannosaurus and a styracosaurus that was used for the cover of the September-October issue of USPS' Philatelic Catalog.

Gurche also used color for effect. He painted a lowering red sky over the tyrannosaurus to give "sort of an evil, menacing feel" to the picture. And he offered CSAC a radical added touch: black borders around the stamps.

"I think paintings tend to be more luminous when they're against a dark background," Gurche explained. "In my case, I really try to paint with light. The skies are infused with light; there's hot light on the landscape. If you want to make that look effective, it works real well to put it on a dark background."

"Everybody kind of liked the black borders," said project manager Brockert. "But we decided it would darken the overall images more than we wanted, and it might do unpredictable things to the perforating pins, and also to the facer-canceler machines that have to read the phosphor signals off the stamps. So the committee said, 'These are nice pieces of art as they are, let's leave them alone.'"

Under Gurche's supervision, Bureau of Engraving and Printing technicians did some touch-up work to the paintings, using the Electronic Design Center's scanner, to prepare them for offset reproduction on the combination D press. (Only the inscriptions were printed in intaglio, on top of the offset.) On the stegosaurus stamp, the heavy shadows on the rocks were lightened to make the intaglio type more legible, and the colors were adjusted to retain the rocks' natural look. With tyrannosaurus, the scanner operator actually "cloned" part of Gurche's painting, extending one of the dinosaurs to fill more space.

"I have a real critical eye," Gurche said, "but I could not tell the difference between what he did, adding a little extra strip on, and my own painting. He added onto it, using information that was already in the painting, and managed to duplicate my style so I couldn't even tell. And I don't think anyone could do that with a paintbrush."

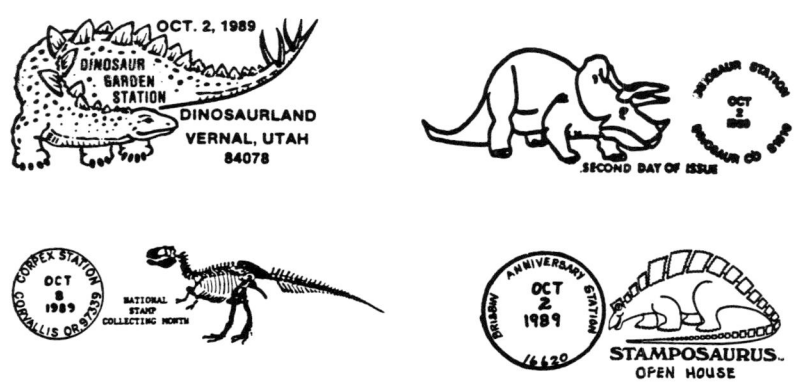

These are a few examples of the many pictorial "dinosaur" postmarks authorized by USPS to publicize National Stamp Collecting Month.

Gurche also furnished USPS with a dramatic painting of a tyrannosaurus battling a styracosaurus, which the Philatelic Sales Division used for the cover of the September-October issue of its *Philatelic Catalog*. However, his busy work schedule prevented him from painting the dinosaur poster that USPS marketed as a related item. That assignment was given to John Dawson, the Idaho artist who designed the block of four Cat stamps issued in 1988.

First-Day Facts

Postmaster General Anthony M. Frank dedicated the stamps October 1 at the Universe of Energy Exhibit in Epcot Center, Orlando, Florida. Bob Matheison, executive vice president of Disney World, was the speaker, and Bob Davis, general manager/postmaster at Tampa, Florida, presided.

Collectors attending the ceremony had to pay the Epcot admission fee ($30.65 for adults, $24.30 for children), which resulted in some angry letters to the philatelic press. However, those wishing only to obtain stamps and first-day cancellations could also get them at the General Mail Facility near the Orlando Airport.

25¢ PRE-COLUMBIAN ARTIFACTS
AMERICA SERIES

Date of Issue: October 12, 1989

Catalog Numbers: Scott 2426   Minkus CM1360   USPS 4469

Colors: brown, dark brown, yellow, magenta, cyan, black

First-Day Cancel: San Juan, Puerto Rico (ceremony canceled)

FDCs Canceled: 215,285

Format: Panes of 50, vertical, 10 across, 5 down. Gravure printing cylinders of 200 subjects (10 across, 20 around) manufactured by Roto Cylinder, Palmyra, New Jersey.

Perf: 10.9 (L perforator)

Selvage Markings: ©United States Postal Service 1989, Use Correct ZIP Code®

Designer: Lon Busch of St. Louis, Missouri

Art Director and Typographer: Richard Sheaff (CSAC)

Project Manager: Joe Brockert (USPS)

Modeler: Richard Sennett (Sennett Enterprises) for American Bank Note Company.

Printing: Stamps printed and sheeted out by American Bank Note Company on a leased Champlain gravure press (J.W. Fergusson and Sons, Richmond, Virginia) under the supervision of Sennett Enterprises (Fairfax, Virginia). Perforated, processed and shipped by ABNC (Chicago, Illinois).

Quantity Ordered: 137,410,000
Quantity Distributed: 137,410,000

Cylinder Number Detail: One group of 6 cylinder numbers preceded by the letter "A" over/under corner stamps

Cylinder Number Combination: A111111

Tagging: block over vignette

The Stamp

On June 20, 1988, two USPS officials flew to Havana, Cuba, to talk stamps with other representatives of member countries of the Postal Union of the Americas and Spain (PUAS).

The topic that drew W.L. (Pete) Davidson Jr. and Donald M. McDowell to Cuba — a country with which the United States has no diplomatic relations and whose own stamps are embargoed by the United States — was the omnibus stamp series that PUAS members planned to issue for the 500th anniversary of Christopher Columbus' discovery of the New World.

PUAS is made up of 23 Western Hemisphere countries from Canada in the north to Argentina and Chile in the south, plus Spain, the cultural homeland of most of Latin America. Founded in 1911 as the South American Postal Union, its mission has been to promote cooperation toward the improvement of the postal services. The United States joined in 1922.

The organization had approved the America stamp project at its 1985 congress, also held in Havana. It recommended that member states issue stamps each year from 1989 through 1992, based on common themes related to America.

The 1989 theme would be pre-Columbian peoples and their customs, images and traditions; 1990 would feature natural surroundings seen by the discoverers; 1991, the discovery voyages, and 1992, the quincentennial of the arrival of Columbus on his first voyage.

The series would be similar in concept to the Europa stamps, issued annually by European nations under the sponsorship of the European Conference of Postal and Telecommunications Administrations.

USPS entered the project with, at best, moderate enthusiasm. In fact, Dickey Rustin, general manager of what was then the Stamp Information Branch, told *Stamp Collector* in 1988 that the United States planned to participate only in the first year. Later, however, USPS changed its mind and let it be known that it would issue stamps in the following years as well.

Attending the five-day Havana meeting were stamp specialists from most of the member countries. Their purpose, as described by Pete Davidson, director of the USPS Office of Stamps and Philatelic Marketing, was to review progress on the omnibus issues, coordinate efforts on design and marketing of the stamps and offer help to countries having research, design or printing problems.

Participants were given recommended specifications for the series, accompanied by sketches for illustration. They were advised, for example, that each stamp should bear a logo created specifically for the series, consisting of the organization's initials and a stylized posthorn. The logo should occupy at least 5 percent of the image area. The word "AMERICA," in capitals, should also appear, in type larger than the country name.

These are sketches furnished by the Postal Union of the Americas and Spain to members to show how the Americas stamps could be designed to incorporate the word "America," which was required to be larger than the country name; the denomination, and the organization logo, which was required to occupy at least 5 percent of the design area.

The initials on the official logo are UPAE, for the Spanish title Union Postale de las Americas y Espana. (The Portuguese acronym, which Brazilians would use, is also UPAE). Don McDowell, general manager of the USPS Stamps Division, suggested that the United States be allowed to use the initials "PUAS," corresponding to the English version of the name. To show what he meant, he sketched a PUAS logo, using a red felt-tipped pen. The other delegates agreed that this would be acceptable.

As it turned out, however, the "PUAS" designation held no more meaning for U.S. stamp users than "UPAE" would have had. There

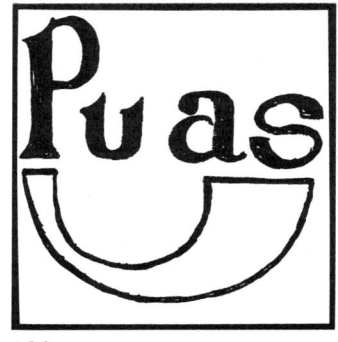

Using a red pen, Don McDowell sketched this alternative logo in which the letters matched the English-language version of the organization name. It was approved for use on the U.S. stamps.

was nothing in the proposed prototype design — or, for that matter, in the designs that USPS eventually prepared and used — to give anyone a clue as to what the logo signifies.

The United States' first America issue consisted of a 25¢ first-class mail stamp, printed by the American Bank Note Company, and a 45¢ international airmail stamp, printed by the Bureau of Engraving and Printing. The airmail stamp is described in a later chapter.

The Design

The decision to use items made by pre-Columbian Indian cultures as the design subjects of the first round of America stamps left the United States at somewhat of a disadvantage, said Joe Brockert, the stamps' project manager.

Designer Richard Sheaff prepared these design essays using various pre-Columbian artifacts. Citizens' Stamp Advisory Committee members liked the sketch using the carved deer head but didn't want a design in a square format.

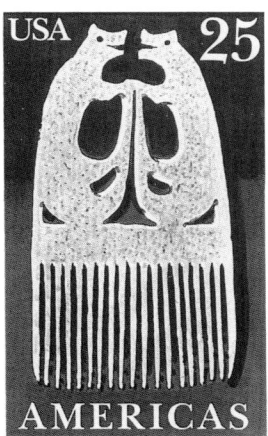

"We don't really have the kind of fancy pre-Columbian artifacts that the Inca and Aztec and other cultures from Latin America are able to show and illustrate," he explained. "We had less colorful and interesting material to select from."

Nevertheless, Art Director Richard Sheaff, in consultation with various museum officials, was able to find several objects that were both appropriate and aesthetically pleasing. "I'm particularly interested in ethnographic art, and I collect African art, so it was a great assignment for me," Sheaff said.

At his studio in Needham Heights, Massachusetts, Sheaff sketched some stamp designs incorporating these specimens, which included: a carved wooden feline figure and a deer's head, both found in Key Marco, Florida, and owned by the Smithsonian Institution; an Iroquois bone comb decorated with two mirror-image bears; the "Repousse Male," a human profile in copper from the Detroit Institute of Art, and a mother-and-child figurine, at least 1,600 years old, unearthed in Illinois and owned by the Milwaukee Public Museum.

The committee generally liked these examples — particularly the "Key Marco cat" — but wanted to see at least one more specimen from the American Southwest. Sheaff did some additional research and returned with the artifact that eventually was chosen for the design of the 25¢ value: a ceremonial wooden statuette owned by the Art Institute of Chicago. In a nice piece of geographical balance, the Key Marco cat was selected for the 45¢ airmail.

Although BEP and the American Bank Note Company could have made gravure plates from color photographs of the artifacts, the Postal Service called in Lon Busch, the St. Louis artist who designed the 1987 Pan-American Games commemorative stamp, to prepare vertically arranged paintings that would fit into typographical layouts supplied by Sheaff.

"Lon's original question was, 'What do you need me for?' " Sheaff recalled. "We wanted Lon to paint them because, although his paintings are all but indistinguishable from photographs, it allowed us to make the areas of color a little simpler and purer and introduce just a notch more color here and there. By using colors that are liked by the (electronic) scanners, we get a cleaner stamp product out of it."

For both stamps the artist worked from photos, including color transparencies, rather than from life. In the case of the 25¢ stamp, that procedure led to the accidental reversal of the image in the stamp design. Ironically, Sheaff lamented, the design team had been very aware of the possibility of a reversal, and had made an effort, both by mail and telephone communication with staff members at the Art Institute of Chicago, to make sure all parties agreed on "which way was right." Despite all the good intentions, the picture on the stamp ended up "flopped." The reversal is evident from black-and-white photos of the artifact (see illustration) and was confirmed by an Art

Institute research assistant who compared the stamp and the actual object.

The artifact was a human male figure from the American Southwest, carved from cottonwood and painted. Radio carbon 14 dating has placed its origin between A.D. 1150 and 1350. It is part of what the Art Institute of Chicago has described as one of the most important groups of ancient North American art objects ever discovered.

The group comprises 10 items that formed a sacred altar created and used by the Mimbres culture that flourished in southern New Mexico 1,000 years ago. The items were found in a small, remote cave in the Cliff Valley near the town of Cliff in New Mexico's southwest corner. Besides the male figure, the cache contained a human female carved from stone and painted, a wood mountain lion, two wooden rattlesnakes, a basketry container, four ceremonial throwing sticks and a set of decorated cotton textiles that were used to wrap the carved figures. The cloth was dated at from A.D. 1400 to 1540, indicating that the artifacts it contained had been quite old before they were hidden away.

This is the painted wooden figure from the Mimbres culture that was depicted on the 25¢ America stamp. Because the artist inadvertently worked from a color transparency that was reversed, the figure as shown on the stamp is a mirror image of the actual figure (note position of hands). Photograph copyright 1989, The Art Institute of Chicago.

Art Institute officials believe the two human figures, or "anthomorphs," represent the deities Sky (male) and Earth (female). The male figure — shown on the stamp — is termed the most impressive human sculptural image ever found from an ancient Pueblo culture, and a forerunner of the kachina figures and kiva sculptures carved by the later Hopi and Zuni tribes.

Around the figure's neck is a necklace of feathers — an obvious sky reference — from 11 different species of birds. All but one, the scarlet macaw, are native to the Cliff Valley area. (The macaw is a Mexican bird, feathers of which were a common trade item in the ancient Southwest.) The figure's chest is painted with turquoise lightning bolts, and the black-and-white pattern of diamond shapes on its belt or skirt is believed to symbolize stars or constellations, as on certain Hopi kachinas and in Navajo ritual sand paintings.

Across the bottom of the stamp design — in the tiniest type seen on a U.S. stamp since the Navajo Art se-tenant block of 1986 — are the words "Southwest carved figure, A.D. 1150-1350." USPS officials had considered being more specific and naming New Mexico as the place where the figure was found, but finally decided that, because New Mexico as a political entity didn't exist at the time the figure was made, "Southwest" would be preferable.

In at least one respect the Postal Service ignored the PUAS design guidelines. The logo of the organization as shown on the U.S. stamp was much smaller than the 5 percent of the total image area that the guidelines called for.

First-Day Facts

USPS had scheduled the first-day ceremony for San Juan, Puerto Rico, on October 12, but canceled it because of the devastation caused by Hurricane Hugo when it swept across the island in late September. The scheduled speakers included Tirso del Junco, a member of the USPS Board of Governors, and Assistant Postmaster General Richard Porras.

However, the Postal Service sold stamps and canceled covers in San Juan October 12. Collectors ordering first-day covers by mail were given the option of obtaining them with the 25¢ and 45¢ stamps separately or in combination.

$3.60 WORLD STAMP EXPO '89 SOUVENIR SHEET

Date of Issue: November 17, 1989

Catalog Numbers: Scott 2433 (souvenir sheet)   Minkus CM1361
Scott 2433a-d (imperf block of 4)
USPS 5532

Colors: red, dark blue, green, orange, gray, black (offset); brown, blue, black (intaglio)

First-Day Cancel: Washington, D.C. (World Stamp Expo '89 stamp show)

FDCs Canceled: unavailable

Format: Imperforate souvenir sheet of 4 stamps. Offset printing plates of 16 subjects (4 across, 4 around); intaglio printing sleeve of 32 subjects (4 across, 8 around).

Perf: imperforate

Selvage Markings: ©USPS 1988, WSE '89 SM, logo SM

Designer and Typographer: Richard Sheaff (CSAC)

Art Director: Jack Williams (USPS)

Project Manager: Joe Brockert (USPS)

Engravers: Andy Shu (BEP, vignette)
Gary Slaght (BEP, lettering and numerals)

Modeler: Jack Ruther (BEP)

Printing: 6-color offset, 3-color intaglio D press (902)

Quantity Ordered: 2,250,000
Quantity Distributed: 2,017,225

Plate/Sleeve Number Detail: no plate or sleeve numbers

Tagging: overall

The Souvenir Sheet

The first of 11 first-day ceremonies held by USPS during World Stamp Expo '89 at the Washington D.C., Convention Center was for a souvenir sheet celebrating the Postal Service-sponsored stamp show. It was placed on sale November 17, opening day.

The sheet was imperforate — the first to be issued in that form since the Sixth International Philatelic Exhibition sheet of 1966 (Scott 1311) — and contained four stamps arranged in a block. At the upper left was a reproduction of the 90¢ Abraham Lincoln stamp of 1869, with carmine frame and black center. The same stamp had been depicted on the 25¢ commemorative issued March 16, 1989, as advance pubicity for World Stamp Expo.

The other stamps on the souvenir sheet were reproductions of three of the so-called trial color proofs of the Lincoln stamp that were issued for display at the International Cotton Exposition in Atlanta, Georgia, in 1881. They showed the design with a blue frame and brown center, a green frame and blue center, and a scarlet frame and blue center. All four reproductions, of the stamp and the proofs, were slightly larger than life size.

Gordon C. Morison, assistant postmaster general, unveiled the design of the sheet more than 11 months in advance, on January 14, 1989, at Aripex '89 in Tucson, Arizona.

The sheet, which was available only at USPS philatelic centers and by mail order, was valid for postage, as was each of the four stamps individually. Unfortunately, the concept of stamps without perforations was too radical for some postal clerks to accept. *Linn's Stamp News* received reports of clerks rejecting the souvenir sheets, and individual stamps cut from them, as unusable. The same thing happened with the two other souvenir sheets issued at World Stamp Expo. "These are only pictures of stamps," one clerk told a *Linn's* reader. "Perhaps," *Linn's* commented, "the USPS should develop a 'New Stamps Not Recognized' postal marking."

At $3.60 face value, the sheet was much costlier than any of the previous 20 souvenir sheets issued by the United States to commemorate major stamp events, beginning with the White Plains sheet for the Second International Philatelic Exhibition in 1926 (Scott 630). The cost of these earlier sheets had ranged from 5¢ (Sixth International Philatelic Exhibition, 1966) to $1.98 (each of the four "presidential" souvenir sheets for Ameripex '86).

Predictably, the high cost of the sheets drew complaints. Some said the 90¢ face value of the individual stamps made them of little practical use. Others, however, noted that 90¢ exactly covered the one-ounce international airmail letter rate (basic 45¢ per half-ounce).

"To the cover collector and the postal historian, the use of a single, unusual stamp to pay a proper franking rate is quite special and desirable," one reader wrote *Linn's*. Another pointed out, equally happily, that 90¢ was the rate for special fourth-class pieces under one pound. "As a volume mailer of video cassettes," he wrote, "I look forward to using the 90¢ stamps on my parcels. I currently have to use weird combinations of Transportation coils."

A study of the rate charts also showed that the $3.60 sheet, plus a 1¢ stamp, would pay the rate for a priority mail piece weighing between four and five pounds and sent to zones 1, 2 or 3. And an individual stamp from the sheet, plus the 25¢ World Stamp Expo commemorative, would pay the 25¢ first-class rate plus the 90¢ return-receipt-requested fee.

Back in 1881, for display at the International Cotton Exposition, the Post Office Department had the American Bank Note Company print proofs of each stamp issued up to that time. This made them

These covers, franked with stamps cut from miniature sheets first issued at World Stamp Expo, were rejected by postal clerks. One wrote "Void — Not Real Stamps" on the envelope; another used a handstamp reading: "RETURN TO SENDER/POSTAGE VOID IF DEFACED/COVERED OR REUSED."

One idea for the souvenir sheet was to adapt this frame essay that had been proposed but not used for the 1869 90¢ Lincoln.

"posthumous proofs," in stamp writer George Brett's phrase, rather than true "trial color proofs."

The proofs were printed on thin white cardboard in varying colors. In the 1869 series, of which the 90¢ Lincoln was a part, the low values were produced in panes of 150, and the bicolor values of 15¢ through 90¢ in panes of 100. After the exposition, these were made available to collectors and were mostly cut into singles.

The 90¢ proofs consisted of 10 different color combinations: black frame with scarlet, brown or green center; scarlet frame with blue center; brown frame with black or blue center; green frame with brown or blue center, and blue frame with brown or green center.

The exposition itself, held in Oglethorpe Park on the northwest edge of Atlanta from October 5 to December 31, 1881, was many things. It was the first world's fair held in the South. It was a friendly Southern answer to the great Centennial Exposition held in Philadelphia five years earlier. It was a proclamation that Atlanta and Georgia were rebounding from the devastation of the Civil War (the city was now a booming commercial center and railroad hub with a population of 37,000, almost double what it had been a decade earlier). It was the herald of the manufacturing era in the former Confederacy, a symbol that cotton was now king industrially just as for decades it had been king agriculturally.

The 286,000 fairgoers from all over the nation who filed through the 11 miles of aisles in the huge exposition building saw exhibits from every state and from seven foreign countries. Three steam engines powered the wide variety of machinery on display. Textiles, agricultural products, livestock and even an art gallery were among the attractions, and the outside was decorated with cotton stalks in every stage of growth. When it was over, the fair showed a profit of $20,000 — an unusual distinction for any exposition — and the building became the home of a cotton factory, the Exposition Cotton Mills.

The Design

The sheet was designed by Richard Sheaff of Needham Heights,

Massachusetts, a design coordinator for the Citizens' Stamp Advisory Committee, who also designed the World Stamp Expo '89 commemorative stamp issued earlier in the year. It was printed on the Bureau of Engraving and Printing's combination D press, with the Lincoln portraits done in intaglio and the rest of the sheet in offset.

The stamp and proof reproductions were shown against a square white background. The rest of the background was gray in color and contained a text block and the show logo.

Once the 90¢ Lincoln stamp of 1869 had been chosen as the motif for the earlier World Stamp Expo commemorative, Sheaff said, it was a natural idea — and one of sure interest to collectors — to use the later Atlanta color proofs on the souvenir sheet.

Before settling on that approach, however, he and CSAC also considered an even more novel notion: that of reproducing an alternative frame design that had been considered in 1869 for the Lincoln stamp and turned down. An essay for such a frame is reproduced in Clarence Brazer's essay-proof catalog and identified as 122E-Cd.

Because the Atlanta color proofs exist in several color combinations, picking the three for the souvenir sheet took some thought. "We had to keep in mind that only three intaglio colors are available on the D press, and of course we wanted the portrait vignette to be intaglio," Sheaff said. "One of the colors had to be black because we were using the stamp in its colors as issued in the upper left. So it became a kind of puzzle: 'OK, we've got four portrait vignettes but only three colors available and these are the colors of the issued stamp and these are the alternatives for the trial proofs, so how can we mix and match these in a way that will also look good?'"

Once the selection was made (the other two intaglio colors chosen were brown and blue), it became the responsibility of BEP craftsmen to find modern offset inks that would correspond as closely as possible to the intaglio proofing inks used in 1881. As a guide for BEP, USPS borrowed a set of actual Atlanta proofs from the collection of Jack Rosenthal of Casper, Wyoming, a member of CSAC and an authority on the stamps, essays and proofs of the period.

First-Day Facts

The first-day ceremony for the souvenir sheet took place at 10:30 a.m., following the grand opening ceremony for World Stamp Expo '89 at 9:45 and the official opening at 10. November 17, appropriately, was Lincoln Day at the show.

Postmaster General Anthony Frank, in his remarks, joked that the 90¢ face value of the stamps on the souvenir sheet didn't "foreshadow our next rate increase." "If our stamps were going to reach 90¢ any time in the near future I'd be wearing a suit of armor," he said. Jack Rosenthal, whose own Atlanta proofs were used to guide the sheet's printers in color selection, was the principal speaker. Other participants included Assistant Postmaster General Morison, who had unveiled the sheet's design many months earlier, and actor Gerald Starr, dressed as Abraham Lincoln.

The souvenir program distributed to attendees consisted of a booklet that included pages for the five adhesive stamp items scheduled to be issued at World Stamp Expo: three souvenir sheets and two blocks of four se-tenant commemoratives. The Lincoln sheet was affixed to the appropriate page and canceled "First Day of Issue."

The same booklet was later used for the first-day ceremonies for the other issues as well, again with the sheet or block affixed to the appropriate page and canceled. For each ceremony a stuffer card, containing the actual dedication ceremony agenda, was placed in the booklet's inside front cover pocket.

Persons who received their first-day ceremony programs by subscription from USPS were sent only one booklet, containing all five items canceled with their respective issue dates.

World Stamp Expo '89 offered this show cancellation November 17-20 and November 24-December 3. Only the date changed.

Besides the standard first-day-of-issue cancellation, numerous other pictorial cancellations were available for the souvenir sheet and other U.S. postal items issued at World Stamp Expo.

For example, the Universal Postal Union Congress offered a cancellation for each of its scheduled Monday through Saturday meetings, beginning November 13 and ending December 14. In both cases, only the date changed from day to day. Also, each "theme day" at World Stamp Expo had its own unique pictorial cancellation.

The United Nations Postal Administration also held a first-day ceremony on the show's opening day, dedicating its first set in a new series commemorating the Universal Declaration of Human Rights.

25¢ CLASSIC MAIL DELIVERY (BLOCK OF FOUR)

Date of Issue: November 19, 1989

Catalog Numbers: Scott 2434-37 (stamps)   Minkus CM1362-65
Scott 2437a (block of 4)   USPS 4470

Colors: magenta, yellow, cyan, black (offset); dark blue (intaglio)

First-Day Cancel: Washington, D.C. (World Stamp Expo '89 stamp show)

FDCs Canceled: unavailable

Format: Panes of 40, square, 8 across, 5 down. Offset printing plates of 160 subjects (10 across, 16 around); intaglio printing sleeve of 320 subjects (10 across, 32 around).

Perf: 10.9 (Eureka off-line perforator)

Selvage Markings: ©United States Postal Service 1988, Use Correct ZIP Code®

Designer: Mark Hess of Katonah, New York

Art Director and Typographer: Richard Sheaff (CSAC)

Project Manager: Jack Williams (USPS)

Engraver: Michael Ryan (BEP, lettering and numerals)

Modeler: Jack Ruther (BEP)

Printing: 6-color offset, 3-color intaglio D press (902)

Quantity Ordered: 164,000,000
Quantity Distributed: 163,824,000

Plate/Sleeve Number Detail: Left-side panes — one group of 4 offset plate numbers over/under corner stamps; one intaglio sleeve number over/under adjacent stamps. Right-side panes — offset/intaglio numbers in reverse positions.

Plate/Sleeve Number Combinations: 2112-1, 2122-1, 3223-1, 3232-1, 3234-1, 4345-1, 4356-1

Tagging: overall

The Stamps

"In a world of faxes and fiber optics, the mails still represent the most intimate means by which ... people reveal their thoughts, their hopes and their dreams."

With these and other words equally reassuring to the ears of people in the mail business, President George Bush welcomed delegates from 170 world postal administrations to the 20th Universal Postal Congress in Washington November 13.

Six days later, USPS released its first postal item directly saluting the Postal Congress. It was a se-tenant block of four 25¢ stamps depicting what the Postal Service called "Classic Mail Transportation" methods — a stagecoach, a steamboat, a Curtiss JN-4H (Jenny) biplane and an early automobile.

The stamps were issued at the Washington Convention Center, site of both the Postal Congress and USPS-sponsored World Stamp Expo '89 held in conjunction with it. The original schedule of first-day ceremonies at World Stamp Expo called for this block to appear November 20 and the 39¢ Montgomery Blair aerogramme to be issued November 19. Later, USPS switched the two.

On November 28 the same four Classic Mail Transportation stamps were released in the form of an imperforate miniature sheet. During the show, the Postal Service also issued a companion set of four Future Mail Transportation stamps in the two formats (see separate chapters).

The designs of the Classic Mail Transportation stamps and miniature sheet had been unveiled more than a year ahead of time, on October 27, 1988, at UPU headquarters in Bern, Switzerland, where the agency's Consultative Council for Postal Studies was holding its annual meeting. Associate Postmaster General Edward E. Horgan Jr. officiated at the unveiling.

Once before, in 1975, USPS issued a block of stamps featuring vintage methods of mail transportation (Scott 1572-1575). In this case, the stamps also illustrated modern communications methods.

The following week, on November 4, Assistant Postmaster General Gordon C. Morison presented the four designs to a U.S. audience at the Chicagopex '88 stamp show in Chicago.

The methods of transportation shown on the four stamps cover a period from the middle of the 18th century to the first quarter of the 20th. Mail transportation has been a popular subject of stamp design over the years, and each of these four modes had been postally illustrated at various times in the past.

In fact, two of them — the stagecoach and the Jenny biplane — were shown on a similar se-tenant block of four commemoratives that was issued in 1975 to mark the 200th anniversary of the independent American postal service (Scott 1572-1575). The Jenny, of course, was the plane that flew the nation's first scheduled airmail flights in 1918, and was depicted on the first three U.S. airmail stamps (Scott C1-3).

The automobile shown on the UPU block is almost a dead ringer for the one on the 15¢ parcel post stamp of 1912 (Scott Q7). And steamboats — five different ones — were pictured on a booklet pane that was issued earlier in 1989.

Today, the smooth flow of mail across national boundaries is taken for granted. That's because of the work of the Universal Postal Union, a specialized agency of the United Nations composed of 169 member countries. Before the UPU was created, however, the situation was chaotic.

"In 1862, the United States had separate bilateral postal agreements with each of eight foreign governments," wrote Rita Moroney, USPS historian, in her 1963 booklet *Montgomery Blair, Postmaster General*. "Rates were arrived at via a complex formula that took account of (1) domestic rates in the United States; (2) 'sea postage' for maritime transport; (3) the transit rate assessed by each country through which the article passed, and (4) domestic rates in the country of delivery.

"Sea postage and transit rates were based on the route and the nationality of the vessels carrying the mail. ... An article to Australia might travel by any one of six routes, with postage varying from 5¢ to $1.02 per half ounce. Adding to the confusion of rates and routes were variations in units of weight, in the progression of rates and weights, and in maximum weights and thicknesses. Most onerous of all was the complicated accounting system needed to cover receipts, which ranged from an equal division among the countries involved, to almost every conceivable fractional division."

At the suggestion of a subordinate, John A. Kasson, Postmaster General Blair wrote to postal representatives of several other nations suggesting a "general congress ... to facilitate the international, social and commercial correspondence, by which national prosperity is so much affected." As a direct result, delegates from 15 countries assembled in Paris May 11, 1863. Kasson, who represented the United States, estimated that these 15 nations had a total population of more than 400 million and sent 95 percent of the world's correspondence.

The conference agreed on 31 articles. During the next decade, the United States, Switzerland, Belgium, Italy and others followed these articles in new postal agreements. Under Blair's direction, the United States also revised existing postal arrangements to bring them into accord with the principles agreed on at the convention. Most of these changes dealt with rate reductions; there remained a lack of uniformity and complicated accounting procedures.

But the reform movement had been launched and now had a momentum of its own. In 1873, at Germany's suggestion, the government of the Swiss Confederation invited the European countries, the United States and Egypt to send representatives to a new postal convention in Bern. At Russia's behest, the meeting was postponed until September 15, 1874. Twenty-two states attended this first Postal Congress and adopted the following revolutionary principles:

"1. That a common postal territory, regulated by a single treaty, should be accepted internationally.

"2. That every country should guarantee to every other country the right of transit of mail by land or sea.

"3. That the burden of providing for the conveyance of mails should rest with the country of origin; that all intermediate services used by such country be paid for at fixed rates; and

"4. That each country should keep all of its postage collections, on both prepaid and unpaid correspondence, so as to sweep away the great mass of detailed international accounts."

The treaty incorporating these principles, signed at Bern October 9, 1874, founded what was first called the General Postal Union. Lands beyond Europe, except for Asiatic Russia and Turkey, Egypt and the United States, weren't covered.

In 1878 a second full Congress, in Paris, revised the treaty to admit any country, state or colony that would agree to carry out the stipula-

One of three airmail stamps (Scott C42-44) issued in 1949 to commemorate the 75th anniversary of the Universal Postal Union.

tions of the convention. The organization was then renamed the Universal Postal Union.

The rules to which member countries conform are set out in a convention, or international treaty. Congresses are held every five years to re-examine the convention and determine what changes are necessary or desirable. A special Congress can be convened if requested by two-thirds of the member countries.

The last previous Congress held in the United States was also in Washington, in May and June 1897. Fifty-six countries sent 103 delegates to that meeting more than nine decades ago.

Many nations issued stamps to commemorate the 75th anniversary of the UPU, in 1949, and the 100th anniversary, in 1974. The United States marked the 75th anniversary with a set of three airmail stamps (Scott C42-44) and celebrated the centennial with a se-tenant block of eight (Scott 1530-1537) reproducing works of art that incorporate a letter-writing theme.

The Design

The decision was made early in the planning stages that the stamps and/or souvenir sheet USPS would issue for the UPU Congress would show mail delivery methods. Details were left to be worked out.

Art Director Richard Sheaff researched and prepared a block of nine sketches featuring mail transportation worldwide. These included such exotic subjects as a mail-carrying "Dak" runner of India approaching a lurking tiger, and a postrider of Europe's famous and long-lived Thurn and Taxis postal system. The sketches each bore the slogan "Letters are universal," a phrase reminiscent of the "Letters mingle souls" inscription USPS had used on its UPU centennial commemoratives in 1974.

"The discussion went round and round," recalled project manager Jack Williams, "and the feeling was, 'If we can pick our design subjects worldwide, which countries do we pick? Whichever they are, we leave the rest of the countries meeting here unrepresented.'

"So we decided to limit ourselves to U.S. mail delivery methods."

At that point the committee suggested that the stamps depict delivery methods of the future as well as the past. Accordingly, Sheaff produced another group of sketches covering a continuum — past,

These sketches were made in the early stages when CSAC was considering a block of stamps showing mail transportation methods around the world.

present and future — with the "present" designs showing such things as a World War II military mail call.

After further consideration, the Citizens' Stamp Advisory Committee and the Postal Service decided that instead of one issue of setenant stamps, they preferred two separate sets, clearly divided between past and future. This turned out to be the final resolution of the question.

To design the stamps for the past — which became the Classic Mail Transportation block — USPS chose Mark Hess, a graphic artist whose pictures had appeared on the covers of *Time* and *Newsweek*. Hess had never done a stamp before, but Richard Sheaff admired his clean style and knew he had experience with historical subjects.

The artist was supplied with reference material, including a number of photographs from the National Philatelic Collection at the Smithsonian Institution. Working with these design sources, he developed four stamp images.

Jack Williams then showed the sketches to James Bruns, curator of the National Philatelic Collection and an authority on postal transportation. Bruns suggested several changes in the interest of accuracy.

The main problem he identified was with a sketch showing a U.S. Navy man-of-war anchored offshore while in the foreground a man in a rowboat was receiving a mailbag for delivery to the ship. The ship

This was one of art director Richard Sheaff's earliest concept sketches for a block of nine stamps depicting historical methods of mail transportation worldwide.

was under full canvas, which isn't the way sailing vessels enter a harbor and definitely not the way they ride at anchor. The distance between vessel and dock seemed to be an unreasonably long row. Among lesser matters, the mailbag wasn't authentic. Hess modified his sketch in an effort to deal with these points.

Ultimately, however, after a series of discussions, Williams and Sheaff agreed that a steamboat on an inland waterway would be a more appropriate representation of U.S. mail delivery methods than a naval vessel, which would carry mail only to overseas points and only as an incidental function.

Bruns provided some steamboat pictures, including one of the 19th-century packet *Chesapeake*, which Hess used as a guide in creating a new design. He included in his painting a man pushing a handcart full of mail from the boat, a detail that was also based on a picture from the National Philatelic Collection.

The artist's first rendering of the steamboat showed smoke billowing from the stacks, which would be an unnatural sight with a docked boat. In his final painting he eliminated the smoke and showed steam being vented from the boiler instead. Left unchanged in his final version was a brick walkway over the river levee, although Bruns had

This earlier version of the water-transportation stamp of the Classic Mail Transportation block was replaced by a design depicting a mail-carrying steamboat.

questioned whether permanent paving of that kind would be used on an earthen floodwall.

The other designs required only minor alterations. Mail-carrying Jennies had a mail compartment in place of the front cockpit, but Hess's original sketch showed two open cockpits. It also showed wording on the plane's fuselage that had no basis in historical fact.

A rear view of a 1906 Columbia automobile used to transport mail. A front view of the same model car was shown on the Classic Mail Transportation block of four. Photo courtesy of the Smithsonian Institution.

This Mark Hess sketch of a pony express-type rider didn't make the "final four."

The artist made the appropriate changes. He also removed some anachronistic touches he had included in his painting of the curbside collection vehicle, which was based on a photo from USPS archives of a 1906 Columbia automobile in Baltimore.

The stagecoach design was used essentially as Hess first painted it. The stage was a Concord, named for the New Hampshire city where it was manufactured. These well-built stages, first used to carry mail and passengers in the Civil War era, were still in service in the Dakotas as late as World War I.

The Classic Mail Transportation stamps were of the square, 40-to-a-pane size first used on the Australia bicentennial commemorative of 1988. They were printed on the Bureau of Engraving and Printing's combination D press, with the image in offset and the "USA 25" inscription superimposed in intaglio.

USPS reproduced each of the four designs on maximum cards that

A view of a Concord stagecoach, circa 1894, identical to the coach shown on the Classic Mail Transportation block of four. Photo courtesy of the Smithsonian Institution.

were placed on sale at World Stamp Expo on its opening day, November 17. Canceled sets of the cards, each bearing the appropriate stamps and postmarked November 19, were available at the show November 27.

First-Day Facts

Virginia Noelke of the Citizens' Stamp Advisory Committee spoke at the first-day ceremony. Gordon C. Morison, assistant postmaster general, dedicated the stamps. A special guest appearance was made

The UPU Congress offered this pictorial cancellation for each of its scheduled Monday through Saturday meetings, beginning November 13 and ending December 14. The design, featuring the UPU Congress' unique ZIP code, was the same each day, with only the date changing.

by "Buffalo Bill Cody," played by Eric V. Sorg.

November 19 was Old West Day at World Stamp Expo. Also issuing stamps that day were San Marino, which unveiled stamps honoring the city of Washington; the Commonwealth of Dominica and Turks and Caicos Islands, which held a joint ceremony for seven sheetlets of six stamps recognizing U.S. presidents, and the Federal Republic of Nigeria.

$1 CLASSIC MAIL DELIVERY SOUVENIR SHEET

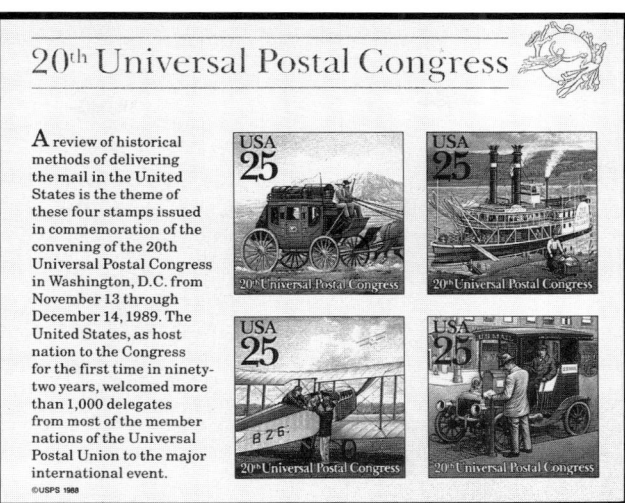

Date of Issue: November 28, 1989

Catalog Numbers: Scott 2438 (souvenir sheet)   Minkus CM1366
Scott 2438a-d (imperf block of 4)
USPS 5530

Colors: magenta, yellow, cyan, black (offset); gray, black (intaglio)

First-Day Cancel: Washington, D.C. (World Stamp Expo '89 stamp show)

FDCs Canceled: unavailable

Format: Imperforate souvenir sheet of 4 stamps. Offset printing plates of 16 subjects (4 across, 4 around); intaglio printing sleeve of 32 subjects (4 across, 8 around).

Perf: imperforate

Selvage Markings: ©USPS 1988

Designer: Mark Hess of Katonah, New York

Art Director and Typographer: Richard Sheaff (CSAC)

Project Manager: Jack Williams (USPS)

Engravers: Michael Ryan (BEP, lettering and numerals)
Gary Slaght (BEP, UPU lettering)
Gary Chaconas (BEP, logo)

Modeler: Jack Ruther (BEP)

Printing: 6-color offset, 3-color intaglio D press (902)

Quantity Ordered: 2,400,000
Quantity Distributed: 2,047,200

Plate/Sleeve Number Detail: no plate or sleeve numbers

Tagging: overall

The Souvenir Sheet

On November 28, USPS issued an imperforate souvenir sheet of four 25¢ stamps to honor the 20th Congress of the Universal Postal Union that was then in progress at the Washington Convention Center in Washington, D.C.

The sheet reproduced in block form the same se-tenant block of four Classic Mail Transportation stamps that had been issued in perforated panes of 40 nine days earlier (see previous chapter).

The designs of both the souvenir sheet and the perforated version of the block of four had been unveiled October 27, 1988, at a meeting in Bern, Switzerland, of the UPU's Consultative Council for Postal Studies.

The souvenir sheets, which were available only at USPS philatelic centers and by mail order, could be used intact on mail to pay $1 in

This essay by Richard Sheaff contemplated a single miniature sheet with eight stamps showing a continuum of mail transportation methods, from past through present to future (including a jet-propelled letter carrier!)

postage or cut apart and used as four separate stamps. However, as was noted in a previous chapter, there were reports of postal clerks rejecting the sheets and stamps as being "only pictures of stamps" and not valid for postage.

The Design

Richard Sheaff, art director for the Classic Mail Transportation stamps, was the designer of the souvenir sheet. The Bureau of Engraving and Printing printed the sheets on its combination offset-intaglio D press, as it had done with the perforated panes of 40. In both versions, the Mark Hess-designed stamps were identical.

An additional intaglio color — gray — was provided for the sheet to reproduce the title "20th Universal Postal Congress" and UPU logo across the top.

A descriptive text appeared in a column of type to the left of the block. This text, like that which appeared on the Future Mail Transportation souvenir sheet, was drafted by project manager Jack Williams and revised into final form after being reviewed at various levels in the Postal Service.

As originally planned, the Universal Postal Congress would have ended on December 15, and the design of the souvenir sheet that was unveiled in 1988 contained that date in its text. Later the closing date was changed to December 14, and the text on the sheet was changed accordingly.

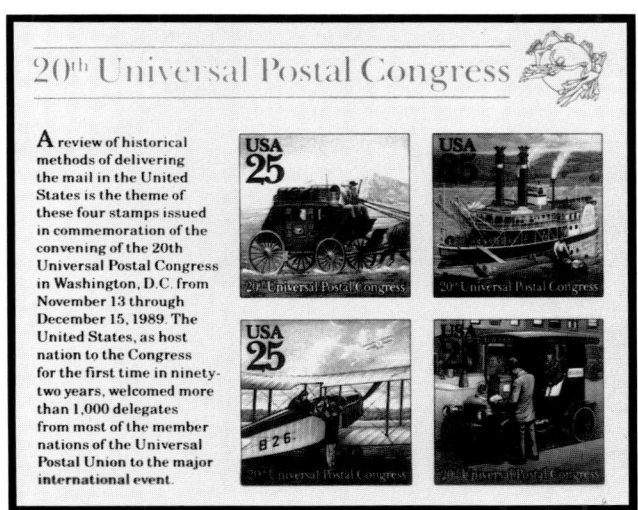

After the closing date of the Universal Postal Congress was moved back to December 14, the text block on the souvenir sheet as it was first unveiled by the Postal Service had to be changed accordingly.

First-Day Facts

The date of issuance of the souvenir sheet was originally announced for November 27. Later USPS switched dates between this sheet and a se-tenant block of four stamps depicting Future Mail Transportation that had been scheduled for issuance November 28.

November 28, when the sheet made its appearance, was Transportation Day at World Stamp Expo.

R.E.G. Davies, curator of air transport at the National Air and Space Museum, spoke at the first-day ceremony. John G. Mulligan, senior assistant postmaster general, dedicated the souvenir sheet. Also taking part in the program was an old-time "airmail pilot," played by Bob Benn.

SPECIAL STAMPS

Special stamps differ from commemorative stamps in that they are issued for use on specific occasions and not to honor persons, places or events. They differ from definitive stamps in that they don't remain on sale for many years at a time or until they are rendered obsolete by a postal rate change.

Only four special stamps were issued in 1989. They were the two annual Christmas stamps, one in a "traditional" design and the other "contemporary," each — for the first time — issued in booklet as well as sheet form. The contemporary version was made by two different printers, one for the booklet, the other for the sheet, which was also a first for the Postal Service.

Three special stamps that USPS had announced for 1989 were deferred until 1990 or later. One was the Love stamp. Although its design was revealed at the ceremony welcoming in 1989 in Washington, D.C., as had become customary, it was later bumped from the year's stamp program, and so 1989 became the first year since 1983 that no new Love stamp was issued. The other two postponed specials were Special Occasions stamps in the form of a booklet, a follow-up to the four-variety Special Occasions booklet of 1988.

25¢ CHRISTMAS MADONNA AND CHILD (SHEET STAMP)

Date of Issue: October 19, 1989

Catalog Numbers: Scott 2427   Minkus 922   USPS 5541

Colors: yellow, pink, red, purple (offset); black (intaglio)

First-Day Cancel: Washington, D.C. (National Gallery of Art)

FDCs Canceled: 395,321 (sheet and booklet)

Format: Panes of 50, vertical, 10 across, 5 down. Offset printing plates of 300 subjects (15 across, 20 around) and intaglio printing sleeve of 600 subjects (15 across, 40 around).

Perf: 11.25 by 11.2 (Eureka off-line perforator)

Selvage Markings: ©UNITED STATES POSTAL SERVICE 1989. USE CORRECT ZIP CODE®

Designer, Art Director and Typographer: Bradbury Thompson (CSAC)

Project Manager: Jack Williams (USPS)

Engravers: Thomas Hipschen (BEP, vignette)
Gary Slaght (BEP lettering and numerals)

Modeler: Peter Cocci (BEP)

Printing: 6-color offset, 3-color intaglio D press (902)

Quantity Ordered: 625,000,000
Quantity Distributed: 609,465,000

Number Detail: Left-side external panes — one group of 4 offset plate numbers over/under corner stamps; one intaglio sleeve number over/under adjacent stamps. Right-side external panes — offset/intaglio numbers in reverse positions. Internal panes — one group of 4 offset plate numbers alongside corner stamps; one intaglio sleeve number alongside adjacent stamps.

Plate/Sleeve Number Combinations: 1111-1, 2211-1, 2221-1, 3342-1, 4453-1, 5564-1, 6675-1

Tagging: block over vignette

The Stamp

In 1989, for the 28th consecutive year, Christmas mailers were offered special stamps to use on their holiday letters and cards. And for the 20th consecutive year, they had their choice of a "traditional," or religious-oriented, design, and a "contemporary," or secular, design.

For the first time, however, they had another option. They could buy their traditional and contemporary Christmas stamps in either sheet or booklet form. All four varieties made their debut October 19.

All four were of the same size, larger than a definitive but smaller than a standard commemorative. This size, introduced with the 1988 Christmas stamps, was a compromise. It responded to the complaints of mailers who thought the definitive-size stamps were too small to properly present the designs. But it still saved paper and ink, a significant consideration with press runs of close to one billion stamps.

Like the 1988 Christmas stamps, the 1989 stamps that were issued in sheet form were printed in sheets of 300, divided into six panes of 50 (10 across by five deep). The 1989 stamps were similar to the 1988s in another way: The traditional versions were produced by a combination of offset and intaglio on BEP's D press, rather than by the gravure method that was used to print all Christmas stamps from 1970 through 1987 (and that continued to be used for the contemporary versions).

"The committee decided that you really need intaglio to bring out the detail in the Old Masters' paintings," explained Jack Williams, USPS project manager of the 1988 and 1989 Christmas stamps.

The Design

As in the past, Bradbury Thompson, a design coordinator for the Citizens' Stamp Advisory Committee, extracted a detail from a Renaissance art masterpiece to serve as the design for the traditional Christmas stamp.

This year's artist of choice was Lodovico Carracci (1555-1619), a native of Bologna, Italy, who became the premier painter of his city and founded the first academy of art where aspiring painters studied all the subjects necessary to their profession. In *The Dream of St. Catherine of Alexandria,* the work on which the stamp is based, the Madonna's head is inclined as she gazes over the shoulder of the Christ child on her lap. The painting, done on canvas around 1590, hangs in the National Gallery of Art in Washington.

The design followed a formula Thompson had used for the contemporary stamps since 1986. The image was in a rectangle that also enclosed the denomination and "USA," with the word "CHRIST-MAS" in red capitals on white across the top and the artist's last name and "National Gallery" in upper- and lower-case across the bottom.

First-Day Facts

Deputy Postmaster General Michael S. Coughlin dedicated both sheet and booklet versions of the traditional stamp in a ceremony at

This is the full painting by Lodovico Carracci, **The Dream of Saint Catherine of Alexandria,** *from which the madonna and child were extracted for the stamp design. The full painting shows Saint Catherine herself and two angels.*

the National Gallery of Art in Washington. The principal speaker was Diane De Grazia, the National Gallery's curator of Southern Baroque painting.

USPS allowed collectors to prepare or order combination covers bearing both the traditional and contemporary Christmas stamps. These were available with either a Washington postmark or a postmark from Westport, Connecticut, the first-day city for the contemporary Christmas stamp.

$5 CHRISTMAS MADONNA AND CHILD BOOKLET

Date of Issue: October 19, 1989

Catalog Numbers: Scott 2427 (stamp)   USPS 6619 (booklet)
Scott 2427a (pane of 10) USPS 6621 (unfolded pane)
Minkus 923

Colors: yellow, pink, red, purple (offset); brown (intaglio)

First-Day Cancel: Washington, D.C. (National Gallery of Art)

FDCs Canceled: 395,321 (sheet and booklet)

Format: Two panes of 10 stamps each arranged vertically 2 by 5. Offset printing plates of 300 subjects (15 across, 20 around) and intaglio printing sleeve of 600 subjects (15 across, 40 around).

Perf: 11.2 by 11.2 by imperforate (Eureka off-line perforator)

Selvage Markings: Sleeve number on binding stub of each pane. Registration mark remnants on 17% of all binding stubs. ©United States Postal Service 1989 on inside of front cover. Universal Product Code (UPC) printed on outside of back cover.

Designer and Typographer: Bradbury Thompson (CSAC)

Art Director and Project Manager: Jack Williams (USPS)

Engravers: Thomas Hipschen (BEP, vignette)
Gary Slaght (BEP, lettering and numerals)

Modeler: Peter Cocci (BEP)

Printing: 6-color offset, 3-color intaglio D press (902). Booklet covers printed on a 6-color Goebel Optiforma offset press (043) in magenta, yellow, cyan and black. Booklets formed on standard bookbinding equipment.

Quantity Ordered: 15,000,000 (booklets)
387,000 (unfolded panes)

Quantity Distributed: 14,479,500 (booklets)
333,000 (unfolded panes)

Plate/Sleeve Number Detail: One sleeve number on each pane binding stub

Sleeve Number: 1

Tagging: block over vignette

The Stamp

USPS issued its 1989 Christmas stamps in booklet as well as sheet form to make it easier for holiday mailers to buy the stamps through self-service vending equipment in postal lobbies, shopping malls and commuter stops, as well as at supermarkets and other retail outlets in the stamps-on-consignment program.

Both the traditional and contemporary booklets contained two panes of 10 stamps each and sold for $5.

Because the Christmas stamps were made in a special size, somewhat larger than a normal definitive, the booklet panes themselves were wider (by just under one-eighth of an inch) and longer than the usual panes.

A variety of markings could be found on the binding tabs of the traditional booklets. Each tab contained the engraved sleeve number 1. There were five different configurations involving partial color bars and an electric-eye register control (crow's foot) marking. There were also tabs that were blank except for the sleeve number; these were actually the most common. In all, 16 different tab combinations could be found in the two-pane booklets.

Following a practice begun with the Steamboats booklet earlier in the year, USPS offered individual booklet panes, complete with numbered tabs and unfolded, through the Philatelic Sales Division.

USPS also utilized the unfolded, tabbed panes on its Christmas stamp souvenir pages, as it had promised. Previously, when making up the Steamboats booklet souvenir pages, USPS personnel had removed the tabs, not realizing that collectors would want intact panes.

The Design

The booklet variety of the traditional Christmas stamp depicting the Carracci madonna and child was identical to the sheet stamp in appearance, except that each copy from a booklet had at least one straight edge.

The cover of the booklet, printed by offset, bore a full-color enlarged reproduction of the design of the stamps inside. Jack Williams, project manager, called it an example of "truth in packaging."

Williams explained that the decision to have the cover reflect the contents stemmed from complaints received in 1988 after the 25¢ Jack London definitive stamp was issued in booklet form. For that booklet cover, BEP artist Frank Waslick painted a scene evocative of the London novels, showing a wolflike animal in the foreground watching a dog team pull a sled through the Arctic snow. Some customers, however, were unhappy that the stamps inside bore no such dramatic picture — merely a portrait of Jack London.

The traditional Christmas stamp's booklet cover bore the words "Season's Greetings," which complemented the word "Christmas" in the stamp-design reproduction on the cover. Originally, the Postal Service had planned to use only the single word "Greetings" on the cover, and in fact illustrated the "Greetings" version in its news release on the Christmas stamps.

The back of the cover was used to promote the Philatelic Sales Division's 1989 Commemorative Mint Set. A coupon for ordering the set appeared on the opposite side, beneath the folded stamp pane.

First-Day Facts

Information on the first-day ceremony is included in the chapter on the traditional Christmas stamp, sheet version.

First-day cover customers were given 60 days rather than the usual 30 to submit stamped covers, or unstamped covers plus remittance, for first-day cancellations. For covers that they prepared themselves, stamp collectors could affix single stamps from booklets. For covers on which the Postal Service affixed stamps, however, only full panes were affixed at a cost of $2.50.

USPS also permitted collectors to prepare or order combination covers bearing full panes from both the traditional and contemporary Christmas booklets. These were available with either a Washington postmark or a postmark from Westport, Connecticut, the first-day city for the contemporary booklet.

25¢ CHRISTMAS GREETINGS (SHEET STAMP)

Date of Issue: October 19, 1989

Catalog Numbers: Scott 2428   Minkus 920   USPS 5540

Colors: red, yellow, magenta, cyan, black

First-Day Cancel: Westport, Connecticut (Arts Center)

FDCs Canceled: 345,931 (sheet and booklet)

Format: Panes of 50, horizontal, 5 across, 10 down. Gravure printing cylinders of 300 subjects (15 across, 20 around).

Perf: 10.9 (L perforator)

Selvage Markings: ©United States Postal Service 1989, Use Correct ZIP Code®

Designer: Stevan Dohanos of Westport, Connecticut

Art Director and Typographer: Bradbury Thompson (CSAC)

Project Manager: Jack Williams (USPS)

Modeler: Richard Sennett (Sennett Enterprises) for American Bank Note Company

Printing: Stamps printed and sheeted out by American Bank Note Company on a leased Champlain gravure press (J.W. Fergusson and Sons, Richmond, Virginia) under the supervision of Sennett Enterprises (Fairfax, Virginia). Perforated, processed and shipped by ABNC (Chicago, Illinois).

Quantity Ordered: 900,000,000
Quantity Distributed: 900,000,000

Cylinder Number Detail: One group of 5 cylinder numbers preceded by the letter "A" alongside corner stamps on 4 external panes. One group of 5 cylinder numbers preceded by the letter "A" over/under corner stamps on 2 internal panes.

Cylinder Number Combination: A11111

Tagging: overall

The Stamp

As was noted in the chapter on the traditional Christmas stamp, the 1989 issues represented a first — the first time the Christmas stamps had been issued in both sheet and booklet forms.

But the contemporary Christmas stamp featured a first of its own. It was the first U.S. stamp of any kind to be printed in two different formats by two different security printers.

The American Bank Note Company, which had been supplying various stamps for USPS under contract for several years, produced the sheet version of the contemporary stamp. The Bureau of Engraving and Printing, which has been in the booklet-forming business far longer than ABNC, did the booklet version.

Both used gravure printing. However, ABNC used an additional color (magenta) for the sheet stamp, besides the red, cyan, yellow and black utilized by both printers. So the two versions are readily distinguishable from each other in surface appearance. They can also be told apart, of course, by the fact that the sheet stamps are fully perforated and the booklet stamps have at least one straight edge.

The 1880s sleigh drawn by Walter Brooks for this 1983 Transportation series coil (Scott 1900) is very similar to the gift-laden sleigh on the 1989 Christmas stamp.

The Design

The contemporary Christmas stamp marked a sentimental return to an old field of endeavor for Stevan Dohanos of Westport, Connecticut. Dohanos, whose many covers for *The Saturday Evening Post* rank second only to Norman Rockwell's for recognizability, was a former chairman and design coordinator of the Citizens' Stamp Advisory Committee. For a quarter of a century he supervised the artwork on more than 300 U.S. stamps and personally designed some 26 others — including five showing the U.S. flag and nine previous Christmas stamps — plus four postal cards. The Hall of Stamps at USPS headquarters in Washington, opened in 1984, is dedicated to him.

Dohanos' design for the 1989 contemporary Christmas stamp was reminiscent of the se-tenant block of four he had done for Christmas in 1970, which featured antique toys against a plain white background (Scott 1415-1418). Like those, the new design was also based on an antique toy; in this case, a sleigh, owned by the New York State Historical Association in Cooperstown, New York.

The upholstered sleigh has red runners curving upward into an S-

This antique toy sleigh, 3 feet 4 inches long and 16 inches wide, by an unidentified craftsman, was the model for the design of the 1989 contemporary Christmas stamp. Photo courtesy of the New York State Historical Association in Cooperstown.

shape at the front, with a yellow arabesque pattern decorating the side of the coach section. Dohanos added gaily wrapped gift packages made out of pieces of paper to his original painting. The design is also remindful of a 5.2¢ Transportation series coil stamp issued in 1983 for use on non-profit mail (Scott 1900). The coil shows a real sleigh from the 1880s.

A comparison of the sheet stamp, printed by ABNC and using the extra color, and the booklet stamp, printed by BEP, discloses several subtle differences. On the sheet stamp, the green package has a black ribbon; in the booklet, the ribbon is dark green. On the sheet stamp, there are a light blue package and two orange packages; in the booklet version, the same packages are dark blue and magenta. The red runners on the sleigh are thinner on the sheet than in the booklet.

Varieties

In January 1990 it was disclosed that a pane of the contemporary Christmas stamps with the horizontal perforations missing had been purchased at a post office in Florida. The buyer, a non-collector, reportedly used 10 of the stamps on Christmas cards before selling the remainder to a stamp collector. Stanley Kopkin of Tropical Stamps Inc., Fort Lauderdale, told *Linn's Stamp News* that 18 vertical pairs, imperforate between, from the pane were later sold to Eydie Gorme, the popular singer, for an undisclosed price. Gorme had been a stamp collector for slightly more than two years, Kopkin said, and specialized in U.S. stamps, plate blocks and errors. Her collection included a copy of the $1 Candleholder invert of the Americana series, the dealer said.

Singer Eydie Gorme purchased 18 vertical pairs, imperforate between, of the Greetings stamp.

First-Day Facts

The dedication ceremony was held at the Westport Arts Center in Westport, Connecticut, hometown of stamp designer Stevan Dohanos. USPS said this was the first time a place of issue was chosen to honor anyone involved in the design or production of the stamp.

Dohanos' fellow stamp designer, Paul Calle of Ridgefield, Connecticut, was among the speakers. The stamp was dedicated by Kenneth J. Hunter, associate postmaster general.

$5 CHRISTMAS GREETINGS BOOKLET

Date of Issue: October 19, 1989

Catalog Numbers: Scott 2428 (stamp)　　USPS 6618 (booklet)
Scott 2428a (pane of 10) USPS 6620 (unfolded pane)
Minkus 921

Colors: red, cyan, yellow, black

First-Day Cancel: Westport, Connecticut (Art Center)

FDCs Canceled: 345,931 (sheet and booklet)

Format: Two panes of 10 stamps each arranged horizontally 5 by 2. Gravure printing cylinders of 300 subjects (15 across, 20 around).

Perf: Imperforate by 11.2 (Eureka off-line perforator)

Selvage Markings: 4 cylinder numbers on binding stub of each pane. Registration mark remnants on 17% of all pane binding stubs. ©United States Postal Service 1989 on inside of front cover. Universal Product Code (UPC) printed on outside of back cover.

Designer: Stevan Dohanos of Westport, Connecticut

Art Director and Typographer: Bradbury Thompson (CSAC)

Project Manager: Jack Williams (USPS)

Modeler: Peter Cocci (BEP)

Printing: Stamps printed on 7-color Andreotti gravure press (602). Booklet covers printed on a 6-color Goebel Optiforma offset press in magenta, yellow, cyan and black. Booklets formed on standard bookbinding equipment.

Quantity Ordered: 20,000,000 (booklets)
387,000 (unfolded panes)
Quantity Distributed: 19,795,500 (booklets)
333,000 (unfolded panes)

Cylinder Number Detail: One group of 4 cylinder numbers on each pane binding stub.

Cylinder Number Combinations: 1111, 2111

Tagging: overall

The Stamp

The contemporary Christmas booklet was printed by the Bureau of Engraving and Printing, unlike the sheet version, which was produced by the American Bank Note Company.

As with the traditional Christmas booklet, the size of the pane was longer and slightly wider than usual, reflecting the slightly larger size of the individual stamps.

Cylinder numbers were found on the binding tab of each booklet pane, but the tabs contained several other markings as well. There were five different configurations incorporating partial color bars and an electric-eye register control (crow's foot) marking. A sixth type of pane, the most common, had no markings other than the cylinder numbers. Eighteen different combinations of tabs were available in the two-pane booklets for each of the two cylinder number combinations (1111 and 2111). Therefore, a complete set of known tab varieties required 36 contemporary booklets.

In a practice begun with the Steamboats booklet earlier in the year, USPS offered, through the Philatelic Sales Division, individual booklet panes, unfolded and with numbered tab attached.

The Design

The design of the booklet stamp was identical to that of the sheet version, although BEP used one fewer process color on its gravure press than ABNC did. The readily discernible color differences between the two varieties were noted in the preceding chapter.

BEP reproduced the contemporary Christmas stamp on the cover of the booklet, as it did with the traditional Christmas stamp. This was done to forestall the kind of criticism some customers had leveled at previous booklet covers that bore pictures differing from those on the stamps inside.

The word "Christmas" also appears on the booklet cover. That word wasn't used on the stamp itself; since 1978, USPS has inscribed its contemporary Christmas stamps with the neutral "season's greetings" or, more recently, just "greetings."

Like the traditional Christmas stamp booklet cover, the cover for the contemporary Christmas stamp bore an advertisement on the back for USPS' 1989 Commemorative Mint Set and a coupon on the reverse for ordering it.

Varieties

At least three errors in the stamps or booklet covers were reported.

A Wilmington, Delaware, postal customer bought a booklet in which a miscut on the second, or bottom, pane had caused the single row of horizontal perforations to move all the way to the bottom edge of the pane, which is normally a straight edge. There were no perfs between the top and bottom row of stamps, and the result was five vertical pairs imperf between. The booklet was scheduled to be sold at auction in February 1990 by dealer Jacques Schiff.

In Arlington, Texas, a food store that carried stamps sold a woman a booklet in which the second, or bottom, pane had the red color omitted. This eliminated the sleigh's runner and some of the packages, and gave a different hue to the cushion on the sleigh. Jacques Schiff had this booklet also, on consignment.

Examples of the booklet cover with the yellow color omitted were found. Leslie Bistline of Hyndman, Pennsylvania, told *Linn's Stamp News* that he had purchased 10 such booklets. All lettering and packages that are green on a normal cover are blue on the error covers. On those found by Bistline, the remaining red and blue colors were misregistered, and there was a faint doubled appearance of all red areas.

First-Day Facts

Information on the dedication ceremony can be found in the chapter on the contemporary Christmas stamp, sheet version.

DEFINITIVES

Years in which postal rates change are big years for new definitive stamps. But even for a non-rate change year, 1989 was light in this category. Only six definitives were issued in 1989, and one of them was a reissued Transportation coil stamp with a new service inscription. Not since five stamps in the Americana series constituted 1979's entire output of definitives had fewer appeared in a single year.

For the first time since the popular Transportation coil series was launched in 1981, there were no face-different additions to the set. And only two new entries in the Great Americans series were made.

The important event of the year was the issuance of a new self-adhesive stamp — labeled "EXTRAordinary" by the U.S. Postal Service — that was sold at a markup over the 25¢ face value. How well the public received it during a 30-day test period in 15 cities would influence whether, and to what extent, the Postal Service would follow up with other self-adhesives.

25¢ FLAG OVER YOSEMITE (PHOSPHORED PAPER)

Date of Issue: February 14, 1989

Catalog Numbers: Scott 2280   Minkus 891a   USPS 7737 (coils of 100s)

Colors: red, blue, green

First-Day Cancel: Yosemite National Park, California (Yosemite Village)

FDCs Canceled: 118,874

Format: Initially in coils of 100; later in larger size coils. Printing sleeves of 864 subjects (18 across, 48 around) and 960 subjects (20 across, 48 around).

Perf: 9.8 (Goebel stroke perforator for coils of 100; Huck rotary perforator for larger coils)

Designer and Model: Peter Cocci (BEP)

Art Director: Joe Brockert (USPS)

Project Manager: Joe Brockert (USPS)

Typographer: Bradbury Thompson (CSAC)

Engravers: Thomas Hipschen (BEP, vignette)
    Dennis Brown (BEP, lettering and numerals)

Printing: 3-color intaglio C press (901)

Quantity Ordered: 9,000 (coils of 10,000)
Quantity Distributed: 5,270 (coils of 10,000)

Sleeve Number Detail: One sleeve number on every 48th stamp for sleeves 10, 11 and 13

Sleeve Numbers: 2, 3, 5, 6, 7, 8, 9, 10, 11, 13

Tagging: overall (phosphored paper)

The Stamp

On February 14, the U.S. Postal Service issued its first full-production definitive stamp on phosphored paper. It was the 25¢ Flag Over Yosemite coil stamp that had been originally issued on regular paper May 20, 1988.

The new stamp, like the old, made its debut at Yosemite National Park, California. This time no dedication ceremony was held.

A form of phosphored paper had previously been used for the 22¢ Flag Over the Capitol test coil of 1987 and on Official Mail stamps beginning in 1988.

Unlike the 1987 test coil, the Yosemite stamp didn't carry the letter "T" (for test) at the bottom edge of each stamp. Nevertheless, the new variety can be distinguished from the old with little difficulty.

Under ultraviolet light, the new stamp glows in a uniform fashion. The effect has been likened to the splotchy, sometimes faint, overall tagging applied by the letterpress station on the Bureau of Engraving and Printing's old Cottrell press. The earlier Yosemite stamp had its phosphor ink applied in a block over the printed image.

Under ordinary light, the paper on the newer stamps appears somewhat whiter and the colors brighter than on the original. The visible contrast between old and new varieties is less striking, however, than was the case with the Flag Over Capitol test coil, because the Yosemite phosphored paper wasn't the same as that used for the Flag test.

With that stamp, and the 1988 Official Mail stamps, the phosphor was added as a coating after the paper's manufacture. For Yosemite, the paper was treated with phosphor. The latter paper is cheaper, costing roughly half as much as the paper with phosphor coating.

BEP began testing the phosphored paper at the end of 1988. During initial press runs it was found that the phosphor was too heavy. BEP personnel complained that the phosphor was flaking off during printing, and printers expressed concern that the "flying phosphor" might be toxic. (Tests showed that it wasn't.)

BEP also tried another approach. Regular Flag stamp paper was run through the Andreotti gravure press and a phosphor coating applied. The rolls were then put on the C press, where the 25¢ Yosemite design was printed over the gravure phosphor coating. After printing, the intaglio Flag inks began to flake, and that ended the experiment.

A BEP spokesman told *Linn's* Washington correspondent Charles H. Yeager that the problem of excessive phosphor was solved by returning all rolls of the phosphored paper to the paper supplier. The supplier apparently scuffed or brushed the rolls to remove loose phosphor particles. Subsequent test printings using this "phosphor-treated" paper produced stamps acceptable to the Postal Service, and regular production runs began.

Some collectors believed at first that they could distinguish the block-tagged Yosemite from the new phosphored paper stamp in a plate number single or strip because the original variety was printed from sleeves 1 through 5. However, a phosphored example was later found printed from sleeve 5, and later both types were found from some of the higher-numbered sleeves.

A prime reason for testing the phosphor-coated paper in 1987 was to reduce revenue loss from the reuse of "cleaned" stamps. Because the phosphor-carrying lacquer sometimes prevents cancel ink from penetrating into stamp paper, USPS had a problem with people who succeeded in removing the ink and illegally reused the stamps. With phosphor already on the paper, the lacquer is unnecessary and the cancel ink can more easily penetrate the paper.

In addition, USPS said, phosphored paper reduces manufacturing costs and improves stamp quality.

News of the stamp, its date and its place of issue was first disclosed in the January 26 issue of the *Postal Bulletin*. At the same time, the periodical reported that the 25¢ Bread Wagon coil stamp of 1986 was no longer available and would be phased out. The official USPS announcement of the new Yosemite variety was made February 10, four days before it went on sale.

USPS gradually replaced the conventionally tagged coil with the prephosphored one. At first, it was available primarily at philatelic centers and post offices with dedicated philatelic windows.

The Design

The stamp was identical in appearance to the earlier version. Peter Cocci's design depicted Half Dome, one of the landmarks of Yosemite National Park, with the Merced River in the foreground. It was produced in three-color intaglio on BEP's C press in rolls of 100 and later in larger size coils.

Varieties

Like most modern coils, the phosphored Yosemite stamp was found in imperforate form. In July 1989, one dealer offered imperforate pairs of both the prephosphored and block-tagged varieties of the stamp for $29.95 each.

First-Day Facts

Only a handful of collectors came to Yosemite February 14 to prepare covers on the official release date. One was Ed Denson, an authority on plate number coil first-day covers, who obtained FDCs canceled with the Yosemite post office's red round-dater.

Reportedly, several post offices placed the new coils on sale before February 14, not realizing they were a new variety.

Because of the late announcement of the new stamp, USPS extended the deadline for ordering first-day cancellations from the standard 30 days to 60 days. This expanded grace period — together with

USPS' liberal policy of replacing damaged covers — led to some abuses by cover collectors. The abuses, in turn, led to a change in the Postal Service's policy on cover replacements.

Reportedly, only stamps from sleeve number 8 were available at Yosemite February 14. During the grace period, sleeve numbers 5, 6 and 7 showed up on phosphored paper, and copies were used on first-day covers.

About two weeks after the April 15 deadline passed, sleeve number 9 of the phosphored Yosemite stamp appeared. Several plate number coil dealers asked for grace-period extensions and serviced FDCs with number 9s. Individual collectors also created number 9 covers.

As an experiment, *Linns's Stamp News* writer Wayne Youngblood, who had received some damaged Yosemite covers long after his normally processed ones arrived, affixed strips of stamps from sleeve number 10 to his replacement covers for cancellation. Sleeve number 10 wasn't even used for printing until mid-July, five months after the issue date and three months after the grace-period deadline. Reporting on his test in the September 11 issue of *Linn's,* Youngblood said the three sleeve 10 covers reached him in perfect condition August 28 — with the February 14 first-day cancellation.

Such covers, which could have been created by anyone with a damaged cover (including those who damaged the covers themselves for this purpose), had a market value of several hundred dollars each, Younblood wrote.

"In its desire to be accommodating and fair to collectors, the USPS has created instant rarities," he concluded. "Collectors should know that although the covers described ... are scarce, they were not created according to standard practices. ..."

USPS reacted quickly after learning of the problem. Henceforth, said Bob Brown, manager of the Philatelic Sales Division, collectors returning damaged first-day covers for replacement would get exactly what they traded in. For instance, if a cover had a coil stamp with a number 2 on it, the owner would get back a cover with a number 2. If the stamp had no number, ditto for the replacement. Collectors could still submit replacement covers by affixing their own stamps, but they would be required to affix stamps identical in plate number status to the ones present on their original covers.

7.1¢ TRACTOR (NEW SERVICE INSCRIPTION) TRANSPORTATION SERIES

Date of Issue: May 26, 1989

Catalog Numbers: Scott 2127a   USPS P938 (coil of 500)
Minkus 917   USPS P939 (coil of 3000)

Colors: red, black

First-Day Cancel: Rosemont, Illinois (Compex '89 stamp show)

FDCs Canceled: 202,804

Format: Coils of 500 and 3,000. Printing sleeve of 936 subjects (18 across, 52 around).

Perf: 9.8 (Huck rotary perforator)

Designer: Ken Dallison of Indian River, Ontario, Canada

Art Director and Project Manager: Jack Williams (USPS)

Typographer: Bradbury Thompson (CSAC)

Engravers: Gary Chaconas (BEP, vignette)
Robert Culin, Sr. (BEP, original lettering and numerals)
Gary Slaght (BEP, new service inscription)

Printing: 3-color intaglio B press (701)

Quantity Ordered: 59,000 (coils of 500)
15,000 (coils of 3000)
Quantity Distributed: 59,850 (coils of 500)
23,168 (coils of 3000)

Sleeve Number Detail: One intaglio sleeve number on every 52nd stamp

Sleeve Number: 1

Tagging: untagged

The Stamp

An old Transportation coil stamp with a new service inscription made its appearance May 26 at Compex '89, the Chicago area's largest stamp show.

It was the 7.1¢ Tractor stamp, bearing the inscription "Nonprofit/5-Digit ZIP+4" in two lines, and issued to meet the needs of non-profit mailers who use ZIP+4 and presort to the first five digits.

Both inscription and vignette were printed in intaglio from a single printing sleeve. USPS calls this kind of inscription a "precancel," because stamps so inscribed aren't tagged and don't normally go through post office facer-canceling machines.

In traditional philatelic parlance, however, the word "precancel" described an inscription overprinted on a previously printed stamp using a letterpress process.

The original 7.1¢ Tractor stamp, issued February 6, 1987, at Sarapex in Sarasota, Florida, was used primarily by non-profit mailers who presorted their mail to five digits. It bore the intaglio inscription "Nonprofit/Org."

It was simultaneously issued in tagged form without the inscription for the benefit of collectors, in keeping with the then-current USPS practice of issuing bulk-rate stamps in two varieties — with and without the service inscription or precancel.

Shown here is the original 7.1¢ Tractor stamp with the "Nonprofit Org." inscription, issued in 1987.

Beginning in 1988, however, USPS stopped issuing unprecanceled varieties of these stamps. Accordingly, the new 7.1¢ Tractor stamp appeared in only one form.

Both of the earlier versions of the Tractor stamp, with and without inscription, were withdrawn from sale by the Philatelic Sales Agency February 28, 1989.

The Tractor wasn't the first Transportation coil to be put back to work with a new service inscription after what had appeared to be a permanent retirement.

In 1988 the 10.1¢ Oil Wagon stamp, originally issued in 1985 for third-class mail presorted to five digits, was reissued with a new inscription for third-class mail presorted to the carrier route. In the case of the Oil Wagon, however, both the first and second service inscriptions were "traditional" precancels — that is, overprints. The reason was that the stamp's design arrangement left no large white area into which an engraved inscription could be squeezed.

The re-employment of both the Oil Wagon and Tractor stamps was made possible by the 1988 postal rate overhaul, which created new uses for certain rates that had previously been assigned to other categories of mail.

The new structure increased the non-profit five-digit rate to 7.6¢ and assigned the 7.1¢ rate to non-profit five-digit mail using ZIP+4, which was a new category.

USPS said all philatelic centers would sell the Tractor stamp, but that as a limited-use item it wouldn't be available at all post offices.

The Design

Except for the service inscription, the new Tractor stamp was identical with the original. It featured Ken Dallison's drawing of a 1920s John Deere machine.

For the revised service inscription, USPS typographer Bradbury Thompson designed a bold sans-serif typeface. On the earlier version, Thompson's service inscription had appeared in the same Roman type with serifs that he had used for the wording on the basic stamp.

As frequently happens when multicolor intaglio stamps are printed from a single sleeve, so-called ink contamination was common on this stamp, with the black inscription showing traces of the red ink used to print the tractor image.

First-Day Facts

Shortly after the official opening of Compex '89 at the Holiday Inn O'Hare in Rosemont, Illinois, W.L. (Pete) Davidson, director of the USPS Office of Stamps and Philatelic Marketing, dedicated the new stamp. Speakers included Charles Berg, president of Compex '89, and Richard E. Drews, chairman of the American Philatelic Society's Chapter Activities Committee.

First-day covers bore the Rosemont postmark. Collectors were reminded that covers bearing a Tractor stamp would have to carry at least 17.9¢ additional postage to meet the 25¢ first-class mail rate. For covers serviced by USPS, the charge was 26¢, and USPS affixed a pair of Tractor stamps plus one 11¢ Stutz Bearcat stamp of 1985 — a stamp that was also designed by Ken Dallison.

$1 JOHNS HOPKINS
GREAT AMERICANS SERIES

Date of Issue: June 7, 1989

Catalog Numbers: Scott 2194A   Minkus 918   USPS 1090

Color: blue

First-Day Cancel: Baltimore, Maryland (Convention Center)

FDCs Canceled: 159,049

Format: Panes of 20 stamps, vertical, 5 across, 4 down. Printing sleeve of 320 subjects (10 across, 32 around).

Perf: 11.2 by 11.1 (Eureka off-line perforator)

Selvage Markings: ©USPS 1989

Designer, Art Director and Typographer: Bradbury Thompson (CSAC)

Project Manager: Joe Brockert (USPS)

Engravers: Gary Chaconas (BEP, vignette)
Dennis Brown (BEP, lettering and numerals)

Modeler: Frank Waslick (BEP)

Printing: 3-color intaglio unit of the 8-color gravure/intaglio A press (702)

Quantity Ordered: 120,000,000
Quantity Distributed: 86,520,000

Sleeve Number Detail: One sleeve number alongside each corner stamp of sheetlet

Sleeve Number: 1

Tagging: block over vignette

The Stamp

A $1 stamp in the Great Americans series was issued June 7 to honor Johns Hopkins, the 19th-century merchant and banker whose $7 million gift was used to establish the hospital, university and medical school bearing his name.

The stamp was first announced by USPS on October 28, 1987, more than a year and a half before its issuance. It wasn't until February 23, 1989, however, that it was disclosed that the denomination would be $1 and that the Hopkins stamp would replace the first Great Americans stamp of that value, which pictured Dr. Bernard Revel and was issued in 1986.

The Hopkins stamp was the 45th face-different stamp in the Great Americans series, which began December 27, 1980, with a 19¢ value honoring Sequoyah. In this respect the Great Americans far exceeds any other set ever issued by the United States for general postal use. (The current Transportation series of coils has a comparable number of varieties, but most are in bulk-mail denominations that can be used only by holders of permits.)

In selecting Hopkins as a stamp subject, the Citizens' Stamp Advisory Committee again fell back on an indirect method of paying tribute to an educational institution on its anniversary. The committee has a rule against stamps or postal cards that honor a specific college, but in the past has frequently found a way to accomplish that end without specifically breaking the rule.

Years ago colleges and universities got full-fledged commemorative stamps. The first of these was Washington and Lee University, whose bicentennial was marked by a 3¢ stamp in 1949 (Scott 982). Columbia University received a bicentennial stamp in 1954 (Scott 1029), when its former president, Dwight D. Eisenhower, was in the White House. A 1955 stamp for the founding of the first land-grant schools named both Michigan State College and Pennsylvania State University (Scott 1065).

But the 1956 issue for Princeton's bicentennial (Scott 1083) embodied a subtle change. The stamp noted only the 200th anniversary of Nassau Hall, the university's oldest building. And a 1958 Freedom of the Press commemorative (Scott 1119) issued in connection with the 50th anniversary of the first school of journalism, at the University of Missouri, carried no reference to the school.

In 1968, CSAC revised postage stamp criteria it had developed a year earlier. "Commemorative stamps shall not be issued for ... schools or institutions of higher learning since so many are reaching significant anniversaries," it said. "Due to the restrictions which must of necessity be placed on the stamp program, it would be most difficult to single out one anniversary for commemoration to the exclusion of the many others."

In fact, Dartmouth College was "singled out" the next year, with a stamp not specifically for the school but for the 150th anniversary of the landmark Dartmouth College case, argued by Daniel Webster before the U.S. Supreme Court. The stamp depicted Webster and Dartmouth Hall (Scott 1380).

Other oblique ways of honoring colleges were found. In 1981, the Professional Management commemorative (Scott 1920) portrayed Joseph Wharton, founder of the Wharton School of Business at the University of Pennsylvania, on its centennial. It was issued at the school.

And in 1983, a definitive — not a commemorative — stamp was issued for Thomas Gallaudet, American pioneer in education for the deaf. He founded the American School for the Deaf at West Hartford, Connecticut, in 1816, and the privately operated Gallaudet University in Washington, D.C., bears his name.

Gallaudet was honored in the Great Americans series (Scott 1861), and two years later so was Abraham Baldwin, the "father" of the state university movement as the founder of the school that became the University of Georgia (Scott 1850).

Thus, when the oldest university in the United States, Harvard, celebrated its 350th anniversary in 1986, a precedent was available — and was utilized. Harvard was offered a 56¢ stamp in the Great Americans series portraying John Harvard, who left half of his estate and his library to found the institution (Scott 2191).

The $1 stamp for Dr. Bernard Revel noted the centennial of Yeshiva University, which he founded (Scott 2194), and a 2¢ stamp picturing Mary Lyon, pioneer in women's education at the college level, covered the 150th anniversary of Mount Holyoke College in 1987 (Scott 2169).

Early in 1989, the U.S. Postal Service used still another approach in honoring Georgetown University on its 200th anniversary. It issued a 15¢ postal card that ostensibly celebrated the preservation of Healy Hall, Georgetown's administration building. (See 15¢ Healy Hall Postal Card.)

A stamp to accompany the Johns Hopkins centennial had been the objective of a major lobbying campaign that was coordinated by Elaine Freeman, director of public affairs for the Johns Hopkins Medical Institutions, and enthusiastically supported by Dr. Steven Muller, president of the university and a stamp collector himself.

Items were inserted in periodicals, newsletters, letters from the president and deans and other mailings, asking alumni and friends to write to the postmaster general and CSAC. "We also turned to some of our faculty, staff and trustees and even former patients whom we knew had contacts in Washington that would be of help to us," Freeman said.

One who was particularly helpful, she added, was Dr. Patrick Walsh, chairman of the Johns Hopkins department of urology, who had developed "some very innovative surgical procedures related to surgery on the prostate which leave patients with their potency and continence intact." Several business executives and at least one member of Congress who had benefited from these innovations took up the cause of a Johns Hopkins stamp, Freeman said, and helped win the endorsement of members of the House Post Office and Civil Service Committee.

All the effort paid off, and the stamp was approved in 1987 by Postmaster General Preston R. Tisch. The Johns Hopkins community was pleased with the attractive stamp that resulted, Freeman said. "Our preference would have been a commemorative stamp, but that was not to be," she said. "The next best and obvious thing was to have it as part of the Great Americans series. I would have also preferred a 25¢ stamp rather than a $1, but other than that, it's very nice."

The $1 Revel stamp that the Johns Hopkins stamp replaced had been uniquely noteworthy. In 1987 collectors — to say nothing of USPS and the Bureau of Engraving and Printing — were startled to learn that its engraver had concealed a tiny Star of David in Revel's beard.

USPS didn't withdraw the Revel stamps, but chose not to reprint them. In the April 6, 1989, issue of the *Postal Bulletin*, postmasters were informed that BEP had depleted its stock of Revels and all unfilled requisitions would be converted to the Hopkins stamp once it was issued. Meantime, the *Bulletin* said, if necessary postmasters should provide customers with pairs of 50¢ stamps.

The May 15 USPS announcement said the Hopkins stamp would be issued in standard panes of 100. This turned out to be incorrect. The stamp was released in panes of 20 stamps, five across by four deep, with a single-digit sleeve number in each corner of the selvage and a 1989 USPS copyright symbol at the top or bottom of each pane.

These 20-stamp panes were introduced with the $5 Bret Harte Great Americans stamp of 1987. At that time, USPS said all future high-value definitives would be released in this format. The 20-stamp panes provided 20 times as many plate number blocks of four per 100 stamps as the standard format and thus reduced the number of leftover stamps that had to be destroyed after plate blocks were removed for collectors, as USPS explained it.

Johns Hopkins was the son of a prosperous Quaker tobacco farmer in Maryland. In 1807 his father's adherence to a new Quaker policy led him to free all his slaves, and suddenly young Johns — it was a family name — was forced to drop out of school at age 12 and go to work in the fields.

At 17 he was hired by his uncle, a wholesale grocer in Baltimore, and he soon proved his ability as a shrewd merchant. He saved enough capital to set himself up in business as a supplier of whiskey, tobacco and other staples. The enterprise grew and prospered, and in

1847 he was named president of the Merchants' National Bank of Baltimore and a director of the Baltimore & Ohio Railroad. By the time he died, he owned 15,000 shares of B&O stock.

As he grew older, Hopkins pondered the problem of disposing of his considerable fortune "for the good of humanity." The idea of bestowing his name on both a university and a hospital appealed to him, and in 1867 a charter was obtained and a board of trustees appointed.

Of his estimated $7 million estate, he stipulated that half was to go toward the university, of which a school of medicine would be a part, and half to the hospital. It would be the first hospital subject to the authority of a university, with the medical school as an adjunct. Eventually the hospital and the university would have separate boards of trustees.

In March 1873, Hopkins set down in a letter to the trustees his vision of an up-to-date hospital with a first-class staff and a physically beautiful setting, and in which "the indigent sick of this city and its environs, without regard to sex, age or color, who may require surgical or medical treatment ... (or be) stricken down by any casualty, shall be received into the hospital, without charge." He died of pneumonia nine months later at 78, never to see the ground broken.

Construction and development proceeded slowly. The first classes were held in 1876 and the hospital was not opened until May 1889 — the event whose centennial observance was accompanied by the Johns Hopkins stamp.

The medical school opened in October 1893 with the help of a $500,000 endowment raised by a group of women on the then-radical condition that women be admitted on the same terms as men. (Dean William Welch confessed that he hesitated to agree to co-education out of a distaste at having to explain "indelicate things" to ladies.)

The women also demanded and got the toughest admission standards ever contemplated for any medical school in the country, including an A.B. degree and knowledge of French, German, Latin, mathematics, chemistry, biology and physics. "We are lucky to get in as professors," physician-in-chief William Osler confided to Welch, "for I am sure that neither you nor I could ever get in as students."

The Baltimore institutions have been responsible for many medical firsts. Doctors at Johns Hopkins were the first to use X-rays in surgery, perform cardiovascular surgery and grow tissue and cell cultures outside the body. They helped develop renal dialysis and improve brain imaging, and they introduced cardiopulmonary resuscitation (CPR). Hopkins' researchers and scientists also developed and refined specialized services such as pediatrics, psychiatry, urology, ophthalmology and oncology.

The Design

Bradbury Thompson, a CSAC design coordinator, designed the

This painting of Johns Hopkins by artist John Dabour, which hangs in the Billings Building of the Johns Hopkins Medical Institutions, was the basis for Bradbury Thompson's Johns Hopkins stamp design.

stamp, using a photograph of an oval head-and-shoulders portrait of Johns Hopkins.

The portrait is an oil painting, measuring about 30 inches by 25 inches, done by John Dabour around 1868. It was donated to the Johns Hopkins Medical Institutions in 1975 by a private owner and hangs in the board room of the old administration building, now called the Billings Building.

First-Day Facts

The Johns Hopkins stamp was issued June 7 at the Baltimore Convention Center at the conclusion of a morning of activities celebrating the centennial of the institutions Hopkins founded. Keynote speaker for the larger ceremony was Louis Sullivan, U.S. secretary of health and human services.

Postmaster General Anthony M. Frank dedicated the stamp. Present for the occasion was his predecessor, Preston Tisch, who had authorized its issuance.

USPS produced no official program for the ceremony.

28¢ SITTING BULL
GREAT AMERICANS SERIES

Date of Issue: September 14, 1989

Catalog Numbers: Scott 2184   Minkus 919   USPS 1038

Color: green

First-Day Cancel: Rapid City, South Dakota (Civic Center)

FDCs Canceled: 126,777

Format: Panes of 100, vertical, 10 across, 10 down. Printing sleeve of 800 subjects (20 across, 40 around).

Perf: 11.2 by 11.1 (Eureka off-line perforator)

Selvage Markings: ©UNITED STATES POSTAL SERVICE 1989, USE CORRECT ZIP CODE®

Designer: Robert Anderson of Lexington, Massachusetts

Art Director: Richard Sheaff (CSAC)

Project Manager: Jack Williams (USPS)

Typographer: Bradbury Thompson (CSAC)

Engravers: Gary Chaconas (BEP, vignette)
Dennis Brown (BEP, lettering and numerals)

Printing: 3-color intaglio unit of the 8-color gravure/intaglio A press (702)

Quantity Ordered: 54,000,000
Quantity Distributed: 44,820,000

Sleeve Number Detail: One sleeve number alongside each corner stamp

Sleeve Number: 1

Tagging: block over vignette

The Stamp

On September 14, USPS issued a 28¢ stamp in the Great Americans series honoring Sitting Bull, the great chief and medicine man of the Hunkpapa tribe of the Sioux, or Dakota, Indians.

The denomination covered the surface rate for postcards sent from the United States to all foreign destinations except Canada and Mexico. Because the rate is relatively little-used, it was the last of the major rates that were adopted in the general revision of April 3, 1988, to be covered with a new definitive or airmail stamp.

The Sitting Bull stamp was the 46th face-different stamp in the Great Americans series and the fourth to depict an Indian leader. The three who preceded him were Sequoyah, a Cherokee (on the first stamp in the series, in 1980) and Sitting Bull's fellow Sioux leaders Crazy Horse (1982) and Red Cloud (1987).

The stamp had had a lengthy wait in the wings. Like most persons depicted in the Great Americans series, Sitting Bull had been put on the "approved" list by the Citizens' Stamp Advisory Committee several years earlier. Plans were made to use his portrait on a 37¢ stamp to meet the two-ounce first-class rate then in effect, replacing the 1982 Robert Millikan stamp of the same denomination. The new stamp was designed and a die engraved.

Before USPS got around to issuing it, however, the two-ounce rate was raised to 39¢ in 1985 and was covered by a new stamp depicting Grenville Clark. When the time finally came to issue the Sitting Bull stamp, the Bureau of Engraving and Printing made a new die, replac-

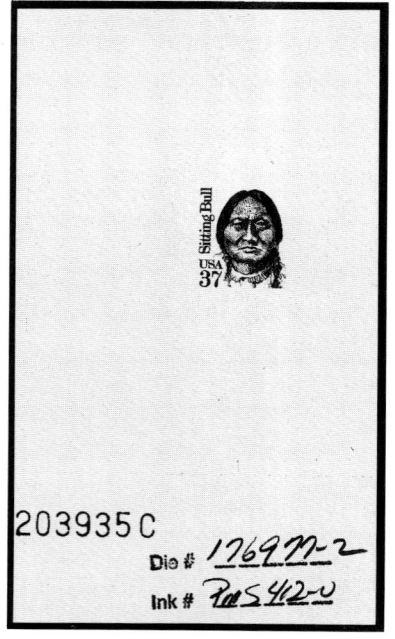

This is a die proof of the original 37¢ Sitting Bull stamp prepared for the Great Americans series. The "37" was removed and replaced by a "28" on a new die.

ing the "37" with a "28." The stamp was announced November 10, 1988, as an addition to the 1989 program, and its denomination was disclosed the following January 11.

Sitting Bull's name is surely the best known of all American Indian appellations. Its owner was born about 1831 on Grand River in what is now South Dakota. He was dubbed "Slow" until, joining his first war party at the age of 14, he distinguished himself by reckless courage in battle. His father then rewarded him with the name "Sitting Bull" — a name the father was said to have received from the Buffalo God himself.

Sitting Bull's first skirmish with white soldiers took place in 1863, and for the next five years he was involved with numerous other fights with the Army, which was invading the Sioux hunting grounds and bringing ruin to an Indian livelihood based on buffalo. In 1866 he became principal chief of the northern hunting Sioux, with Crazy Horse, leader of the Oglala division, as his vice-chief.

Two years later the Sioux made peace with the whites in exchange for a guaranteed reservation north of the North Platte River and the right to hunt off the reservation. But the discovery of gold in the Black Hills brought a rush of miners into the reservation area, and the treaty was violated. Sitting Bull's continued defense of his people's hunting grounds and his refusal to be confined to the reservation led in 1876 to an Army campaign against the Sioux.

Summoned by Sitting Bull, the Sioux, with Cheyennes and some Arapahoes, met in a great encampment, fought and defeated General George Crook's forces, and then, on June 25, on the Little Bighorn River, wiped out five companies of Seventh Cavalry commanded by General George A. Custer. Sitting Bull took no part in the actual battle, but his visions had foretold victory and inspired his warriors.

In May 1877, Sitting Bull led his remaining followers to Canada. But hunger and attrition among the force ultimately forced him to surrender. After 1883 he lived in a remote part of the Standing Rock Reservation in North Dakota.

In 1884 and 1885 he toured with two traveling shows, the second one being the Wild West Show of his friend Buffalo Bill Cody (who was the subject of a 1988 Great Americans stamp). Billed as "the slayer of General Custer," Sitting Bull drew large crowds wherever he went, sold autographed photos and met important people, including President Grover Cleveland. At the end of the season, Buffalo Bill gave to Sitting Bull the horse that the chief had ridden in the show.

Sitting Bull returned to the reservation, where he watched in bitterness as the government pressured his people into bargaining away the Dakota homeland. Refusing to sign any such agreement, he declared: "There are no Indians left now but me!"

Disease and famine added to the misery on the reservations. In their search for a miracle that would restore the old, free Indian life, diehards like Sitting Bull turned to the "Ghost Dance," which stemmed from a faith that the white man's Christ would return to earth in 1891, bring back the Indian dead and the vanished buffalo, and sweep the white invader from the plains. Those who danced the frenetic Ghost Dance would see this new world in their visions.

Whites in the Dakotas were alarmed at the hysteria and hostility that accompanied the strange new ritual. Army reinforcements were dispatched, and efforts were made to outlaw the dance, which further angered the Indians. Worried over Sitting Bull's potential for causing still more difficulty, officials sent Indian police and troops to arrest him. They seized the chief on Grand River, December 15, 1890, and he was killed during a rescue attempt by his warriors. Sitting Bull had always said he would never be an "agency Indian," and he died still preaching resistance to the white man.

In the din and confusion, witnesses said, a truly ghostly event occurred: Sitting Bull's horse, hearing the shooting, thought himself back at Buffalo Bill's Wild West show, and all alone, riderless, went through his tricks as his master lay dead.

The Design

Robert D. Anderson, a portrait artist of Lexington, Massachusetts, designed the stamp, which displayed a full-face portrait based on a photograph by the western photographer D.F. Barry from the National Anthropological Archives of the Smithsonian Institution.

The photograph, taken in 1885 when Sitting Bull was 54 years old, shows him wearing a white buckskin shirt and a single feather in his

Robert Anderson made his pencil sketch for the stamp from this portrait of a stern-faced Sitting Bull made by D.F. Barry.

hair. His long braids hang down his chest, and around his neck hangs a brass and wood crucifix given to him by Father Pierre Jean De Smet, a Jesuit missionary to the Indians. In his hands is a calumet, or ceremonial pipe. For his pencil sketch for the stamp, however, the artist used only the subject's head and his strong, solemn features.

Anderson's previous design credits, all in the Great Americans series, were Sylvanus Thayer (1985), Alden Partridge (1985), John Harvard (1986) and Red Cloud (1987).

First-Day Facts

The Sitting Bull stamp had its first day sale September 14 at the Mount Rushmore Plaza Civic Center in Rapid City, South Dakota. James Holy Eagle, Sitting Bull's grandson, was among the honored guests, who also included Clarence Skye, executive director of the United Sioux Tribes.

Charles W. Murphy, tribal chairman of the Standing Rock Reservation, was the principal speaker. The National Anthem was sung by Debbie Iron Cloud and the Sioux Anthem by M.J. Bull Bear. Peter K. Eichorn, senior assistant postmaster general, dedicated the stamp.

Rapid City was the third announced location for the ceremony, all of them in South Dakota. Mobridge, where Sitting Bull is buried, was originally listed as the first-day city, but the site was changed to Pierre, the state capital (where the South Dakota Statehood commemorative had made its debut earlier in the year) to coincide with a meeting there of the United Sioux Tribes. The Sioux later shifted their meeting to Rapid City, and on June 2 USPS announced that it was changing its first-day site again. The town of Mobridge was represented at the Rapid City event by Carol Schlomer, its postmaster.

25¢ EAGLE & SHIELD PRESSURE-SENSITIVE STAMP

Date of Issue: November 10, 1989

Catalog Numbers: Scott 2431 (stamp) Minkus 924 (booklet)
Scott 2431a (unfolded pane) Minkus 925 (coil)
Scott 2432 (coil stamp) USPS 6609 (pane)
  USPS 609C (coil stamp)

Colors: yellow, red, blue, black

First-Day Cancel: Virginia Beach, Virginia (Vapex '89 stamp show)

FDCs Canceled: unavailable

Format: Unfolded pane of 18, horizontal, 3 across, 6 down; coil of 5,004 stamps. Gravure printing cylinders of 310 subjects (288 pane subjects — 12 across, 24 around, 22 coil subjects around) manufactured by Roto Cylinder, Palmyra, New Jersey.

Perf: die cut, no perforations

Selvage Markings: ©USPS 1989, "Self-adhesive, Do not wet, EXTRAordinary Stamps®, Peel this strip, Fold here" on unfolded pane only. "DO NOT WET, SELF-ADHESIVE" printed on unfolded pane and coil release liner.

Stamp Designer: Jay Haiden of Bryans Road, Maryland
Pane Backing Designer: John Boyd of New York City

Art Director and Typographer: Howard Paine (CSAC)

Design Project Manager: Joe Brockert (USPS)
Technical Project Manager: Joseph Y. Peng (USPS)

Modeler: Richard Sennett (Sennett Enterprises) for American Bank Note Company.

Printing: Printing stock supplied by Fasson, Inc. Stamps and backing paper printed by American Bank Note Company on a leased Champlain gravure press (J.W. Fergusson and Sons, Richmond, Virginia) under the supervision of Sennett Enterprises (Fairfax, Virginia). Fergusson slit the coil stamp row from the web, die cut, stripped and processed into coils, sheeting out the remainder of the web into 288-subject sheets. Printed 288-subject sheets die cut by Labels Systems, Inc. (Bridgeport, Connecticut). Sheets processed into 18-subject unfolded panes by ABNC (Chicago, Illinois).

Quantity Ordered: 5,000,000 unfolded panes
600 coils of 5,004 stamps
Quantity Distributed: 4,080,000 unfolded panes
600 coils

Cylinder Number Detail: Unfolded panes — one group of 4 cylinder numbers preceded by the letter "A" alongside upper left or lower right corner stamp. Coils — no cylinder numbers.

Cylinder Number Combination: A1111 (unfolded pane only)

Tagging: overall

The Sheet Stamp

"Isn't it about time," a *New York Times* reader asked in 1976, "that the Postal Service got into the 20th century by issuing a postage stamp with pressure-sensitive glue to do away with the archaic, unsanitary ... habit of (applying) a stamp that has previously passed through many hands with a solution of saliva from the tongue?"

As the years went by, postal officials came to hear that kind of demand with increasing frequency. People wrote in enclosing examples of the many self-adhesive labels they encountered in everyday life. Stamps made this way would not only be sanitary, they pointed out, but would have other advantages too.

They would stick to envelopes but not to each other. They would be easier to handle, especially for older users. And they would eliminate a problem USPS had been unable to solve: finding a stamp gum whose taste was acceptable to everyone.

Officials took due note of the growing sentiment for pressure-sensitive stamps. They had a good reason, however, for moving cautiously.

In 1974 the Postal Service had issued a self-sticking stamp — not for any of the reasons customers were now citing, but for efficiency. The project was an experiment, and it had been an expensive failure.

The stamp was the so-called Christmas "precancel," a 10¢ item picturing the Dove of Peace weathervane atop Mount Vernon (Scott 1552). It represented a radical move on the part of USPS to speed

The first U.S. self-adhesive stamp, the Christmas "precancel" of 1974, was an experiment.

mail processing during the holiday rush by diverting large quantities of envelopes around the facer-canceler machines.

The self-sticking stamp wouldn't need canceling, officials reasoned, because its adhesive would resist soaking from envelopes. And to make it harder to peel the stamp from an envelope intact, security slits would be die-cut into the design.

To produce the stamps, the Bureau of Engraving and Printing had to buy and lease special equipment. BEP also had to send its gravure stamp paper to a private contractor to have the self-stick adhesive and pull-off paper backing applied.

A total of 213 million stamps were printed and distributed in panes of 50 — at a production cost about five times that of normal stamps. These were sent to five specified postal districts for sale to the public to use on its Christmas mail.

Afterward, officials sat down with their calculators to figure out what happened. What they found was that the operation wasn't cost-effective.

While USPS did realize a saving from bypassing the facer-cancelers with bulk mail, which came in already faced, it lost a larger amount on loose letters that had to be faced by hand. (The stamps weren't tagged because taggant would have dulled the die-cutting equipment.)

Most discouraging was the discovery that despite all precautions, the stamps were being reused. In the sample areas, a loss of $346,000 was attributed to this factor.

Several solvents, including lighter fluid, would loosen the adhesive, but a deft set of fingers often could peel away the stamps without help. One customer even boasted that he had put an envelope in the freezer and had frozen the stamp off.

From a collector's viewpoint, the experiment was a disaster. BEP's paper processor had neglected to apply a buffer or primer coat between stamp and adhesive. In the years since 1974, collectors have reported that the gum has bled through the stamps, causing brown spots to appear on the front. Officials advised that the only sure way to preserve the stamps was to remove the adhesive with a solvent.

Fast-forward to April 1986. By now, said Don McDowell, general manager of USPS' Stamps Division, it was clear the public's call for pressure-sensitive stamps "was a demand that must be responded to."

In a speech at a security printing conference in San Diego, Gordon

C. Morison, assistant postmaster general, did something virtually without precedent. He invited private industry to invent a product for the Postal Service — specifically, a pressure-sensitive adhesive for stamps that could be used effectively.

The adhesive, Morison said, must be strong, yet slow-acting, so customers could reposition the stamps on envelopes. It must have a long shelf life. It must be water-soluble, so collectors could easily retrieve used specimens, and it must not "migrate" through stamp paper and cause discoloration.

"The response was immediate," McDowell recalled. "A group of four companies and the Japanese Finance Ministry stepped forward and said, 'We think we can invent that.'

"We learned that the private sector can do things for you if it believes there is a market and there's a reasonable expectation that it might profit by investing some research and development efforts.

"I had thought the biggest problem would be the water-soluble feature. It took three weeks for the first of these outfits to come forward with a solution, and all of them had done it within eight weeks."

The response told USPS that if it solicited a manufacturing contract for pressure-sensitive stamps, bidders would be able to shop among several suppliers for gummed paper that would meet specifications. This would mean lower costs, plus protection against any cutoff of supplies.

The way was clear for the stamp the public had said it wanted.

"We felt committed by May of 1986 to do it," McDowell said. "By mid-1987 we were talking about doing it in the fall of 1989."

Several other questions had to be answered first, however. What size and shape should the stamps be? Should the corners be rounded or at right angles? Would customers be troubled by stamps without perforations?

To address these and other uncertainties, the Postal Service's advertising consultants conducted market research in late 1987.

Focus groups were convened and given booklets of pressure-sensitive stamps that BEP had offset-printed in eight different combinations of design (using two generic designs), shape and layout. Two of the examples had perfs and the rest didn't. The groups were asked to put the stamps on envelopes.

"The people opened the booklets and said, 'Oh neat! They're like labels,'" McDowell said. "They knew what to do with them. They didn't need an owner's manual.

"The focus groups told us that what people liked best was right-angle corners. They liked the stamps to butt against each other, with no matrix in between. They were comfortable with stamps of conventional size and shape."

The USPS Engineering and Development Center conducted a large test mailing. Forty thousand blank-paper labels were furnished by

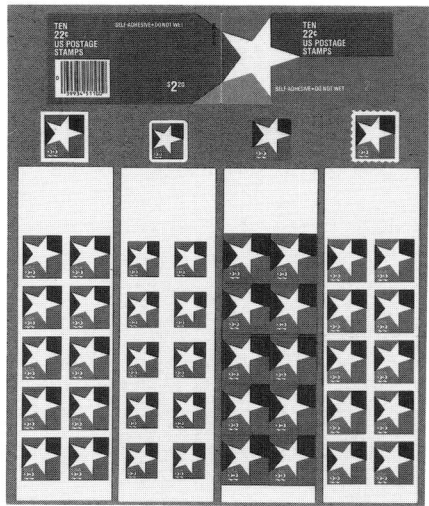 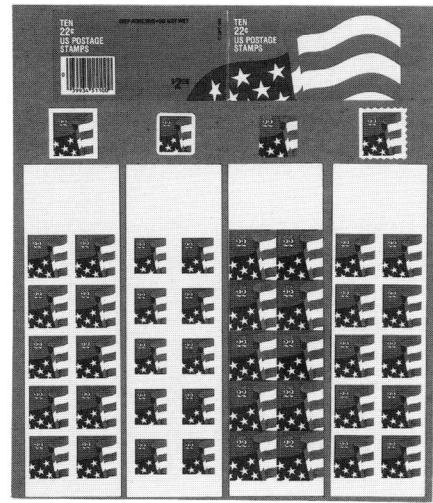

These are the eight different prototypes of a self-adhesive stamp, in two different designs and two different booklet covers, that were given to focus groups in 1987 to test their reaction. Among the variables were size, the presence or absence of spaces between the stamps, and the presence or absence of perforations.

each of the five suppliers that had responded to Gordon Morison's invitation at San Diego. These labels were placed on envelopes alongside regular first-class stamps, and the envelopes were distributed among the Postal Service mail-processing centers and mailed back to headquarters.

"We put 200,000 in the mailstream and got 200,000 back," said McDowell. "Not a single one came off or dog-eared or created a machine jam. That really gave us confidence that these were going to work with the processing equipment."

Three major decisions remained.

One was the printing method. Officials wanted the stamps to be in full color. They decided against using combination offset-intaglio printing because of concern that the heavy pressure required for intaglio would cause the adhesive to flow outward between the stamp and the peel-off paper. So they chose gravure, the same method used on the original Christmas self-stick stamp of 1974.

The second choice was the format. The Postal Service dealt with this one in a novel way.

"It doesn't take a genius," said Don McDowell, "to figure out that if you have a stamp product where you have to have two pieces of paper anyway — stamp and backing — then that's a booklet. Japan did its pressure-sensitive stamp that way. So did Canada."

It occurred to McDowell that by having the stamps cut, shipped and sold in small "sheetlets" that the customer himself could fold into a booklet, a major cost component of the production process — folding — could be eliminated.

"The way you control manufacturing costs is to make things simple," McDowell said. But, he added, "if the customer comes back and says 'I love these stamps but I hate the idea of taking the center strip off and folding the thing, I do not want to be a booklet-forming machine,' it's going to be back to square one."

Finally, there was the choice of printer. The job went to the American Bank Note Company, which was already under contract to furnish booklets to USPS, rather then to BEP.

"The Bureau has no die-cutting, label-making capability," McDowell explained. "Every piece of equipment the Bureau buys for stamps is charged to the Postal Service through the billing rate. We pay for it.

"Now, it makes no sense to us to set the Bureau up in the label-printing business, so to speak, when there is a vast, already-equipped pressure-sensitive label industry out there.

"Will the Bureau eventually get into pressure-sensitives? Probably, but only when we get to something that is so unique that whoever makes it is going to have to incur a capital investment and pass it on to us."

The disclosure that the stamp would be issued in late 1989 came in an unusual way. The stamp was listed in the 1990 edition of *The U.S. Postal Guide to U.S. Stamps,* which went on sale October 1, 1989.

The *Guide* didn't illustrate the stamp, but described its design (eagle and shield), listed the designer (Jay Haiden) and gave the denomination (25¢) and Scott catalog number (2431).

It also stated: "This self-adhesive, issued on foldable liners containing 18 stamps, was to be tested in 15 cities."

On November 9, USPS issued a press release supplying details. The stamp went on sale the next day, November 10, at the Vapex '89 stamp show in Virginia Beach, Virginia.

An initial printing of four million stamps was distributed to 15 cities for a 30-day test marketing period: Atlanta, Chicago, Cleveland, Columbus, Dallas, Denver, Houston, Indianapolis, Kansas City, Los Angeles, Miami, Milwaukee, Minneapolis, Phoenix and St. Louis. The stamps were also sold at philatelic centers.

USPS officially described them as "EXTRAordinary Stamps" (and trademarked the term). Most extraordinary, perhaps, was the disclosure that the stamps would sell at a premium: $5 per booklet, or 50¢ more than the $4.50 face value (roughly 27.7¢ per stamp). The market research, Gordon Morison said in the press release, had "indicated that consumers place a high value on the new features we are offering and feel it is appropriate to charge extra for them."

To find out whether the public as a whole would feel that way was the major purpose of the market test. It wasn't the first time the government had sold U.S. stamps at a markup; from 1900, when the first U.S. stamp booklets were issued, until 1963, all booklets sold for 1¢ over face value. Now, however, the relative surcharge was much larger.

Some criticism was heard. A *Linn's Stamp News* editorial, titled: "EXTRAordinary? No!" called the surcharge a "marketing gimmick" designed to extract money from collectors. "Stamp collectors are looming larger and larger in the profit picture of the USPS," the newspaper said. "If the test marketing ... is successful, we can look for

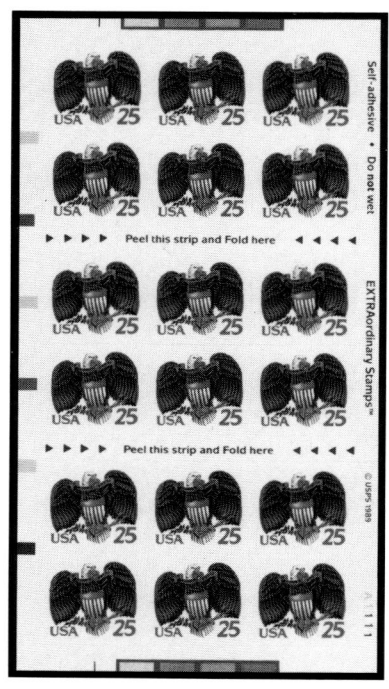

The backing paper for the eagle and shield sheetlet became a booklet cover when folded.

many more USPS 'deluxe' products. Why sell stamps at face value when they can sell them for more?"

Besides issuing the stamps in sheetlet form, USPS also made them available to collectors in "coil" strips of 18, spaced one-fourth of an inch apart on the liner. These also sold for $5, at philatelic centers only.

Post offices in the test cities promoted the stamps with cardboard stand-up signs on the counters. And customers who bought them early in the test period were given questionnaires asking their reactions to the stamps and to the sales price.

They found the sheetlets to consist of three "blocks" of six stamps each, three across by two deep. The stamps were almost square, measuring 0.87 by 0.96 inches overall, and die-cut, with straight edges on all four sides. Each block of six was surrounded by a peelable selvage or matrix containing marginal markings. The two horizontal strips on either side of the center block bore the instructions "Peel this strip and fold here."

The upper side of the backing paper — the side in contact with the stamps — had a silicone layer to allow easy separation. The paper bore the message: "Do Not Wet ★ Self-Adhesive," in blue capitals, repeated in diagonal parallel lines. In an intact sheetlet, the stamps and selvage completely conceal this message.

The other side of the liner became the booklet cover when the sheetlet was folded. Printed in red and blue, it carried an enlarged reproduction of the stamp design, diagrams showing how to form the booklet and peel the stamps, and a message promoting the "EXTRAordinary" theme.

The stamps were printed from 310-subject gravure cylinders. On the printed sheets, the vertical row on one side was the coil strip. It was slit off before the printed web was sheeted out, die cut and processed into sheetlets or panes. The remainder of the sheet consisted of four panes across by four panes down. The cylinder number combination, A1111, alternated from upper left to lower right on adjacent panes, with color dashes between.

Collectors found that used stamps did indeed separate readily from their envelopes in water, although rather than floating free they had to be peeled off after soaking. The water-soluble material was actually a separate layer between the stamp and the self-adhesive, so that the latter remained on the envelope paper after the stamp was removed.

Unfortunately, there were reports that some postal clerks were rejecting the unfamiliar-looking imperforate stamps as invalid for postage (which was particularly aggravating considering that the stamps had sold for more than face value).

The Design

To design the eagle and shield stamp, art director Howard Paine

The 13¢ Americana stamp of 1975 (Scott 1596) also depicted a multicolor eagle and shield.

suggested Jay Haiden of Bryans Road, Maryland, a specialist in airbrush work, which adapts well to the gravure printing process. It was Haiden's first stamp design.

His eagle resembled a sculpture, with sharply defined, stylized feathers on the outspread wings. Gold was the predominant color. The eagle clutched in its beak a ribbon bearing the motto "E Pluribus Unum," but because both the beak and ribbon were rendered in the same gold shade the artwork lacked definition at this important point.

The booklet cover was designed by John Boyd of New York City.

The eagle and shield motif is part of the Great Seal of the United States and as such has appeared on all stamps that have reproduced the Seal, such as the 6¢ American Legion commemorative of 1969 (Scott 1369) and the current series of Official Mail stamps.

The eagle and shield alone, apart from the Seal, has also appeared in various forms in stamp designs, as early as the 30¢ value of the 1869 series (Scott 121) and as recently as the Senate Bicentennial commemorative of 1989, which is described in a previous chapter. The forerunner that most closely resembles the self-adhesive stamp design is the 13¢ Americana definitive of 1975 (Scott 1596).

First-Day Facts

In his speech at the November 10 first-day ceremony at Vapex, Gordon Morison responded to some of the criticism of recent USPS issues and marketing programs.

"We've got to find new collectors to strengthen the hobby," Morison said. He said stamps designed to be widely popular, and other USPS products, were intended to bring non-collectors into philately and to turn casual collectors into serious ones. He said USPS must issue colorful topical stamps, as well as "strange products" such as pins, T-shirts and posters, because "traditional promotions" have not been as successful as the Postal Service would like in creating new stamp collectors.

Morison himself is a serious collector whose exhibit of Iceland postal stationery, entered under the name William Goodson, won a vermeil medal at Vapex.

The principal speaker at the ceremony was Daniel Ertzberger, president of the Virginia Philatelic Federation Inc.

Because of the late notice, first-day cover collectors were given two months to submit their covers instead of the normal one-month grace period.

Collectors who wished to have USPS affix stamps to first-day covers were instructed to send their self-addressed envelopes to the Philatelic Sales Division in Washington, with 25¢ for each stamp wanted. Interestingly, that meant the stamps were sold to these collectors at a discount that wasn't available to any other customer.

The Coil Stamp

The "coil version" of the pressure-sensitive Eagle and Shield stamp raised some unprecedented questions for collectors. Is it a separate variety? If so, how should it be collected?

The basic stamp is the same one USPS offered for sale to the general public in 15 test cities. Instead of being issued in sheetlets of 18 stamps that customers could fold into booklets, it was sold in strips of 18 at philatelic centers only. There was no separate first day sale or ceremony.

As sold, the two versions were readily distinguishable from each other. Whereas the sheetlet stamps abutted one another on their peel-off liner, the strip stamps were spaced one-fourth of an inch apart on their backing paper, which was 1¼-inch wide. However, individual stamps from the two versions, once separated from their backing, couldn't be told apart.

A used copy of the Eagle and Shield stamp was by definition minus its liner, meaning that for collectors of used stamps there could be but one collectible variety. But saving mint specimens — in the case of the coil, in singles, pairs or strips — wasn't necessarily a permanent answer to the question of differentiation. Over a long period of time, USPS officials acknowledge, mint copies will dry and separate from their liners, leaving the collector with two unconnected elements.

The decision to create the self-adhesive stamp in strips as well as sheetlets was prompted by a concern voiced by Bob Brown, who as manager of USPS' Philatelic Sales Division runs the first-day cover processing operation.

When Brown learned of plans for the new stamp, he realized immediately what a problem it would pose for his employees. They would have to do their job by hand, taking sheetlets of stamps, peeling them one at a time from their liners and affixing them to envelopes submitted by collectors. The same procedure would have to be followed in preparing first-day ceremony programs and souvenir pages.

"We immediately concluded that wasn't such a good idea," said Don McDowell, general manager of the Stamps Division.

"However, we were already in the process of looking at the pressure-sensitive label industry. We had seen the automatic affixing of labels off coil rolls. So we said, 'Hey, if we just print ourselves a coil along one side of the web of stamps, and we lay it out with the intervals between the stamps corresponding to the industrial standards that off-the-shelf label affixing machines work with, we can handle it efficiently.'"

Once the decision was made to create this "variety," a quick follow-up decision was made to offer it to collectors. The reason, McDowell explained, is that during philately's "sorting-out" process, when it will decide just how to collect pressure-sensitive stamps, USPS is obligat-

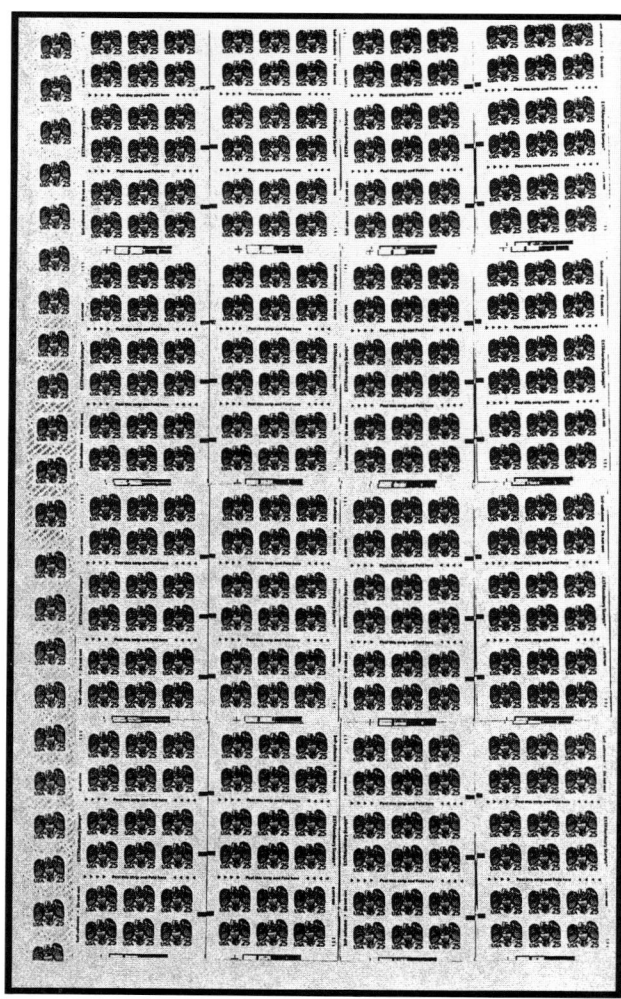

A mock-up of how the 25¢ Eagle and Shield self-adhesive layout may look.

ed to "let collectors have all the things to play with possible."

"So I said, OK, I'm going to sell coils during this test period, and if anybody wants 18 stamps off a strip for the same $5 that gets you 18 stamps in a booklet, that's fine," he said.

The coil stamps were printed on the same 310-subject sheets as the sheetlet/booklet stamps, but along one side. The coil strip was slit off before the rest of the sheet was processed into sheetlets. It contained no printing cylinder number.

Because the stamps on the strip were set apart from each other, and the matrix on the coil version had been stripped away, it was possible with an intact strip to read the message printed on the upper side of the liner: "Self-Adhesive ★ Do Not Wet," repeated in a series of parallel diagonal lines.

On the back side of the backing paper for the coil strip were color registration targets for the booklet covers that were printed on the adjacent part of the web. These markings consisted of a red outer box and blue inner box. They appeared at approximately six-stamp intervals on the coil.

A rough etched-in cut mark in red also appeared on the back, at 22-stamp intervals. These roughly lined up with the top and bottom edges of the 288-subject printed sheets of panes.

$32.25 EXPRESS MAIL (BOOKLET)

Date of Issue: June 19, 1989

Catalog Numbers: Scott 2122 (stamp)   USPS 6608 (booklet)
Scott 2122a (pane of three)   USPS S608 (single stamp)

Colors: yellow, magenta, cyan, black

First-Day Cancel: none

FDCs Canceled: unavailable

Format: One pane of 3 horizontal stamps. Gravure printing cylinders of 78 subjects (6 across, 13 around).

Perf: Imperforate by 9.9 (Goebel booklet machine stroke perforator)

Selvage Markings: 5 cylinder numbers and registration markings on each pane binding stub. ©United States Postal Service 1985 on inside of booklet cover. Universal Product Code (UPC) on outside of back cover.

Stamp Designer: Young and Rubicam of New York City
Booklet Cover Designer: Joe Brockert (USPS)

Art Director and Project Manager: Jack Williams (USPS)

Typographer: Bradbury Thompson (CSAC)

Stamp Modeler: Jack Ruther (BEP)
Booklet Cover Modeler: Jack Ruther (BEP)

Printing: Stamps printed on 7-color Andreotti gravure press (601). Covers printed and booklets formed on a Goebel booklet machine.

Quantity Ordered: 750,000 booklets
Quantity Distributed: 750,000 booklets

Cylinder Number Detail: One group of 5 cylinder numbers on each pane binding stub

Cylinder Number Combination: 22222

Tagging: untagged

The Stamp

On April 29, 1985, the U.S. Postal Service placed on sale an Express Mail stamp with a $10.75 denomination that covered the then-new half-pound rate for overnight domestic service. The stamp was issued in booklets of three.

In 1988, the rate for the service was reduced to $8.75. On October 4 of that year a new Express Mail stamp at that denomination was introduced. Unlike its predecessor, it was printed in mini-sheets of 20.

On February 28, 1989, the obsolete $10.75 Express Mail stamps and booklets of 1985 were removed from sale by the Philatelic Sales Agency. A few months later, however, USPS announced that the $10.75 stamp had been reissued for use with a new reduced half-pound rate for Express Mail International Service that was effective July 1.

Like the original version, the stamp was produced in booklets of three (although the announcement erroneously described the original as having been made in sheet form). The booklet cover was changed to reflect the new role for the stamp. But, the Postal Service said, because the old and new stamps themselves were identical, first-day cancellations weren't offered.

A few enterprising stamp collectors and first-day cover dealers were able to obtain first-day cancellations anyhow — along with evidence that the stamps being canceled were genuine reissues rather than from the original batch.

The date on their covers was June 19, 1989, the day on which the stamps went on sale at the L'Enfant Plaza post office in Washington, D.C., and other locations. The covers bore panes of three with binding stub selvage attached bearing the gravure cylinder numbers 22222. This proved them to be different from the original $10.75 stamps, which bore a group of five gravure cylinder numbers (11111), one for each color used. This group of numbers is printed on the binding stub of the pane.

The denomination area on the $10.75 stamps is the easiest place to tell the old and new versions apart. The older stamp (top) has a much grainier appearance. The newer version has a much smoother application of the ink.

The old and new versions of the $10.75 Express Mail booklet panes. The copyright notice appears on the new version of the booklet.

Later, it turned out that the new and old stamps themselves differed, after all.

As described by Wayne Youngblood of *Linn's Stamp News,* the new stamps "are printed on a whiter-looking paper stock. The overall appearance of the stamp is much glossier than the old.

"The black on the new stamp is a more solid and intense color than the old. The overall appearance of the design is much crisper.

"The biggest difference between the two stamps is in the denomination, however. The magenta color of the denomination of the older version has a much grainier appearance and has large color dots. The denomination of the new version has a smooth and solid application of the magenta color."

The proof sheets were later examined. The magenta screen was removed on the later stamps, leaving only the special red. Two screens were used on the older version in the denomination.

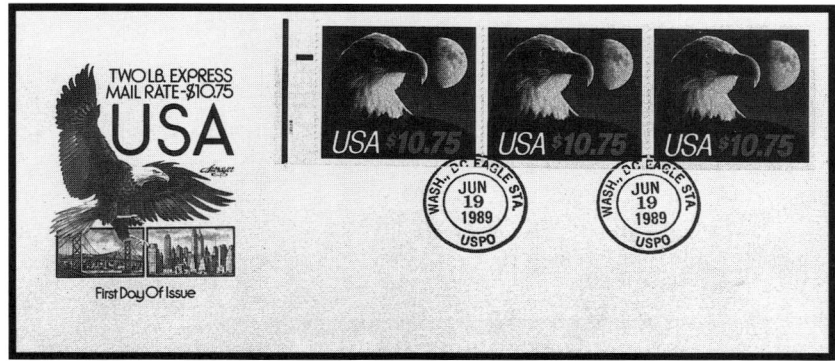

This Artmaster cover was canceled on the day the reissued $10.75 stamps were placed on sale. (The cachet inscription, "Two lb. Express Mail Rate — $10.75," was a mistake. The domestic two-pound rate was $12.)

Collectors who sought to buy the reissued stamps at their post offices had to double-check to make sure that's what they were getting, however. The June 10, 1989, *Postal Bulletin* advised: "Post offices with inventories of the 1985 $10.75 Special Issue booklet stamps may place them back on sale. Since the 1985 booklet cover version refers to the obsolete domestic rate, offices must sell the 1985 stamp version without the booklet cover."

USPS' Express Mail International Service guaranteed one-day service to Canada, two days to Europe and three days to the Pacific Rim and elsewhere.

Late in 1989, eight major competitors of USPS charged in a lawsuit that the $10.75 international Express Mail rate was too low.

At the time of the last rate overhaul, April 3, 1988, the half-pound rate for that service was set at $18, except to Canada and Great Britain, which were $13 and $15, respectively.

For a promotional period from April 25 to July 1, 1989, the rate dropped to a flat $8.75, the same as domestic Express Mail. After July

These are two unused essays for the new international Express Mail booklet cover, prepared by USPS' Joe Brockert. One of them features a two-color rendering of the basic stamp design and is similar to the cover used with the original 1985 booklet of three $10.75 stamps.

1, it was set at $10.75. Most companies' international rates at that time were more than $20.

The plaintiffs, who included United Parcel Service, Air Forwarding Inc., Federal Express, DHL Airways Inc. and an industry association, the Air Courier Conference of America/International Committee, charged "unfair and illegal competition" by USPS. They contended that the $10.75 international rate was being subsidized by other USPS services that are protected from private competition by the Private Express Statues. They argued that the rate was set without review by the Postal Rate Commission.

Postmaster General Anthony Frank, commenting on the suit, said the new rates "benefit the American householder and smaller businesses who don't qualify for the volume discounts offered to major corporations by these international couriers."

"At issue here," Frank said, "is why these giants in the industry, who enjoy a lion's share of the corporate international market, should be so concerned with the Postal Service's initiative to lower its rates — especially given our meager share in that marketplace."

The Design

The stamp was of the same design created by the Young & Rubicam ad agency for the 1985 stamp, showing a bald eagle's head with a half-moon hanging in the night sky overhead.

Joe Brockert, USPS program manager, stamp design, designed the cover for the new booklet, which emphasized the words "Express Mail International" and included a stylized eagle from the Express Mail envelope and the $32.25 price of the full three-stamp booklet.

The back of the cover bore a Universal Pricing Code (UPC) symbol and Express Mail International Service advertising. The inside of the cover provided instructions for mailing with the new stamps.

$2.40 MOON LANDING (PRIORITY MAIL)

Date of Issue: July 20, 1989

Catalog Numbers: Scott 2419   Minkus CM1352   USPS 1102

Colors: red, yellow, blue, black, dark blue (offset); black (intaglio)

First-Day Cancel: Washington, D.C. (National Air and Space Museum)

FDCs Canceled: 208,982

Format: Panes of 20, vertical, 4 across, 5 down. Offset printing plates of 80 subjects (8 across, 10 around); intaglio printing sleeve of 160 subjects (8 across, 20 around).

Perf: 11.1 by 11.25 (Eureka off-line perforator)

Selvage Markings: ©UNITED STATES POSTAL SERVICE 1988 in left and right selvage

Designer: Christopher Calle of Ridgefield, Connecticut

Art Director and Project Manager: Jack Williams (USPS)

Typographer: Bradbury Thompson (CSAC)

Engravers: Kenneth Kipperman (BEP, vignette)
Dennis Brown (BEP, lettering and numerals)

Modeler: Ronald Sharpe (BEP)

Printing: 6-color offset, 3-color intaglio D press (902)

Quantity Ordered: 35,000,000
Quantity Distributed: 30,630,000

Plate/Sleeve Number Detail: One intaglio sleeve number alongside corner stamps of each pane; one group of 5 offset plate numbers alongside adjacent stamps.

Plate/Sleeve Number Combinations: 11111-1, 11112-1, 11113-1, 11114-1, 11124-1, 11211-1

Tagging: overall

The Stamp

With its first Priority Mail stamp, USPS achieved two objectives. It promoted the Priority Mail service, which promises two-day delivery between all major markets and three-day delivery elsewhere. And it celebrated the 20th anniversary of man's first landing on the moon.

The denomination was $2.40, the rate for Priority Mail items weighing from 12 ounces to two pounds. The place of issue was the National Air and Space Museum in Washington July 20, 1989, in conjunction with a major federal observance of the moon-landing anniversary.

The stamp bore no Priority Mail designation and was valid for all categories of postage. Nor did it carry an anniversary inscription. By USPS criteria, a 20th anniversary isn't an appropriate occasion for a commemorative; besides, USPS issued the stamp as a definitive that would be available as long as the $2.40 rate was current.

However, the design itself made the issue's commemorative nature unmistakable. It depicted two astronauts — obviously Apollo 11 crew members Neil A. Armstrong and Edwin E. "Buzz" Aldrin Jr. — standing on a cratered lunar surface, planting an American flag.

USPS had been considering a special stamp for Priority Mail for some time. At one point, officials asked wildlife artist Chuck Ripper of Huntington, West Virginia, to prepare some sketches. But Ripper's offering — a rendition of a pheasant in flight — ended up not on a Priority Mail stamp but squeezed into a small format and used on a 25¢ definitive in booklets (see *Linn's U.S. Stamp Yearbook, 1988*). For Priority Mail, a space theme was chosen.

Space had been a popular topic for U.S. stamps in the past, but with the troubles that beset the U.S. space program in the 1980s, particularly the tragic loss of the space shuttle *Challenger* in January 1986, there was little to commemorate postally. The $2.40 Priority Mail stamp was the first true space-theme stamp to come from USPS since the eight-stamp Space Achievement block in 1981.

The landing of Armstrong and Aldrin on the moon while their fellow crewman, Michael Collins, orbited overhead in the *Columbia* command module climaxed years of intense research, testing and training by the National Aeronautics and Space Administration as it drove itself to deliver on President John F. Kennedy's 1961 vow that

This 10¢ airmail stamp was issued to celebrate the first moon landing in 1969. It was designed by Paul Calle, father of Christopher Calle, who designed the 1989 anniversary stamp.

Chris Calle's space poster shows an astronaut descending from the lunar lander to the moon's surface and is surrounded by inset pictures showing aviation and space pioneers and vehicles.

the United States would put a man on the moon and return him safely during the decade.

On July 20, 1969, while the world watched and listened via television and radio, the two astronauts descended to the lunar surface in their landing module. Then came Commander Armstrong's electrifying announcement from 235,000 miles away in space: "The Eagle has landed." Some 6½ hours later, when Armstrong descended the ladder to become the first human in history to set foot on an extraterrestrial body, he radioed home another memorable message: "That's one small step for a man, one giant leap for mankind."

The event was commemorated by the U.S. Post Office on September 9, 1969, with a 10¢ airmail stamp that set an all-time record for first-day covers canceled (8,743,070) and quickly became very popular with the general public. The stamp, designed by Paul Calle of Ridgefield, Connecticut, depicted an astronaut stepping from the ladder of the lunar lander onto the moon's surface with the blue globe of Earth hanging in the black sky above.

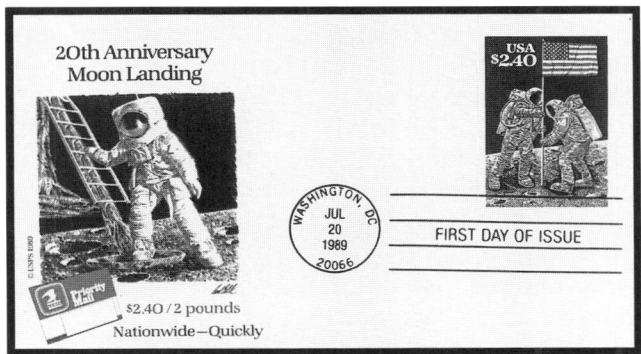

Paul Calle designed the cachet promoting Priority Mail on this official USPS first-day cover.

In a public-relations masterstroke credited to Julian Scheer, NASA's assistant administrator for public affairs, the stamp was printed from plates made from a master die that was carried to the moon and back with the Apollo 11 astronauts. As an extra touch, a die proof of the stamp attached to an envelope was hand-canceled by the astronauts on the moon.

Designer Calle was a veteran member of NASA's Fine Arts Program, whose purpose was to capture on canvas the drama of the Mercury, Gemini and Apollo missions. He was the only artist present with the Apollo 11 crew members on the morning of their launch.

For the 20th anniversary stamp project, the Citizens' Stamp Advisory Committee turned not to Paul Calle but to his artist son Christopher, with whom the senior Calle shares a studio in Ridgefield. It did so knowing, as one official put it, that Paul would inevitably be "peeking over his shoulder." Chris Calle needed no outside help, however; he was a veteran stamp designer in his own right, and between them the Calles had designed more than two dozen stamps for USPS.

The father-and-son team also produced two ancillary products in connection with the Priority Mail stamp.

One was a space poster, featuring a Chris Calle painting of an astronaut just prior to setting foot on the moon. A border of red, white and blue surrounded the figure, along with a number of other portraits and pictures tracing the development of flight, and reproductions of the 1969 and 1989 Moon Landing stamps. The item, which sold for $10, was the third in a series of stamp-related posters commissioned by USPS. Its predecessors had featured the Classic Cars (1988) and Lou Gehrig (1989) stamps.

USPS also made an unusual venture into the first-day cover market by offering what it called a "souvenir envelope" bearing the new stamp, the July 20 first-day cancellation and a cachet designed by Paul Calle. Some 450,000 covers were offset-printed by the Government Printing Office and offered for sale for $3.50.

The Postal Service justified this step, in direct competition with private cachetmakers and first-day cover providers, as a means of promoting Priority Mail. It was not the first time USPS had prepared and sold cacheted covers; for the $9.35 Express Mail stamp of 1983, it arranged with NASA to fly a total of 260,899 covers aboard the space shuttle *Challenger*, and later sold these to collectors for $15.35 each. Because the stamp release date was moved up after the covers had been postmarked, however, these were actually "third-day covers" rather than FDCs.

Several other nations also commemorated the 20th anniversary of the moon landing, including the Republic of the Marshall Islands, which issued both stamps and a $5 silver coin. The latter item was extensively advertised on television in commercials featuring Astronaut Michael Collins.

These essays by Christopher Calle incorporated wording pertaining to the lunar landing anniversary that USPS decided was unnecessary on the finished stamps.

The Design

The stamp was in the extra-large format of the Express Mail and Migratory Bird Hunting and Conservation stamps. Like those items, it was printed in a combination of offset and intaglio on the Bureau of Engraving and Printing's D press. Unlike them, however, it was issued in panes of 20 rather than 30.

Paul Calle had kept the thick file of art and photographs he had made during Apollo training sessions in the 1960s, and he turned these over to Chris for reference. As his father had done in 1969, Chris based his sketches on these photographs of the astronauts in practice maneuvers on Earth.

Calle made concept sketches showing only one astronaut (as in his father's 1969 stamp) and with commemorative inscriptions in the design. But the committee wanted two astronauts to be depicted this time, and USPS officials decided that the stamp should be bare of type except for the basic "USA $2.40."

After Calle turned in his finished painting, "The Bureau did a beautiful job with it," said Jack Williams, art director and project manager. "They smoothed out the dark blue background, and made it all one nice solid blue. They de-emphasized some shading lines on the flag a little bit so it wouldn't look as if the flag was soiled or covered with moon dust.

"Then the engraver (Kenneth Kipperman) did quite a bit of work, etching lines in and around the feet and legs, bringing out the craters a little more sharply, hyping up the highlights in the helmet, and providing a little more gray in the moon's blue, to make it closer to the actual coloration of the soil."

Although the astronauts on the new stamp were obviously Armstrong and Aldrin (just as the figure on the 1969 airmail was clearly Armstrong), the Postal Service wouldn't admit to breaching the law forbidding the portrayal of living people on stamps. The humans in the stamp designs were enclosed in space suits and helmets and were quite unrecognizable. USPS considered them generic astronauts, not specific individuals.

First-Day Facts

The ceremony at the National Air and Space Museum combined a celebration of the 20th anniversary of the moon landing and dedication of the Priority Mail stamp. It featured an address by President George Bush, and marked his first attendance as president at a stamp first-day ceremony.

The President was introduced by Vice President Dan Quayle. After the stamp was dedicated by Postmaster General Anthony M. Frank, Apollo 11 astronauts Armstrong, Aldrin and Collins spoke briefly.

The program distributed at the ceremony was a hybrid. The principal part was a four-page folder produced by the Smithsonian Institution and NASA and listing the speakers. Inserted was a card, produced by the Postal Service, bearing the stamp and first-day cancel and including two paragraphs of text on the moon landing and the anniversary ceremony.

Subscribers to the USPS first-day ceremony program service received only the card insert. Because it lacked the list of participants, of course, it was something other than a "program" as defined by the American Ceremony Program Society.

A NASA spokesman told *Linn's Stamp News* that NASA produced 1,200 of the folders. At the ceremony 1,000 were distributed and the remaining 200 went to USPS, he said.

Joining to dedicate the Priority Mail stamp on the 20th anniversary of the moon landing were, from left, Vice President Quayle, President Bush, Postmaster General Frank, and Apollo astronauts Neil Armstrong, Michael Collins and Buzz Aldrin.

45¢ FRENCH REVOLUTION BICENTENNIAL AIRMAIL JOINT ISSUE WITH FRANCE

Date of Issue: July 14, 1989

Catalog Numbers: Scott C120   Minkus A120   USPS 4463

Colors: red, blue, silver (offset); black (intaglio)

First-Day Cancel: Washington, D.C. (Jefferson Memorial)

FDCs Canceled: 309,975

Format: Panes of 30, 5 across, 6 down. Offset printing plates of 120 subjects (12 across, 10 around); intaglio printing sleeve of 240 subjects (12 across, 20 around).

Perf: 11.25 by 11.1 (Eureka off-line perforator)

Selvage Markings: ©UNITED STATES POSTAL SERVICE 1989, USE CORRECT ZIP CODE®

Designer: Richard Sheaff of Chestnut Hill, Massachusetts

Art Director and Project Director: Joe Brockert (USPS)

Typographer: Bradbury Thompson (CSAC)

Engravers: Kenneth Kipperman (BEP, vignette)
Dennis Brown (BEP, lettering and numerals)
Kenneth Wiram (BEP, background pattern)

Modeler: Jack Ruther (BEP)

Printing: 6-color offset, 3-color intaglio D press (902)

Quantity Ordered: 40,000,000
Quantity Distributed: 38,532,000

Plate/Sleeve Number Detail: Left-side panes — one group of 3 offset plate numbers over/under corner stamps; one intaglio sleeve number over/under adjacent stamps. Right-side panes — offset/intaglio numbers in reverse positions.

Plate/Sleeve Number Combination: 111-1, 121-1, 122-1, 222-1

Tagging: block over vignette

The Stamp

The U.S. stamp of 1989 that received the greatest amount of public attention was the 45¢ airmail issued to commemorate the 200th anniversary of the French Revolution.

The press found certain aspects of the design to be controversial. As it turned out, most of the controversy was in the eye of the media. Still, the coverage produced a lot of publicity for what was in fact a handsome and interesting postage stamp.

France had been preparing for a long time to celebrate the bicentennial of its revolution, and the subject was a natural for other countries to commemorate with stamps. USPS, in announcing its preliminary 1989 stamp program, included a joint issue with the French. The stamps would be issued July 14, which France celebrates as Bastille Day, the anniversary of the seizure of the notorious Paris prison by revolutionaries.

This joint issue turned out to be the kind in which the countries use different design treatments — although in this case the subject matter was the same. In most of the 20 previous joint issues involving the United States, the designs of the participating countries' stamps were similar, as with the 1988 issues for Australia's bicentennial (with Australia) and the New Sweden tercentenary (with Sweden and Finland).

The U.S. and French stamp designs were unveiled April 14, 1989, by Postmaster General Anthony M. Frank and French Deputy Chief of Mission Michel Lennuyeux-Comnene. They featured three female figures representing the motto of the French Republic: "Liberty, Equality, Fraternity."

The U.S. stamp was a single, picturing all three figures. France's contribution was a triptych — a side-by-side joining of three different stamps, each portraying one of the symbolic figures. Attached to the triptych was a non-postal label promoting Philexfrance '89, the inter-

This is the French triptych issued July 14, 1989, the same day the U.S. stamp made its debut.

national stamp exhibition scheduled for July 7-17 in Paris. The three French stamps also were issued individually, in sheet form; the first one, in fact, had been out for almost a month at the time of the unveiling ceremony in Washington.

The U.S. stamp was an airmail at the 45¢ basic international rate. This marked the third time a U.S. contribution to a joint issue has been an airmail stamp. The others occasions were the Philip Mazzei issue, with Italy, in 1980 (Scott C98) and the New Sweden issue of 1988 (Scott C117).

USPS also sold a souvenir card, which is described in a later chapter, and an eight-page souvenir booklet, *Liberte, Egalite, Fraternite*. The $5.95 booklet included a block of four of the U.S. stamp and the triptych strip of French stamps, each with a July 14 first-day cancellation. Such joint "covers" weren't otherwise available.

The three individual French stamps comprising the triptych were valued at 2.20 francs each, the domestic postage rate. The triptych, with attached label, sold for $1.10 in U.S. currency. The stamps were designed by Roger Druet and engraved by Claude Durrens.

Even in France, which happily welcomed the tourists attracted to its bicentennial celebration, few would argue that the French Revolution was an unalloyed blessing.

It spread the concept of liberty across Europe, it defined France as a modern state, and at its beginning it was seen from abroad as a needed reformation of a corrupt and entrenched system based on privilege. "Bliss was it in that dawn to be alive," the young William Wordsworth said when he arrived on the scene from England. But the Revolution soon came to be viewed as a triumph of excess, a case of lofty motivations leading to catastrophic ends.

Nowadays, historians tend to stress the Revolution's negative features. The Old Regime headed by Louis XVI actually was making some reforms, they point out, when it was struck down. And they focus unforgivingly on the murderous nature of the revolutionary government that followed. Americans of the time, whose own revolution had produced independence and a republic that truly safeguarded the lives, property and rights of its citizens, watched with dismay as the French uprising became a precipitous slide into bloodshed, vengeance and terror. What began with the proclamation of the Rights of Man ended with the guillotine working night and day to dispatch those who ran afoul of the Committee of Public Safety and "the Law of Suspects." The most celebrated victims of this cruel machine were, of course, Louis XVI and his wife, Marie Antoinette. (Louis can be found on, of all places, a U.S. stamp. The 13¢ French Alliance bicentennial commemorative of 1978, Scott 1753, depicts a porcelain sculpture of the king and the American envoy, Benjamin Franklin.)

The difference between the two revolutions, wrote Alexander Hamilton, "is no less great than that between liberty and licentiousness."

Thomas Jefferson, corresponding with John Adams years afterward, mourned that "your prophecies ... proved truer than mine; and yet fell short of the fact, for instead of a million, the destruction of eight or ten millions of human beings has probably been the effect of these convulsions."

Eventually Napoleon seized power, established a dictatorship and embroiled France in extended warfare that ended with Waterloo and the restoration, for a time, of the Bourbon monarchy.

Louis XVI, the unfortunate monarch who was beheaded during the French Revolution, is shown with Benjamin Franklin on this 1978 U.S. commemorative (Scott 1753) showing a 1785 sculpture by Charles Gabriel Sauvage in Du Pont Winterthur Museum in Delaware.

The Design

The images of Liberty, Equality and Fraternity on the U.S. stamp and the three individual French stamps were based on engravings by an unknown French artist that are in the collection of the Carnavalet Museum, a Paris institution that dates to the 1500s.

Liberty is seated, holding a tablet and a spear topped by the Phrygian cap adopted by the revolutionaries as "the red cap of liberty." Equality, also seated, holds a balance and the fasces, the Roman symbol of authority. Fraternity stands with what appear to be hearts in her left hand, her right hand protectively over two young children who are embracing each other.

Richard Sheaff of Needham Heights, Massachusetts, a design coordinator for the Citizens' Stamp Advisory Committee, designed the U.S. stamp, working closely with the Bureau of Engraving and Printing craftsmen in the process. The printing was a combination of offset (red, blue and silver) and intaglio (black) on BEP's D press, in the extra-large size used for the $8.75 Express Mail stamp of 1988 and the

On this preliminary pencil sketch the much-discussed nipple on Fraternity is very much in evidence. In the final design, the words "Declaration of Rights" were replaced by "French Revolution."

Department of Interior's annual migratory bird stamps. Like these, it was printed 30 stamps to a pane, five across by six deep.

Three aspects of the design attracted the attention of the press. The first related to the appearance of one of the female figures, the second to the color of one of the allegorical cherubs and the third to the arrangement of the background colors.

The publicity began when *Newsweek,* in its issue December 19, 1988, ran a brief story under the headline: "Someone's Been Fooling With Miss Liberte."

The story reported that the forthcoming U.S. stamp for the French Revolution would picture Liberty, Equality and Fraternity — which was accurate — but then implied that the image of Liberty would be the bare-breasted warrior woman from a well-known painting by Eugene Delacroix. "Officials revealed," *Newsweek* said, "that the stamp will lack a small detail: The breast that tumbles from the torn blouse will not have a nipple."

The official explanations for this anatomical anomaly, the magazine continued, were "as confusing as a garden maze at Versailles." According to *Newsweek,* W.L. (Pete) Davidson of USPS said the nipple disappeared when the picture became stamp-size: "We're talking about miniaturization." Hugh Kasley, assistant to the assistant director for operations at BEP, said he had "orders" to remove the nipple — from whom, *Newsweek* didn't say. And Dickey Rustin, head of the Stamp Support Branch, said the French had "brushed out the central part of the nipple (on their stamp), and we followed suit."

"Did the French really tamper with their own national symbol? *Mais non,"* the magazine concluded. " 'After all,' said a French official, 'a pretty drawing of a naked woman is always beautiful.' "

When the designs of the two countries' stamps were unveiled, it turned out that the figure involved in *l'affaire mammaire* wasn't Liberty, after all, but Fraternity, whose right breast peeped out from under her draped garment. France's stamps, which reproduced the old engraving in color, did show a nipple. The U.S. stamp, which rendered all three female figures in a simplified, colorless form that made them resemble classic statuary, had some shading lines on the underside of the breast — but was nippleless.

"The Bold and the Bashful" was the head over Bill McAllister's stamp column in *The Washington Post* after the designs were published. And *The New York Times* quoted one reader as saying the absence of a nipple was "in the realm of the ridiculous," given the prevalence in contemporary culture of "nudity, sex and violence."

If in fact the omission was a calculated act on the part of USPS, no one was making a clean breast of it. Kim Parks of the Stamp Support Branch called the *Times* reader's comment "silly" and attributed the streamlining of Fraternity's figure to the need to reduce it to stamp size. And because this particular stamp assignment gave wide inter-

There was no sign of prudery in the Post Office Department's depiction of an Indian maiden on this newspaper stamp of 1896 (Scott PR125).

pretive latitude to the engraver, designer Sheaff told *The Times,* decisions such as the inclusion or non-inclusion of a "tiny, tiny dot" had been left up to that particular craftsman, Kenneth Kipperman.

Finally, when the stamps themselves made their appearance, it became quite clear that the controversy was much ado about virtually nothing. A good magnifying glass was needed to determine that the French stamp did indeed show a nipple and the U.S. stamp didn't. Not that the BEP's Kipperman couldn't have provided the detail if he had chosen to do so; the same glass would also reveal some virtuoso engraving. On both the French triptych and U.S. stamp, the tablet held by the Liberty figure bears the minuscule but legible wording of the first article of the French constitution.

(Ironically, Kipperman once got in trouble at BEP for adding an alien detail to a stamp design. Unbeknownst to his supervisors, he engraved a tiny Star of David in the portrait on the $1 Bernard Revel definitive of 1986, Scott 2194. Its subsequent discovery became one of the major philatelic news stories of the decade.)

It's also interesting to note that U.S. postal officials of an earlier era — the era we call "Victorian" — could never have been accused of any prudish hangups. In the 1870s, the Post Office Department issued newspaper stamps in an extra-large size bearing pictures of "Peace," Hebe and an Indian maiden, all unashamedly topless — and anatomically correct. And the 2¢ Pan-American Exposition commemorative of 1901, which depicts a locomotive, has as part of its frame two female figures whose bosoms are as undraped as their logical connection to the rest of the design is unclear.

The second question raised about the French Revolution stamp involved the color of the cherubs.

In the original engraving of Fraternity that was the design source, one of the two infants that embrace at the woman's feet is white and the other black, a symbol of interracial brotherhood. On the multicolored French stamp, the racial difference is obvious. But the marble-statue treatment of the U.S. stamp shows both figures in a neutral white. Wrote *New York Times* stamp columnist Barth Healey: "The loss of symbolism has left the (Postal) Service open to charges that it is defacing art to avoid scarring the sensibilities, if that is the word, of racists." Healey didn't suggest, however, that any such charges actually were made.

The third question arose because designer Richard Sheaff placed each of his female figures against a colored panel. These were red, white and blue, with the whole overlaid with a cycloid pattern in metallic silver. Taken together, the panels resembled the French tricolor, only in reverse.

The Times' Healey quoted a reader who said the reversal of colors would "scream from every stamp" and expressed the hope that USPS would not be "ridiculed by a stamp which will mainly be used for letters to Europe." Healey also found a French Embassy official who expressed puzzlement over why the colors were arranged as they were.

But the stamp wasn't a flag, as USPS had taken pains to point out in its original April 19 news release.

"The colors were chosen to reflect the fundamental democratic principles common to the two nations and the long-standing ties between them," the release said. "Because the configuration of elements in the U.S. stamp suggests a flag, the Postal Service intentionally chose a red/silver/blue sequence to avoid having the design misconstrued as a representation of the blue/white/red French tricolor," Obviously, that effort wasn't altogether successful.

In fact, there were some reports in circulation that the arrangement of colors had indeed been a mistake by USPS and that the explanation contained in the April 19 release was an attempt to rationalize *fait accompli.* USPS officials insist it didn't happen that way, however.

(Coincidentally, at about the same time the color controversy was being aired, writer Arthur Cyr, discussing in *The Wall Street Journal* the reaction to the U.S. Supreme Court's decision upholding the right of people to burn the U.S. flag as a political statement, noted that other countries, including France, were much less reverential about their flags. "As France celebrates the bicentennial of its revolution," Cyr wrote, "the *tricolore* is showing up on many souvenirs, including boxer shorts.")

These essays placed the figures of Liberty, Equality and Fraternity into niches in a marble wall. One showed the figures in color; the other gave them a statuary treatment, the same as on the finished stamp.

In preparing his design for the stamp, Richard Sheaff sketched several variations for CSAC's consideration, using photocopies as well as drawings of the three figures. One variation had the figures in ovals; this was similar to the French treatment, but it would have resulted in smaller images. Different combinations of wording were tried and rejected, including "France & USA" and "Declaration of Rights."

Some essays included two dates, 1789 and 1989, but CSAC decided that the year of issue was unnecessary to make the point that the occasion was a bicentennial. It was a similar preference for typographical minimalism that had led the committee to drop the "1989" from the Washington, North Dakota and South Dakota statehood stamps issued earlier in the year.

What USPS ultimately delivered to BEP to be made into a finished stamp was Sheaff's final committee-approved sketch (at this stage, Fraternity still had a nipple) plus die proofs of the French stamps that were supplied by French officials.

"It was an interesting stamp in that it never was really designed," Sheaff said. "From these pieces, it was sort of designed as a process of giving instructions to the Bureau, having them try some things, experiment with what could be engraved and not engraved and so on, and show them to me and the others and we'd say, 'Yes, but now let's try this or try that.' We never did do the kind of slick-looking finished design we customarily do.

"The Bureau should be credited in substantial part with the design of the stamp."

BEP also developed the silver pattern used so effectively on the finished product. The pattern was first engraved, using a geometric lathe, a device that produces variations of loops. An offset plate was then made from the engraving.

If the stamp as printed has any drawback, it is that the names of the three figures, printed in metallic silver, are difficult to read, particularly "Equality," which is on a white background.

"It all depends on how you hold it with respect to the light," said Joe Brockert, the stamp's project manager and art director. "We felt it was preferable to printing the names in black, which wouldn't have been very legible against the blue, or reversing it, which wouldn't have

This essay presented the three figures in ovals, similar to the treatment used on the three separate French stamps. The wording "France & USA Airmail" was replaced by "French Revolution/USAirmail."

looked good on the silver background. Or we could 'mix and match' colors and backgrounds, which would look really bad." In this case, CSAC concluded that perfect legibility wasn't essential, Brockert said.

First Day Facts

The U.S. stamp and French triptych were issued simultaneously in Washington and Paris on July 14.

The Washington ceremony was held at the Jefferson Memorial. Featured speakers included former Chief Justice Warren E. Burger, chairman of the Commission on the Bicentennial of the U.S. Constitution; Postmaster General Anthony M. Frank; Charles Mathias Jr., chairman of the American Committee for the Bicentennial of the French Revolution, and Emmanuel de Margerie, ambassador of France to the United States. Excerpts were read from the Declaration of the Rights of Man and the U.S. Constitution.

The ceremonies in Paris were held in conjunction with Philexfrance '89 at the Parc des Expositions de Paris at the Porte de Versailles. A "premiere" of the U.S. issue was held on the evening of July 13, and the stamp was placed on sale the next day.

In Washington, the French triptych was sold at the main post office, the Philatelic Center at USPS headquarters, the first-day ceremony site and by mail order from the Philatelic Sales Division. It wasn't available at other philatelic centers.

The first-day cancellation policy for France's triptych was much more restrictive than for previous joint issues. France's first-day cancellations were available only on a handback basis and only at Philexfrance '89. Also, at the request of the French postal administration, USPS declined to apply the U.S. first-day postmark to the French stamps, either alone on cover or in combination with the U.S. airmail stamp. Covers bearing French stamps would be returned unserviced, the Postal Service announced.

45¢ PRE-COLUMBIAN ARTIFACTS AIRMAIL AMERICA SERIES

Date of Issue: October 12, 1989

Catalog Numbers: Scott C121   Minkus A121   USPS 5575

Colors: orange, brown, green, dark brown

First-Day Cancel: San Juan, Puerto Rico (ceremony canceled)

FDCs Canceled: 93,569

Format: Panes of 50, vertical, 10 across, 5 down. Gravure printing cylinders of 200 subjects (10 across, 20 around).

Perf: 11.1 (Eureka off-line perforator)

Selvage Markings: ©United States Postal Service 1989, Use Correct ZIP Code®

Designer: Lon Busch of St. Louis, Missouri

Art Director and Typographer: Richard Sheaff (CSAC)

Project Manager: Joe Brockert (USPS)

Printing: 7-color Andreotti gravure press (601).

Quantity Ordered: 35,000,000
Quantity Distributed: 39,325,000

Cylinder Number Detail: One group of 4 cylinder numbers over/under corner stamps

Cylinder Number Combination: 1111

Tagging: overall

The Stamp
The first series of America stamps to be issued by USPS as part of the omnibus issue sponsored by the Postal Union of the Americas and Spain (PUAS) featured pre-Columbian artifacts and comprised a 25¢ first-class mail stamp and a 45¢ airmail stamp. The story of how the project originated can be found in the chapter on the 25¢ item.

The Design
The Citizens' Stamp Advisory Committee provided regional balance in its design selections for the two America stamps by choosing an artifact from the Southwest for the 25¢ stamp and one from the Southeast for the 45¢ airmail. The subject of the airmail stamp was a small wooden figure with a human body and cat's head made by the Calusa Indian tribe of South Florida.

The figure, owned by the Smithsonian Institution's National Museum of Natural History, is called the "Key Marco cat" because it was found at Key Marco, a shell island on Florida's Gulf Coast south of Naples that the Calusa used as a ceremonial site. Its discoverer was archaeologist Frank Hamilton Cushing, who headed an expedition in 1896 sponsored jointly by the Smithsonian's Bureau of American Ethnology and the University of Pennsylvania.

Among the specimens Cushing excavated were a remarkable number of wood, cordage and other organic artifacts, whose preservation over the centuries apparently resulted from their immersion in muck, where they were protected from exposure to oxygen. Most of his finds were later divided between the Smithsonian and the University of Pennsylvania Museum in Philadelphia.

The Key Marco cat "is probably the most famous archaeological specimen in our collections," said Dr. Bruce Smith, curator in the Smithsonian's Department of Anthropology. Only about six inches tall, it is the sole wooden cat figure from its period and region to be found, and is said to resemble ancient Egyptian or Babylonian art more closely than any other specimen so far found in America.

Its discoverer, Frank Cushing, described it as a "man-like being in the guise of a panther." "Its dignity of pose may fairly be termed 'heroic,' and its conventional lines are to the last degree realistically treated," he wrote. "It is observable that not only the legs and feet, but also even the paws, which rest so stoutly upon the thighs or knees of the sitting or squatting figure, are cut off, unfinished; bereft, as it were, of their talons.

"And this, I would note, is quite in accordance with the spirit of primitive sacerdotal art generally — in which it was ever sought to fashion the form of a God or Powerful Being in such wise that while its aspect or spirit might be startlingly shown forth, the powers associated with its living form might be so far curtailed, by the incompletion of some of its more harmful or destructive members, as to render

The Key Marco cat, excavated from the muck on an island off the Florida Gulf coast more than 90 years ago.

its use for the ceremonial incarnation of the God at times, safe, no matter what his mood might chance, at such times, to be."

Experts have been unable to precisely date the item, and this uncertainty is reflected in the descriptive line USPS placed on the stamp, which reads "Southeast carved figure, A.D. 700-1450."

Artist Lon Busch made a painting for the Bureau of Engraving and Printing to use in making the gravure printing plates. He worked from photographs and verbal instruction from Art Director Richard Sheaff, who visited the Smithsonian with Joe Brockert, project manager for the stamp, and personally inspected the artifact.

As it turned out, the color of the cat in Busch's painting, and on the stamp, is a lighter brown than that of the actual object. Lightening the color made it possible to display details on the figure, Sheaff explained, adding: "We didn't want to have just a blob on the stamp." Besides, said the Smithsonian Institution's Dr. Smith, "We actually don't know what the color was originally. The color on the stamp may be close to what the cat looked like before it was submerged for 500 years or so in a bog."

As this was written the Key Marco cat wasn't among the items on display at the Smithsonian, but there are plans to exhibit it again once the museum's North American Indian area is remodeled, Dr. Smith said. That could take five years or more depending on Congress' willingness to fund the project, he added.

First-Day Facts

As mentioned in the chapter on the 25¢ America stamp, the first-day ceremony scheduled for October 12 in San Juan, Puerto Rico, was canceled because of the damage caused by Hurricane Hugo.

$1.80 FUTURE MAIL DELIVERY SOUVENIR SHEET

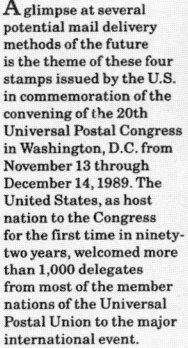

Date of Issue: November 24, 1989

Catalog Numbers: Scott C126 (souvenir sheet) Minkus A122
Scott C126a-d (imperf block of 4)
USPS 5531

Colors: magenta, yellow, cyan, black (offset); gray, light blue (intaglio)

First-Day Cancel: Washington, D.C. (World Stamp Expo '89 stamp show)

FDCs Canceled: unavailable

Format: Imperforate souvenir sheet of 4 stamps. Offset printing plates of 16 subjects (4 across, 4 around); intaglio printing sleeve of 32 subjects (4 across, 8 around).

Perf: imperforate

Selvage Markings: ©USPS 1988

Designer: Ken Hodges of Los Alamitos, California

Art Director and Typographer: Richard Sheaff (CSAC)

Project Manager: Jack Williams (USPS)

Engravers: Michael Ryan (BEP, lettering and numerals)
Gary Slaght (BEP, UPU lettering)
Gary Chaconas (BEP, logo)

Modeler: Jack Ruther (BEP)

Printing: 6-color offset, 3-color intaglio D press (902)

Quantity Ordered: 2,400,000
Quantity Distributed: 1,944,000

Plate/Sleeve Number Detail: no plate or sleeve numbers

Tagging: overall

The Souvenir Sheet

On November 24, USPS issued an imperforate souvenir sheet of four 45¢ airmail stamps to honor the 20th Congress of the Universal Postal Union that was in progress at the Washington Convention Center in Washington, D.C.

The occasion was Space Day at World Stamp Expo '89, the USPS-sponsored stamp show that was held concurrently with the UPU Congress. On hand for the occasion were Edwin E. "Buzz" Aldrin Jr., the former U.S. astronaut who was the second man to walk on the moon, and Gherman S. Titov, the Soviet cosmonaut who was the second man into space and the first man to orbit the earth more than once.

Reflecting the theme of the day, the U.S. souvenir sheet contained a se-tenant block of four stamps depicting what the Postal Service called "Future Mail Transportation" methods — three of which had outer-space settings.

These were the first U.S. stamp designs other than cartoons or allegories to depict objects or procedures that weren't based on present or historical reality. The vehicles on the four stamps were logical extrapolations, rather than anything that existed in that form when the stamps were issued.

They consisted of a hypersonic airliner soaring through space, a shuttle involved in a mid-space mail transfer at a space station, a surface rover vehicle delivering to a space colony and a mail-delivering hovercraft driving along the highway on a cushion of air.

The same four stamps also were printed as a perforated se-tenant block of four and distributed in panes of 40. The perforated version was issued three days after the souvenir sheet, on November 27. (See separate chapter.)

In its tentative schedule of first-day events for the UPU Congress-World Stamp Expo postal issues, released May 16, 1989, USPS had placed the perforated version of the Future Mail Transportation stamps in the November 24 slot and set aside November 28 for the souvenir sheet. Later, the two were switched. Still later, the date of issue of the perforated version was advanced a day, to November 27.

The Future Mail Transportation stamps and souvenir sheets were companion pieces to a similar se-tenant block and souvenir sheet depicting "Classic Mail Transportation" methods. These were issued November 19 and 27, respectively.

Like the Classic Mail Transportation items, the designs for the Future Mail Transportation stamps and sheet were unveiled months ahead of their issue date at UPU headquarters in Bern, Switzerland.

The Classic designs were made public October 27, 1988, at a meeting of UPU's Consultative Council for Postal Studies. The Future designs were disclosed April 26, 1989, during the UPU's Executive Council meeting. In both cases the official who did the honors was Associate Postmaster General Edward E. Horgan Jr.

The souvenir sheets could be used intact on mail to pay $1.80 in postage or cut apart and used as four separate stamps. However, unlike the perforated panes, the sheets were available only at USPS philatelic centers and by mail order.

The Design

The chapter on the Classic Mail Transportation block of four describes how the basic decision of USPS and the Citizens' Stamp Advisory Committee to issue stamps showing mail delivery methods evolved into a plan for two separate sets depicting historical and future mail transportation vehicles.

As it had done with the Classic Mail Transportation stamps, USPS assigned the Future Mail design job to a first-time stamp designer: Ken Hodges of Los Alamitos, California.

"Ken knows a lot about the aerospace industry and NASA because he works with them," explained Richard Sheaff, the art director. "We talked specifically about what kind of vehicles he would do — a hovercraft, a hypersonic transport plane, a lunar rover and so on.

"We told him what we wanted was the industry's best guess, at least insofar as he could interpret it, of what these kinds of vehicles might look like. We didn't want any specific manufacturer's concept, but something that would strike the technology people as being in the right ballpark."

After Hodges delivered his paintings, he was asked to make only small modifications. The most important was to add the U.S. flag to each of the four vehicles, "to add a touch of color and 'Americanize' them," said Jack Williams, project manager. A brownish background on the hovercraft stamp was changed to blue-green to be consistent with the other stamps.

When the final designs were published, someone complained that the flag on the hypersonic transport plane was reversed. USPS replied, correctly, that the design was accurate; the proper procedure for painting a flag on an aircraft fuselage is for the field of stars to be closest to the front.

The stamps used on the imperforate souvenir sheet were identical to those issued in perforated panes of 40. Art Director Sheaff designed the souvenir sheet, arranging the elements in a manner similar to those on the slightly larger World Stamp Expo '89 (Lincoln) souvenir sheet, which he also designed and which was issued on the stamp show's opening day.

The Bureau of Engraving and Printing printed both versions of the stamps on its combination offset-intaglio D press. The intaglio portion was used to print the inscription "USAirmail 45" in light blue on each stamp. An additional intaglio color — gray — was provided for the sheet to reproduce the title "20th Universal Postal Congress" and UPU logo across the top.

The UPU logo, which was also featured on some of the other postal items issued for the 20th Congress, is based on the well-known statue at UPU headquarters in Bern. The bronze-and-granite statue, a sphere of the world around which five messengers, representing the five continents, are exchanging letters, was designed by Rene de Saint Marceau of Paris, the winner of a UPU-sponsored competition, and dedicated in 1909. It has been shown on scores of UPU-related stamps of the world, including one of the U.S. airmails issued in 1949 for the organization's 75th anniversary (Scott C42).

A descriptive text appeared in a column of type to the left of the imperforate block. The text was drafted by project manager Williams and then revised into final form after being reviewed at various levels in the Postal Service.

First-Day Facts

For "Buzz" Aldrin, it was the second time in just over four months that he had participated in a first-day ceremony. He and Apollo 11 commander Neil Armstrong, his companion on the first moon landing, had taken part in the dedication July 20 of the $2.40 Priority Mail stamp marking that event's 20th anniversary.

At the same November 24 ceremony at which the Future Mail Transportation sheet was issued, the Soviet Union issued a similar imperforate souvenir sheet of four stamps. The Soviet stamps depicted the Soviet interplanetary automatic Lunakhod space station, a space-suited U.S. astronaut making the first landing on the moon, and two different representations of a possible future manned mission to Mars, one of which showed a Soviet cosmonaut and American astronaut jointly surveying the surface of the red planet.

"The great future that exists for both (nations) is in space," Aldrin said. "I am dedicating the rest of my life ... to ensuring that we have a space program in our future. The fact that philately has embraced the space program is very warm to my heart."

Said Titov: "Today Soviet-American relations in the area of space research have developed from competition to collaboration. The two countries' knowledge of outer space complement and enrich each other. ... Today we have unprecedented chances for success."

Also participating were Soviet Ambassador Yuri Dubinin (who said "We are all a little bit philatelists"), Deputy U.S. Postmaster General

The Soviet Union issued this souvenir sheet of four space stamps on November 24, Space Day, as part of a joint ceremony at which the U.S. Future Mail Transportation souvenir sheet was also dedicated.

Michael S. Coughlin and Soviet Director General of Posts Boris P. Boutenko.

Nine days later, at the Malta summit meeting, President George Bush presented Soviet President Mikhail Gorbachev with a black leather, gold-lettered presentation folder containing the two countries' souvenir sheets, along with a cover bearing the U.S. sheet postmarked December 3 aboard the *USS Belknap,* the Navy cruiser that served as Bush's at-sea summit headquarters. The folder also included copies of the 10 other U.S. stamps and postal stationery items issued at World Stamp Expo.

Space Day at World Stamp Expo saw another first-day ceremony, when the Republic of the Marshall Islands issued a se-tenant sheet of 25 stamps that showed high points of space exploration from Robert Goddard's successful launch of a liquid rocket to the flight of the space shuttle *Discovery,* in 1988. On the same day the Republic of the Maldives unveiled stamps based on NASA photographs celebrating the Apollo 11 moon mission, and Sweden introduced two new booklets, one paying tribute to Nobel laureates (including five Americans) and the other containing Christmas stamps.

45¢ FUTURE MAIL DELIVERY AIRMAIL (BLOCK OF FOUR)

Date of Issue: November 27, 1989

Catalog Numbers: Scott C122-25 (stamps) Minkus A123-26
Scott C125a (block of 4) USPS 5576

Colors: magenta, yellow, cyan, black (offset); light blue (intaglio)

First-Day Cancel: Washington, D.C. (World Stamp Expo '89 stamp show)

FDCs Canceled: unavailable

Format: Panes of 40, square, 8 across, 5 down. Offset printing plates of 160 subjects (10 across, 16 around); intaglio printing sleeve of 320 subjects (10 across, 32 around).

Perf: 10.9 (Eureka off-line perforator)

Selvage Markings: ©United States Postal Service 1988, Use Correct ZIP Code®

Designer: Ken Hodges of Los Alamitos, California

Art Director and Typographer: Richard Sheaff (CSAC)

Project Manager: Jack Williams (USPS)

Engraver: Michael Ryan (BEP, lettering and numerals)

Modeler: Jack Ruther (BEP)

Printing: 6-color offset, 3-color intaglio D press (902)

Quantity Ordered: 107,000,000
Quantity Distributed: 106,360,000

Plate/Sleeve Number Detail: Left-side panes — one group of 4 offset plate numbers over/under corner stamps; one intaglio sleeve number over/under adjacent stamps. Right-side panes — offset/intaglio numbers in reverse positions.

Plate/Sleeve Number Combinations: 1111-1, 1112-1, 2223-1, 2233-1, 2243-1, 2263-1

Tagging: overall

The Stamps

In its tentative schedule of first-day events for the UPU Congress-World Stamp Expo postal issues, released May 16, 1989, the U.S. Postal Service had placed the perforated version of the Future Mail Transportation stamps in the November 24 slot and set aside November 28 for the souvenir sheet.

Later, the two dates were switched — meaning that for the first time a U.S. stamp would appear as a souvenir sheet before it came out in regular perforated form. Still later, the date of issue of the perforated version was advanced a day, to November 27.

USPS also produced a set of four maximum cards, each depicting one of the four Future Mail Transportation stamps. These went on sale at World Stamp Expo on its opening day, November 17. Canceled sets of the cards, each bearing the appropriate stamp and postmarked November 27, were available at the show on the latter date.

The Design

The same four Ken Hodges designs that appeared on the souvenir sheet were also used for the perforated panes of 40. These consisted of a hypersonic airliner soaring through space, a shuttle involved in a mid-space mail transfer at a space station, a surface rover vehicle delivering to a space colony and a mail-delivering hovercraft driving along the highway on a cushion of air.

Varieties

A pane of the stamps was found in Colorado with the light blue intaglio ink (the 45¢ denomination and "USAirmail") missing. The finder reportedly believed the value was intentionally left off to trick people into using 45¢ stamps as 25¢ stamps. The pane was sold intact in a private transaction through the Jacques Schiff firm in Ridgefield, New Jersey.

First-Day Facts

November 27, when the Future Mail Transportation block was issued, was Aviation Day at World Stamp Expo.

Participating in the dedication ceremony were Dick Rutan and Jeana Yeager, the team that set the world distance record by flying *Voyager* on a non-stop, non-refueled flight around the world, and Astronaut Henry Hartsfield, a long-time stamp collector. The stamps were dedicated by Assistant Postmaster General Thomas E. Leavey.

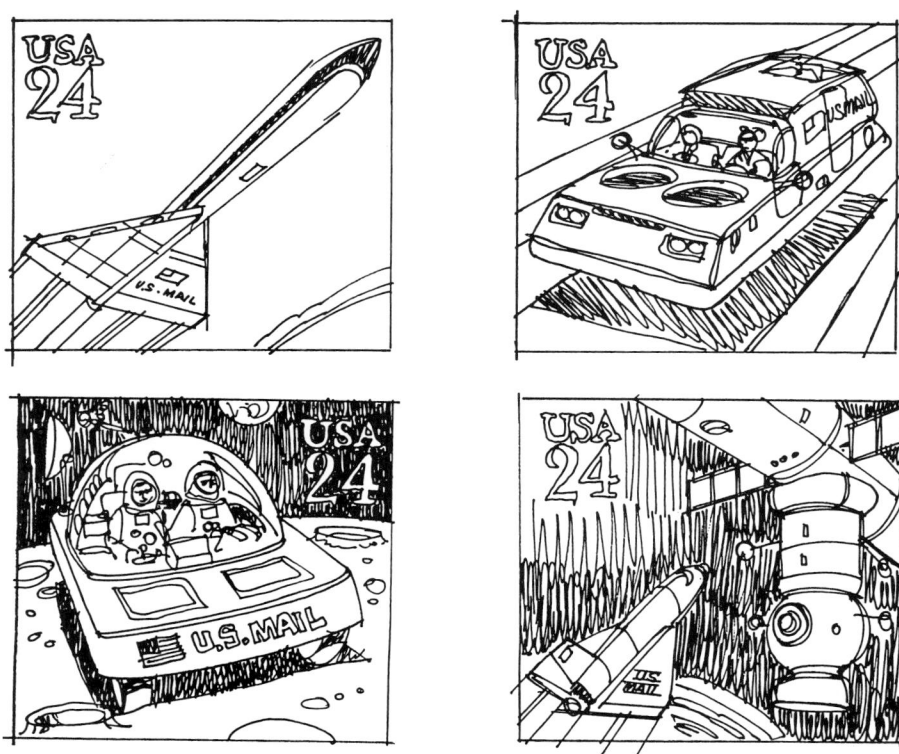

These four sketches by art director Richard Sheaff showed artist Ken Hodges the kind of design that was wanted for the Future Mail Transportation block.

1¢ OFFICIAL MAIL

Date of Issue: July 5, 1989

Catalog Numbers: Scott O143   Minkus OF139   USPS 5550

Colors: blue, red, black

First-Day Cancel: Washington, D.C. (no ceremony)

FDCs Canceled: 113,381

Format: Panes of 100, vertical, 10 across, 10 down. Offset printing plates of 400 subjects (20 across, 20 around).

Perf: 11.2 by 11.1 (Eureka off-line perforator)

Selvage Markings: ©UNITED STATES POSTAL SERVICE 1982

Designer and Typographer: Bradbury Thompson (CSAC)

Art Director and Project Manager: Joe Brockert (USPS)

Modeler: Peter Cocci (BEP)

Printing: 6-color Goebel Optiforma offset press (043)

Quantity Ordered: 15,000,000
Quantity Distributed: 6,700,000

Plate Number Detail: no plate number

Tagging: overall (phosphored paper)

The Stamp

A new 1¢ Official Mail stamp was announced in March and issued July 5 in Washington. It was the 16th in the current Official Mail series, which was introduced in 1983.

The government refers to the stamps as "Penalty Mail" stamps, because of the inscription they carry: "Penalty for Private Use $300." They are created for use on official correspondence in order to make each agency accountable and ensure that appropriate postage will be collected by USPS.

The Bureau of Engraving and Printing printed the first 11 stamps of the series on its intaglio presses. In 1988, however, it switched to less-costly offset lithography for Officials, and all four new varieties produced that year were made by offset on pre-phosphored paper.

Before that time, USPS hadn't printed many stamps by the offset process because of fear that they could be easily counterfeited. However, when phosphored paper proved to be practical as a method of tagging stamps, officials concluded that this feature by itself would provide a satisfactory security factor.

Additionally, BEP used an engraved die proof in the photographic process of manufacturing the offset plates, something counterfeiters would be unlikely to duplicate. Most significant was that Officials are invalid for use on private mail, thus eliminating virtually any incentive to counterfeit them.

The new 1¢ stamp replaced an earlier, intaglio stamp of the same denomination that was part of the original group of Officials issued January 12, 1983. Supplies of the older stamp were nearly exhausted, the Postal Service explained.

Though most recent new Officials had been issued in coil rolls, the 1¢ was produced in panes of 100, like its 1¢ predecessor. Unlike the earlier version, however, it carried no plate number in its margin. Since 1985, new Official sheet and coil stamps have been issued without plate numbers; before that time, the Postal Service had a continuing problem of disposing of large numbers of excess stamps left after panes or coil rolls were broken to provide collectors with numbered blocks or strips.

A survey by *Linns' Stamp News* in mid-1989 showed that 215 government agencies used what USPS calls "penalty indicia" for postage accounting and that of these, 50 agencies used Official Mail stamps or stamped envelopes. The largest group of the 50, accounting for 92

This is the earlier, intaglio version of the 1¢ Official Mail stamp issued by the U.S. Postal Service in 1983.

percent of the total use of Official Mail stamps, was composed of the Army (41 percent), Navy (23 percent), Department of Public Debt (11 percent), Air Force (10 percent), Soil Conservation Service (5 percent) and Marines (2 percent).

Some agencies that had used Official Mail stamps have abandoned them, going to what USPS calls total accountability. This means that the agencies use standard postage stamps and meters, which must be prepaid, instead of Official Mail stamps or penalty inscriptions on standard envelopes.

The biggest user of Official Mail stamps, the Army, was scheduled to make such a switch by September 15, 1989. The Army explained that there would be less temptation to waste postage if it went to a prepaid basis.

Despite the Army's defection, Jim Stanford, general manager of USPS' Official and International Mail Accounting Division, told *Linn's* that the general use of Official Mail stamps was growing, rather than diminishing.

The Design

The stamp used the design common to all current Official Mail stamps, namely, the central portion of the Great Seal of the United States in dropout white on a blue background, with inscriptions in red and black. It was the work of Bradbury Thompson, design coordinator and typographer for the Citizens' Stamp Advisory Committee.

Like the more recent Officials, however, the stamp's denomination is an unadorned "1" centered under the vignette. This style represented the last stage of a simplification trend.

The original group of Officials bore the wording "USA 1c," "USA 4c" and so on. Then came a 14¢ and 22¢ stamp in 1985 that dropped the "c" symbol. With the 1988 stamps, the "USA" also disappeared from the denomination line.

First-Day Facts

As was customary with Official Mail stamps, no dedication ceremony was held. Only once has the Postal Service held a first-day ceremony for Officials; that was in 1988, when the 15¢ and 25¢ denominations were dedicated at the Texpex '88 stamp show in Corpus Christi, Texas, as a replacement for the 25¢ Honeybee coil definitive, which had been scheduled for release at the show but was delayed by production problems at BEP.

Collectors could obtain first-day cancellations by mail, however. They were required to submit covers bearing their own address in the normal space and, in three lines in the upper left corner, the return address: "U.S. Postal Service/Washington, DC 20066/Official Business." The inscription could be typed, stamped or applied by gummed

The American eagle is shown in the cachet of this first-day cover for the new 1¢ Official issued July 5.

label, but not written in longhand. This satisfied the requirement that Official Mail stamps be used only on mail from a government agency.

Collectors could affix up to 24¢ in uncanceled postage to combine with the new 1¢ Official to cover the 25¢ first-class rate. For envelopes submitted without stamps and accompanied by 25¢ each, the Postal Service added one 20¢ Official stamp and one 4¢ Official to the new 1¢ stamp.

$12.50 MIGRATORY BIRD HUNTING (DUCK) STAMP 1989-90

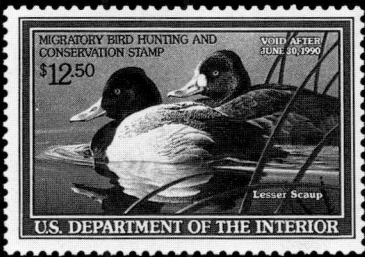

Date of Issue: June 30, 1989

Catalog Numbers: Scott RW56   Minkus RH56   USPS 3320

Colors: magenta, yellow, cyan, black, blue-gray, brown (offset); black (intaglio); black (flexographic back plate)

First-Day Cancel: June 30, 1989, Washington, D.C. (Smithsonian Institution)
July 1, 1989, Lincoln, Nebraska (State Capitol)

Format: Panes of 30, horizontal, 5 across, 6 down. Offset printing plates of 120 subjects (10 across, 12 around); intaglio printing sleeve of 240 subjects (10 across, 24 around); flexographic back plate of 120 subjects (10 across, 12 around).

Perf: 11.2 by 11.1 (Eureka off-line perforator)

Selvage Markings: sleeve number

Designer: Neal Anderson of Lincoln, Nebraska

Coordinator, Federal Duck Stamp Program: Norma Opgrand (Fish and Wildlife Service)

Typographer and Modeler: Ronald Sharpe (BEP)

Engravers: Gary Chaconas (BEP, vignette)
Gary Slaght (BEP, lettering and numerals)

Printing: 6-color offset, 3-color intaglio D press (902)

Quantity Ordered: 4,500,000
Quantity Distributed: 4,299,000

Sleeve Number Detail: one intaglio sleeve number at a pane corner

Sleeve Number: 182531
Flexographic Back Plate Number: 67522

Tagging: untagged

The Stamp

The 1989 Federal Migratory Bird Hunting and Conservation stamp, popularly known as the "duck stamp," was placed on sale June 30 in Washington and on July 1 nationally.

Its price, $12.50, was a new high for the annual stamp, which waterfowl hunters must purchase, sign and carry with their licenses. The first issue, in 1934, sold for $1; since then the cost has risen to $2 (1949), $3 (1959), $5 (1972), $7.50 (1979) and $10 (1987). It is scheduled to increase again, to $15, in 1991.

The stamp depicted a swimming pair of lesser scaup, from a gouache painting by Neal R. Anderson of Lincoln, Nebraska. Anderson's artwork was picked as the best of 681 entries in the 1988 Duck Stamp contest sponsored by the U.S. Fish and Wildlife Service.

The victory made a prospective millionaire of Anderson. Although no cash prize is involved in the contest, the winning artist has the right to market limited-edition prints of the design. These prints are extremely popular among art collectors, bird lovers and sportsmen, and command high prices. The contest can make the reputation of a previously unknown wildlife artist, or powerfully enhance it for an established professional.

Placing second in the competition was Vicky Hipsley of Redlands, California, with an oil painting of a red-breasted merganser. Paul Butala of Southfield, Michigan, was third with his acrylic of a pair of spectacled eiders. A fifth round of judging was required to break a seven-way tie for third place.

Anderson had entered paintings in five previous duck stamp contests, finishing second in 1985 with a pair of redhead ducks and third in 1983 with a single redhead. In those years, artists could depict any

Neal R. Anderson's painting of a pair of lesser scaup that was used as the design for the 1989 duck stamp.

species of North American waterfowl that hadn't appeared on a duck stamp in the preceding five years.

However, this time Anderson and other contestants were required to choose their subjects from among only five waterfowl species, selected by the Fish and Wildlife Service from among a list of nine that hadn't been depicted before. Besides the lesser scaup, they were the spectacled eider, red-breasted merganser, Barrow's goldeneye and black-bellied whistling duck.

In 1990 the lesser scaup was to be dropped and the black scoter added to the list of five eligible species. Thus, through the process of elimination, all 42 species of North American waterfowl will have been portrayed on a duck stamp by 1997.

Neal Anderson studied at Omaha Art School and worked as a commercial artist for 13 years while devoting his free time to painting wildlife. In 1986 he began devoting full time to this genre, specializing in waterfowl. He paints almost exclusively in gouache, producing work that is known for its detail, sharpness and clarity.

Among Anderson's previous honors were wins in the 1984 and 1988 Nebraska Conservation Stamp competitions sponsored by the Nebraska Wildlife Federation, and commissions to paint the 1984 National Arbor Day Stamp, the 1984 Nebraska Trout Stamp and the 1986 Wood Duck Stamp sponsored by Waterfowl USA.

Anderson chose the lesser scaup for his 1989 contest entry because of its availability in his home state. Even so, it wasn't easy finding models. Because of the drought, the ducks are "just gone," said the lifelong resident of Nebraska. "I've never seen it this bad. Several

The turning bars at the top of Bureau of Engraving and Printing's offset/intaglio D press are used only in the production of the annual duck stamp. They turn the web, with the stamp image already printed, so the message can be printed on the gummed side. In this picture the web is moving from left to right through the press.

After the message is applied by flexography to the reverse side of the web, the web goes to a takeup spindle at the end of the press to be wound gum side out for processing into panes.

lakes near my home are dry for the first time since I can remember, and the waterfowl just aren't there."

The fall flight of ducks in 1988 was estimated to be only 66 million, second only to the 1985 all-time low of 62 million ducks. Besides the years of drought in important breeding areas of Canada and the United States, the overall loss of wetland habitat has been a factor in cutting the waterfowl population.

The duck stamp program is designed to counter trends like these. Money from the sale of stamps is deposited in the Migratory Bird Conservation Fund and is used to add acres to the National Wildlife Refuge System. Since 1934, stamp revenues have paid for acquisition of nearly four million acres of wetland. In 1988 alone a total of 65,846 wetland acres were protected through purchase, easement and lease at a cost of nearly $32 million.

Judges in the contest for the 1989 stamp design were Robert Kuhn, a wildlife artist; Joan Allemand, art educator; Jack Lorenz, executive director of the Izaak Walton League; F. John Marshall, attorney and waterfowl art collector, and Tom Paugh, editor-in-chief of *Sports Afield*. Lieutenant General David Grange, a retired Army officer, was an alternate judge.

The Design

Violet, blue and brown predominated in the Bureau of Engraving and Printing's interpretation of Neal Anderson's painting, which was produced on the offset/intaglio D press.

A message ("Take Pride in America/Buy Duck Stamps/Save Wetlands") was printed on the gummed side by flexographic plates. The two-side printing is achieved by use of turning bars on the D press that invert the moving web after the front of the stamp has been printed. One of the problems with this system is the tendency of the still-damp ink on the reverse to offset onto the picture side. Sources said BEP experienced a high rate of spoilage with the 1989 stamps.

Katherine Davalos Ortega, treasurer of the United States, affixes her signature to the duck stamp proof sheet.

First-Day Facts

Three official ceremonies are now held in conjunction with the printing and issuance of the duck stamp. Since 1987, a special ceremony has been staged at BEP in connection with the first printing of the current year's stamps. And, since 1988, two first-day ceremonies have been held, one in Washington, the other in the hometown of the artist.

The 1989 event at BEP took place May 9. On hand to sign the first two sheets were artist Neal Anderson; Secretary of the Interior Manuel Lujan; Nebraska's two senators and three representatives; Katherine Davalos Ortega, treasurer of the United States, and other federal officials and guests.

One sheet of four unseparated panes was displayed at BEP, and the other was sent to the Smithsonian Institution's National Philatelic Collection. Before 1987, BEP furnished die proofs to the Smithsonian of each duck stamp, but now the museum receives the signed production sheet instead.

As for the first-day ceremonies, they were held on different days for the first time, which facilitated the appearance of artist Anderson at both events. The first was held in Washington June 30; the second, in Lincoln, Nebraska, on July 1, which has been the traditional day of release of the duck stamp nationwide.

The Washington ceremony was held at 10 a.m. at the Smithsonian Institution's National Museum of American History. Secretary Lujan was the featured speaker. The stamp was available afterward at a

The special first-day cancellations provided for the June 30 ceremony in Washington and the July 1 ceremony in Lincoln.

temporary Duck Stamp Station post office at the museum, and could be affixed to covers to receive a June 30 cancellation at any post office as long as a first-class postage stamp was placed next to it. At the Duck Stamp Station, a special cancellation was available depicting a reversed image of the pair of ducks in the stamp design.

The Fish and Wildlife Service prepared 5,000 first-day ceremony programs for the June 30 event. Most were distributed free to those attending. The rest were held back for later sale to collectors. Each of those sold bore the duck stamp, a 25¢ postage stamp and the special cancellation, and was priced at $15, $2.25 over the face value of the stamps affixed and canceled.

The July 1 ceremony was held in the rotunda of the Nebraska State Capitol in Lincoln, and a special cancel depicting a flying duck was available for covers. Among the speakers was TV personality Dick Cavett, a Lincoln native. On that same date, the stamp was placed on general sale in post offices and national wildlife refuges.

STAMPED ENVELOPES

Since its introduction in 1853, the U.S. stamped envelope has been an inherently dull item compared to the postage stamp. Printing techniques have been limited and incapable of delivering detail, multiple colors or subtlety. The natural result has been that collectors of envelopes, although dedicated to their specialty, have been relatively few in number.

That may change in the next few years, thanks to the novel envelope with which U.S. Postal Service closed its 1989 program of stamp and stationery issues.

The 25¢ Space Station envelope, featuring the world's first holographic indicium, did more than introduce "3-D" pictures to the mailstream. By showing how standard envelopes could be married to high-quality printing surfaces through a simple adaptation of the old-fashioned window-making process, this envelope has opened the door to a wide range of possibilities. "We think," said Don McDowell, general manager of USPS' Stamps Division, "that one of the really important new frontiers is going to be stationery."

Even before the Space Station envelope appeared, USPS had been in an innovative mode in 1989. It also produced its first envelope specifically for philatelic mail, its first security envelope and its first Love envelope.

In fact, only one envelope-type product issued during the year didn't represent a departure: It was an aerogramme honoring Montgomery Blair, and was one of the mailbag full of new issues with which the Postal Service celebrated World Stamp Expo '89 and the 20th Universal Postal Congress.

25¢ PHILATELIC RETURN STAMPED ENVELOPE

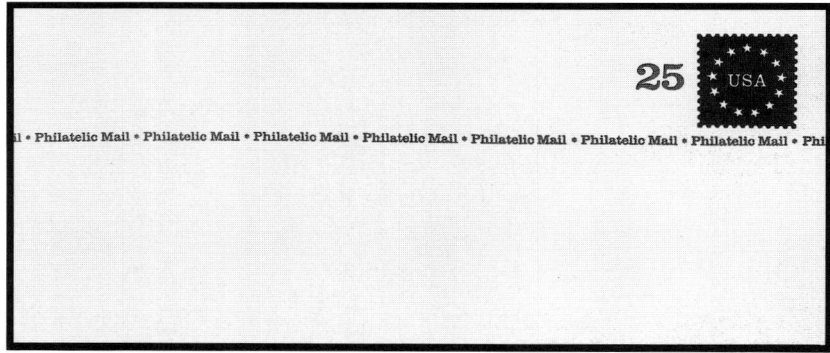

Date of Issue: March 10, 1989

Catalog Numbers: Scott U614   Minkus EN914   USPS 2121

Colors: blue, red

First-Day Cancel: Cleveland, Ohio (Garfield-Perry stamp show)

FDCs Canceled: unavailable

Size: 9

Watermark: star above S in USA

Markings: ©USPS 1989 under flap; "Philatelic Mail" repeated in a single horizontal line of lettering across front and wrapping around to the back on both sides.

Designer and Project Manager: Joe Brockert (USPS)

Art Director and Typographer: Bradbury Thompson (CSAC)

Printing: Westvaco-USEnvelope Division in 2-color flexography on a VH machine

Quantity Ordered: 2,547,500 (plain)
              208,000 (corner card, commercial)

Quantity Distributed: 2,547,500 (plain)
              208,000 (corner card, commercial)

Tagging: rectangle above denomination

The Envelope

The first stamped envelope created specifically for philatelic mail was issued March 10 in Cleveland, Ohio, at a ceremony opening the Garfield-Perry March Party stamp show.

The 25¢ envelope was manufactured in the number 9 size, which at 8⅞ by 3⅞ inches falls between the two standard USPS envelope sizes, number 6¾ and number 10. It was created, as USPS explained in a February 10 announcement, to provide collectors with a way to have covers returned after philatelic cancellations had been applied with the assurance that they wouldn't be overcanceled or damaged.

On January 1, 1989, USPS had begun a one-year test period during which it relaxed its regulations prohibiting the return of postmarked envelopes under cover. During this time, collectors were allowed to submit stamped, self-addressed envelopes along with their philatelic cancellation requests.

"The new envelope provides the final element in a perfect cancellation request kit," USPS said. "A self-addressed Philatelic Mail envelope can be enclosed with covers in a larger envelope and sent to a post office where the covers will be serviced and returned. Of course, the envelope may be used for other purposes as well, such as the exchange of covers between collectors. It may not, however, be used for first-day-of-issue-cancellation requests, because the Philatelic Sales Division already encloses all standard-sized first-day covers in durable clear plastic."

Collectors could have between four and seven number 6¾ covers returned to them in the new envelope, depending on the thickness of the stuffers used, USPS said. For the one-ounce rate of 25¢, the envelope would hold four covers with one postcard-thickness stuffer; five with one corrugated stuffer, or seven covers without a stuffer. Additional postage would be needed if the weight of the envelope, including the canceled covers and other enclosures, exceeded one ounce. As

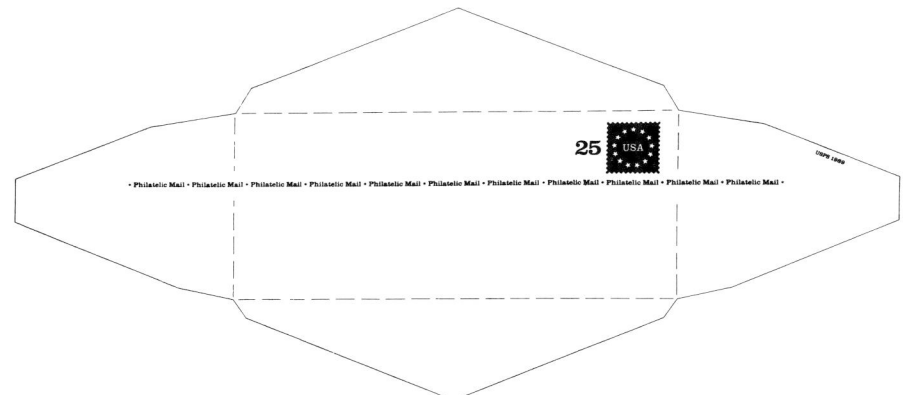

This is an "exploded" view of the Philatelic Mail envelope.

an option, the collector could send more than one Philatelic Mail envelope for the return of more covers.

The number 9 size envelope — which was last used by the Post Office Department in 1953 — was ideal for the purpose, in that number 6¾ envelopes would fit nicely into it and it in turn would fit in a number 10 business-size envelope for mailing to the post office that was offering the desired cancellation.

Envelopes were sold individually at philatelic centers or by mail order from the Philatelic Sales Division for 30¢. They were also available in bulk, imprinted with a return address, at $15.20 per pack of 50 (30.4¢ each) or $136.90 for a box of 500 (27.38¢ each).

Not all collectors were thrilled by the new envelope. One wrote to *Linn's Stamp News* nominating it as the "most unnecessary" item of the year and adding: "The majority (of special postmarks) come back in superb condition. Some postal clerks return my covers in glassine envelopes. The San Bernardino, California, sorting center has even printed a special 'We Care' glassine envelope for that purpose.

"When I place 25¢ (or more) postage on a cover, the stamp pays for its return. I am not going to pay an additional 30¢ for an overpriced envelope for the same purpose."

The Design

Because of the equipment of the Postal Service's stamped envelope supplier, Westvaco-USEnvelope Division, the stamp had to be printed by flexography. USEnvelope can only emboss envelopes made in the two standard sizes.

The stamp was similar to that of the combination embossed-flexo Circle of Stars envelope of 1988. A ring of 13 white stars encircles the letters USA on a dark blue background, with the denomination, 25, printed in red to the immediate left. However, the dark blue stamp background on the Philatelic Mail envelope featured simulated perforations around the outer edge, in contrast to the straight-edged design on the 1988 envelope.

Also distinguishing the new envelope — and providing the security element that is normally afforded by the embossing process — were the words "Philatelic Mail" repeated 11 times in a single horizontal band of red lettering across the front and onto the reverse sides. This wraparound technique was used on the 20¢ Small Business envelope of 1984. Canada has used it as a security device since 1977.

Design credit went to Joe Brockert, program manager, philatelic design for the Postal Service, who was also credited with designing the 1988 Circle of Stars envelope. Brockert make a rough sketch of the envelope to guide Anagraphics Inc., a graphics firm used by USPS, in designing the simulated perforations and typesetting the horizontal band of words.

Brockert's sketch called for an alternating message: "Philatelic

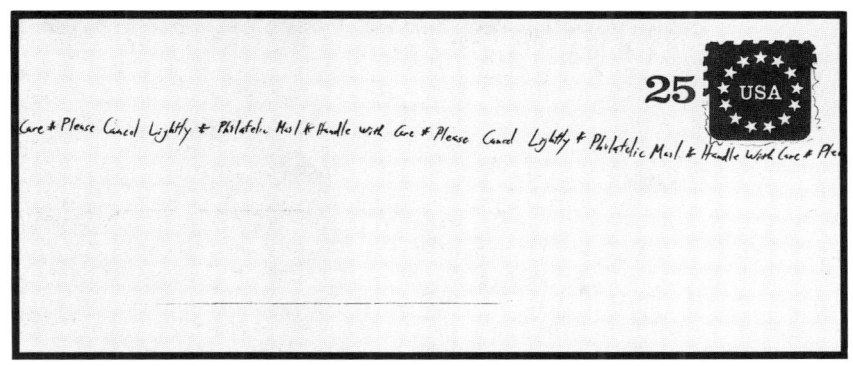

Joe Brockert took a 25¢ Circle of Stars envelope and added "perforations" around the indicium and a hand-lettered line of messages to demonstrate what he had in mind for the Philatelic Mail envelope.

Mail/Handle With Care/Please Cancel Lightly." Later, it was decided to use just the repeating "Philatelic Mail." The other two slogans were dropped, Brockert explained, because the principal interest of the collector using the envelope would be the contents, not the envelope itself. "Besides," he said, "we couldn't do a thing about the fact that an automatic machine somewhere might overcancel the envelope. We thought it might be self-defeating to put all these messages on the outside and call that much more attention to the fact that in the course of normal mail processing it's likely to get canceled more than once."

Officials also originally intended to put on the envelope the following return address: "United States Postal Service/Stamps Divison/U.S. Postal Service Headquarters/Washington, DC 20260-6751." Their idea was that the address would be appropriate for any post office in the country that was returning philatelic mail to a collector. "Then we thought, no, what about the collector who might want to send philatelic mail to other collectors?" Brockert said. "We decided the envelope would be more universally usable if we didn't add a return address."

First-Day Facts

The first-day ceremony was held in the Gold Room of the Masonic Temple Auditorium in Cleveland before an audience of some 350 people. Gordon C. Morison, assistant postmaster general, delivered the address, and guests were introduced by Richard H. Parker, president of the Garfield-Perry Stamp Club. Keith Wagner, executive director of the American Philatelic Society, and Dale R. Pulver, exhibits chairman of the Garfield-Perry March Party, also spoke. Immediately afterward, Morison and Garfield-Perry officials formally opened the show, which is one of the oldest continuing stamp exhibitions in the United States.

25¢ STARS SECURITY STAMPED ENVELOPE

Date of Issue: July 10, 1989 (no window)
December 29, 1989 (windows)

Catalog Numbers: Scott U615 USPS 2154 (no window)
Minkus EN915 USPS 2158 (large window)
USPS 2159 (small window)

Colors: blue, red

First-Day Cancel: Washington, D.C. (no ceremonies)

FDCs Canceled: 33,461 (no window)

Size: 9, with and without windows

Watermark: none

Markings: ©USPS 1989 under flaps; security design inside

Designer and Project Manager: Joe Brockert (USPS)

Art Director and Typographer: Bradbury Thompson (CSAC)

Printing: Westvaco-USEnvelope Division in 2-color flexography on a VH machine

Quantity Ordered: 4,334,000 (plain, no window)
70,000 (plain, corner card, commercial)
200,000 (plain, window)
Quantity Distributed: 4,334,000 (plain, no window)
70,000 (plain, corner card, commercial)
200,000 (plain, window)

Tagging: rectangle above denomination

The Envelope

USPS continued its practice of creating new types of stamped envelopes to meet specific needs when it issued its first-ever first-class security envelope in Washington July 10.

The 25¢ security envelope was issued by the Postal Service for use by mailers wishing to send checks, money orders and important documents. It contained a liner with a light blue pattern to protect the contents from outside detection.

Like the philatelic mail envelope that preceded it by four months, this one was manufactured in the number 9 size, which at 8⅞ by 3⅞ inches falls between the two standard USPS envelope sizes, number 6¾ and number 10. It sold for 30¢, but was also available in boxes of 500 for $136, or 27.2¢ apiece. The envelope could also be ordered from the manufacturer with a pre-printed return address at a cost of $15.20 for 50 and $139.50 for 500.

There had been no indication that a security envelope was being planned before the official announcement was made June 20.

Then, at year's end, USPS made the envelope available with a window, in two different formats — one for use by the general public, the other tailored to the specifications of a single customer. A December 28 news release announced that the window versions of the envelope would be issued the next day in Washington.

The window envelope sold to the general public contained a window measuring 1⅛ inches high and 4¾ inches wide and appearing one inch from the left edge.

A special version of the Security envelope produced for the Arizona Department of Economic Security to meet its mailing needs bore the department's pre-printed return address and contained a window that was 1¼ inches high and 3½ inches wide and placed one inch from the right edge. In both versions, the window was five-eighths of an inch from the bottom.

Except for the windows, the two new varieties were identical to the basic envelope that was issued July 10.

The "Arizona" envelope was offered for public sale only through the Philatelic Sales Division, but without the department's imprinted return address.

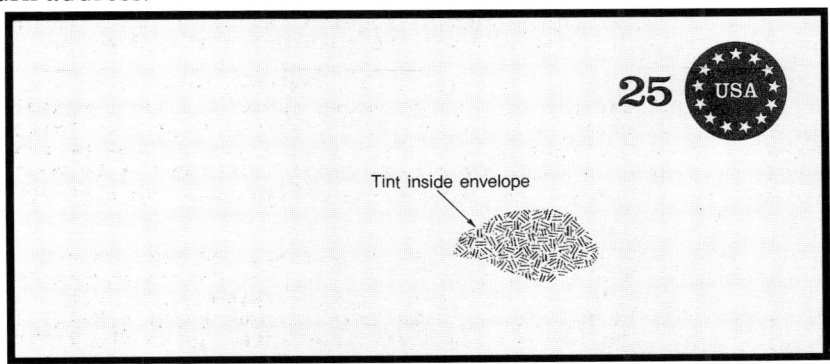

This Postal Service drawing shows the random pattern finally adopted for the interior of the Security envelope.

One proposed variation of the Circle of Stars indicium was this octagonal figure.

The Design

Besides being the same size as the Philatelic Mail envelope, the new envelope was similar to that one in another respect. Its stamp was a variation of the circle-of-stars design that had been introduced in 1988 with the 25¢ first-class mail envelope.

On the 1988 envelope, the blue background behind the 13 white stars was square. For the Philatelic Mail envelope, simulated perforation teeth were added to the design. And for the Security Mail envelope, the blue background was turned into a circle that was concentric with the ring of stars. All three carried the denomination, a red "25," to the left of the blue stamp. In each case, design credit went to Joe Brockert, a USPS program manager for philatelic design.

"We decided, for the sake of postal clerks' sanity if nothing else, to again make the stamp visibly different from the standard circle-of-stars envelope," Brockert said. "When you're rushed, you want to be able to distinguish a security mail envelope from an ordinary envelope without having to open it to see whether it's tinted on the inside or not.

"First we tried changing the stamp to an eight-sided shape, oriented in two ways: one, with a point at the top, and two, in the manner of a stop sign. Finally we settled on the circle. The circle has almost a coinlike quality to it that we kind of liked."

To guide artist John Boyd in preparing a mockup of the security-mail stamp, Brockert took a Philatelic Mail envelope and, using a typist's white correction fluid, covered the simulated perf teeth on the blue square and rounded off the corners to convert it to a circle.

For the security lining of the envelope, USPS considered using a repeating pattern of the eagle from its corporate logo, just as certain credit-card companies work their logos into the interior designs of the return envelopes they enclose with their bills. But on prototype envelopes, the eagles showed through to the outside in recognizable form, which was undesirable, Brockert said.

"It also occurred to us," he said, "that if we used the USPS logo, some people might perceive this as an official envelope to be used only by the Postal Service or to the Postal Service." The random repeating pattern that was finally chosen turned out to be quite satisfactory, he added.

On the original 1988 circle-of-stars envelope, the stamp was printed by a combination of embossing and flexography. However, the equipment owned by Westvaco, the manufacturer, could emboss only on two sizes of envelope, number 6¾ and number 10. Consequently, both the Philatelic Mail and Security Mail envelopes were produced by flexography alone. With the latter envelope, protection against counterfeiting — always a concern of USPS — was enhanced by the presence of the patterned liner.

First-Day Facts

There were no first-day ceremonies for either the non-window or window versions of the envelope, but first-day cancellations were offered in all three cases. Customers were encouraged to buy their envelopes at post offices and philatelic centers, self-address them and send them to the postmaster in Washington, except in the case of the "Arizona" window envelopes. These should be ordered canceled through the Washington post office because of the 30-day time limitation, USPS said.

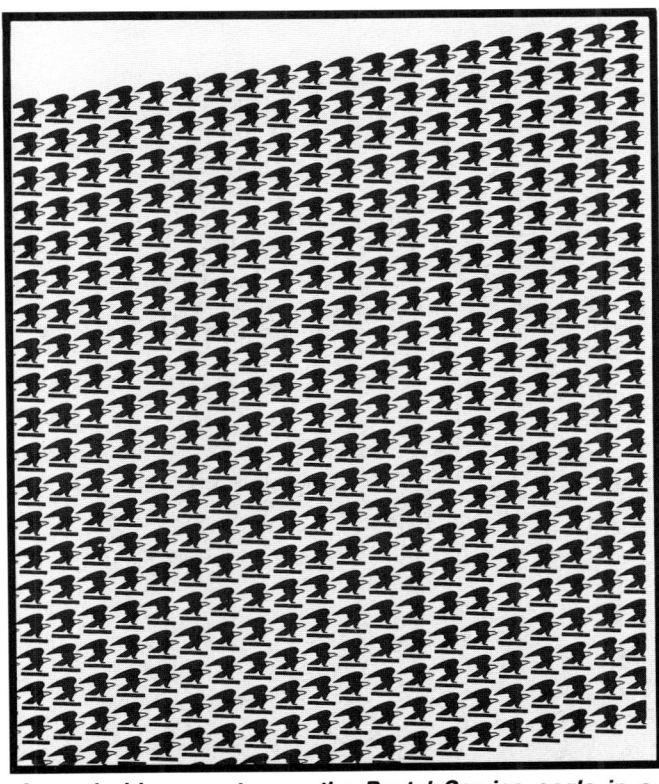

An early idea was to use the Postal Service eagle in a repeated pattern to tint the inside of the Security envelope and provide the desired opaqueness.

25¢ LOVE STAMPED ENVELOPE

Date of Issue: September 22, 1989

Catalog Numbers: Scott U616   Minkus EN916   USPS 2168

Colors: blue, red (offset); blue (flexography)

First-Day Cancel: McLean, Virginia (AFDCS convention)

FDCs Canceled: 69,498

Size: 9

Watermark: none

Markings: ©USPS 1989 under flap

Designer: Tim Girvin of Seattle, Washington

Art Director: Derry Noyes (CSAC)

Project Manager: Joe Brockert (USPS)

Printing: Westvaco-USEnvelope Division in 1-color flexography (diagonal lines) on a VH machine; 2-colors (stamp) on a Jet offset press

Quantity Ordered: 7,376,000 (plain)
27,000 (corner card, commercial)

Quantity Distributed: 7,376,000 (plain)
27,000 (corner card, commercial)

Tagging: rectangle to left of stamp

The Envelope

Following a recently established tradition, USPS unveiled the design for its next Love stamp in a midnight ceremony welcoming in the New Year of 1989 at the old Post Office Building on Pennsylvania Avenue in Washington. Later in the year, USPS announced that the stamp would be issued in 1990 rather than 1989 as planned.

However, in a surprise announcement August 16, USPS disclosed that it would issue its first Love stamped envelope September 22 in conjunction with the American First Day Cover Society convention in McLean, Virginia.

Thus the Postal Service followed a popular stamp series — the Love stamps — with an envelope, just as in 1988 it had expanded its practice of issuing annual Christmas stamps by producing its first-ever Christmas envelope.

The extent and makeup of the potential market for the 25¢ Love envelope was uncertain. It was issued in the number 9 size (3⅞ by 8⅞ inches) appropriate for return envelopes, suggesting that it might be used for RSVPs by persons mailing invitations in a number 10. Authorization to issue odd-size envelopes had been granted to USPS by the Postal Rate commission in March 1988; before that, the Postal Service could only sell number 6¾ and number 10 sizes.

Like other non-standard envelopes issued under the new authorization, this one carried no embossing. The Postal Service's envelope maker, Westvaco-USEnvelope Division, can only emboss envelopes of the two traditional sizes. However, security in this case was provided by narrow, light blue diagonal lines in the background — the first patterned paper to be used on a U.S. stamped envelope.

A two-press operation was used to make the envelopes. They were formed and the diagonal blue lines and copyright symbol were printed by flexography on Westvaco's VH machine. Then the stamps were applied by a two-color offset Jet press in a single-run process.

The envelopes were sold for 30¢ each or $136 (27.2¢ each) for boxes of 500. Customers could also order the envelopes with return addresses printed in dark blue for $15.20 for 50 and $139.50 for 500.

The Design

The design, by Tim Girvin of Seattle, had originally been submitted to the Citizens' Stamp Advisory Committee as artwork for a Love stamp. The committee liked it and put it aside for future use.

When the time came to pick a design for the Love envelope, Girvin's design filled the bill. "We were looking for something that had two qualities," said Joe Brockert, the project manager. "It should be without well-defined borders, and it should be suitable for printing in two colors."

Girvin's design, described as "playful" in the USPS news release, is simply the word "love!" in red lower-case italics, looking as if it was dashed off in freehand with a flat-tipped lettering pen. A blue pen stroke underscores the word, while a vertical blue stroke combines with a small red heart to form the exclamation point.

Stamp designers, finding it difficult to come up with new design themes for Love stamps, have frequently fallen back on using the

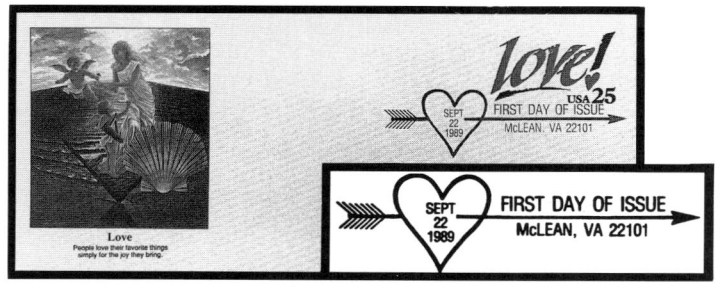

The U.S. Postal Service used this pictorial first-day-of-issue cancellation for the Love envelope.

word itself in various ways. The precedent was set, of course, with the very first Love stamp in 1973, which depicted Robert Indiana's celebrated block-letter sculpture.

Before choosing the pattern for the envelope's paper, the Postal Service examined a large number of prototypes in which Westvaco formed envelopes and printed the indicium on different backgrounds — including such assertive hues as shocking pink, green and a tweed-textured brown. Ultimately Postal Service officials opted for the muted pattern of blue lines.

First-Day Facts

The envelope was dedicated at the McLean Hilton Hotel in a ceremony held in conjunction with the opening of the first joint convention of the AFDCS and the Universal Ship Cancellation Society.

Peter K. Eichorn, senior assistant postmaster general, was the principal speaker. Others participating in the program were Bernard H. Kroll, president of the Robert C. Graebner Chapter of AFDCS; Michael Litvak, president of the American Ceremony Program Society; Jackson Bosley, president of the Universal Ship Cancellation Society, and Pat McMahon, Virginia's director of tourism.

39¢ MONTGOMERY BLAIR AEROGRAMME

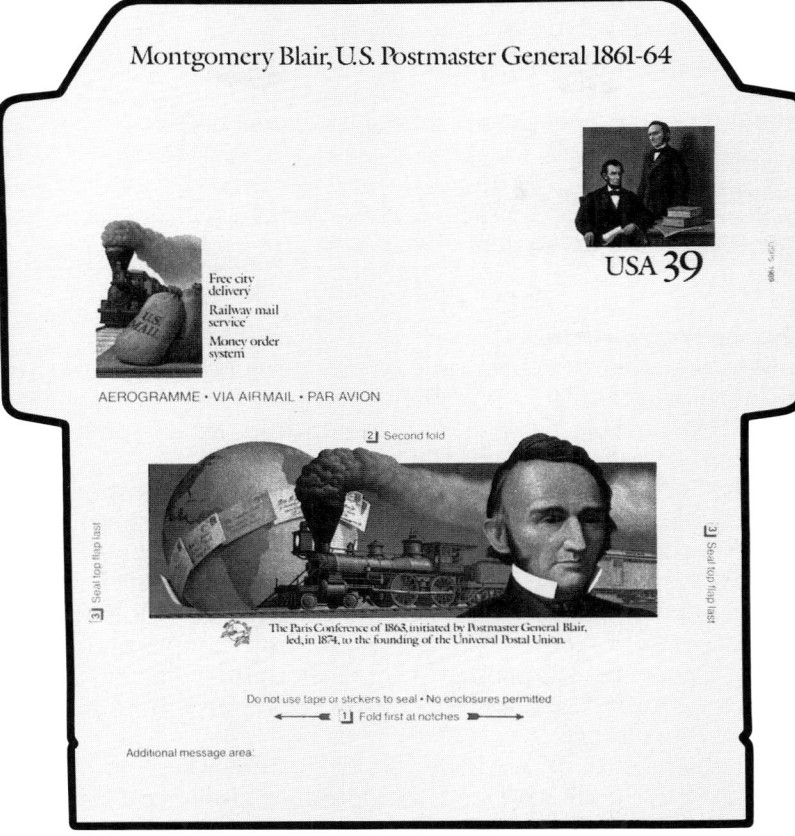

Date of Issue: November 20, 1989

Catalog Numbers: Scott UC62   Minkus A122   USPS 2234

Colors: magenta, yellow, cyan, black

First-Day Cancel: Washington, D.C. (World Stamp Expo '89 stamp show)

FDCs Canceled: unavailable

Size: 7½ by 3 9/16 folded

Format: Die cut into single aerogrammes. Printing plates of 4 subjects (2 across, 2 around).

Watermark: none

Markings: ©USPS 1989 on side flap

Designer: Ned Seidler of Hampton Bay, New York

Art Director and Typographer: Howard Paine (CSAC)

Project Manager: Jack Williams (USPS)

Modeler: Frank Waslick (BEP)

Printing: 6-color Goebel Optiforma offset press (042)

Quantity Ordered: 9,000,000
Quantity Distributed: 4,857,500

Tagging: vertical bar to right of stamp

The Aerogramme

The most clearly appropriate of the many postal items USPS issued during World Stamp Expo '89 and the 20th Congress of the Universal Postal Union was a 39¢ aerogramme honoring Montgomery Blair, President Abraham Lincoln's postmaster general.

Blair, perhaps the most innovative person ever to hold that office, can be called, if not the father of the UPU, then certainly its grandfather. An international postal conference that he sponsored in 1863 led directly, 11 years later, to the formation of the UPU.

USPS dedicated its "Blairogramme" November 20 at the Washington Convention Center, site of the World Stamp Expo stamp show. The aerogramme supplemented, rather than replaced, the 39¢ standard aerogramme of 1988, and was expected to remain in service until the next rate change.

The availability of two different kinds of aerogramme was expected to help USPS deal with conflicting complaints, said Jack Williams, project manager for the Blair item. Some aerogramme users want maximum space for writing their messages and a minimum of colorful designs that tend to show through on the opposite side of the sheet. To them, USPS could offer the standard aerogramme, which has a simple indicium and no other pictorial material. Others prefer air lettersheets with lots of color and pictures — which is an apt description of the Blair aerogramme.

Montgomery Blair is the only postmaster general appointed under the Constitution to be pictured on stamps or stationery, and this was his second appearance. He was previously portrayed on a 15¢ airmail stamp of 1963 (Scott C66) commemorating the 100th anniversary of the 1863 conference, held in Paris.

As another part of that 1963 centennial observance, the Post Office Department issued a booklet on Blair's life and accomplishments by Rita Lloyd Moroney, department historian. USPS reissued the booklet November 13, 1989, in honor of the UPU Congress.

Born May 10, 1813, in Kentucky, Montgomery Blair was a member

Montgomery Blair was honored on this 15¢ 1963 airmail marking the centennial of the first international postal conference.

of a distinguished and colorful political family. His father, Francis Blair, owned the house in Washington that now bears his name. In this house — which was depicted on a Historic Preservation postal card of 1988 — Montgomery Blair lived for a time before moving to suburban Maryland.

A lawyer, he participated in many of the historic cases of his era. He was on the losing side in two of the most notorious of these, arguing on behalf of the slave Dred Scott before the U.S. Supreme Court and helping prepare the defense of abolitionist John Brown against the charge of armed insurrection.

The Blairs supported Lincoln at the 1860 Republican convention, and after his election, Lincoln made Montgomery Blair his postmaster general. Wrote Rita Moroney:

"The department ... was archaic, inefficient, and chronically riddled with troubles. ... There were no official letter-boxes on the streets, except in a few larger cities, no mail railway cars, and free delivery did not exist.

"There was no money order system and little uniformity in international mail procedures. The system of registering letters had been pronounced a failure by Blair's predecessor. ... The department was running deeply into debt. The postal deficit in 1860 ran to about 40 percent of the estimated budget."

Blair moved vigorously to make improvements, introducing new, efficient procedures that soon cut into the deficit. Ironically, it was the major domestic crisis of the age — the Civil War — that did the most to change the red ink to black, by enabling the department to drop hundreds of miles of money-losing Southern rural routes. The cre-

The 100th anniversary of free city mail delivery, one of the major achievements of Montgomery Blair's term as postmaster general, was marked with this commemorative stamp (Scott 1238) designed by Norman Rockwell.

ation of this "war surplus" in the Post Office Department helped make it possible for Blair to financially justify one of his major reforms, free city delivery, which began in 49 post offices July 1, 1863.

Another of his great accomplishments also stemmed from the war, as the need for a safe way for soldiers to send money home led him to create a uniform money-order system and revive the faltering registration system. His third major innovation was the introduction of the railway post office — railroad cars in which mail was sorted and distributed en route, saving as much as 24 hours in processing time.

Of all Blair's work, however, none has had as wide and lasting an impact on world communications as his efforts to bring uniformity to international mail. These efforts, and their consequences, are described in the chapter on the Classic Mail Transportation block of four that was issued to commemorate the UPU Congress.

Blair made enemies among radical Republicans because of his moderate views on postwar reconstruction. He also offended some of his fellow cabinet members by his tactlessness and strongly-expressed opinions. In September 1864, Lincoln, facing a tough re-election campaign and in need of the solid support of his own party, wrote Blair a letter full of praise for his leadership of the Post Office — but asking him to resign. Blair promptly complied. He practiced law after the war and died in 1883 at age 70.

A portrait of Blair, painted by Arthur C. Johnson of Hampton, New Hampshire, was presented to the UPU in 1954 by Post Office officials on behalf of the U.S. government. It hangs in the organization's headquarters building in Bern, Switzerland.

The Design

Artist Ned Seidler of Hampton Bay, New York, incorporated several elements in his aerogramme design.

The indicium, or stamp, portion shows Blair standing to the right of a seated President Lincoln. For the cachet area, Seidler painted a locomotive approaching a station with two mailbags waiting on the platform. To the right of the cachet, in six lines, are the words: "Free city/delivery," "Railway mail/service" and "Money order/system."

The portion of the aerogramme that becomes the back side when folded is dominated by a montage. On the left is a globe circled by a belt of letters, a design idea that is similar to one used on the Blair airmail stamp of 1963. In the center is another locomotive, with cars behind it. To the right is a large portrait of Blair.

Beneath the montage is a small reproduction of the UPU symbol and the two-line inscription: "The Paris Conference of 1863, initiated by Postmaster General Blair,/led, in 1874, to the founding of the Universal Postal Union."

In designing the indicium, showing Lincoln and Blair together, Seidler relied on a famous painting: Francis B. Carpenter's depiction

This is an early version of the aerogramme design, before modifications were made to the indicium, cachet and montage portions.

of Lincoln reading his Emancipation Proclamation to his assembled cabinet. To juxtapose Lincoln and Blair, Seidler had to eliminate the intervening cabinet members — Secretary of the Navy Gideon Welles, Secretary of Interior Caleb B. Smith and Secretary of State William Seward — and move the two men he wanted together.

The painting was made by Carpenter, a New York portrait artist, during a six-month residency at the White House in 1863-64. He spent long hours in Lincoln's office and at cabinet meetings, sketching the principals and the furnishings. Mary Todd Lincoln, familiar with the contentious personalities in the cabinet, sarcastically dubbed the finished painting "The Happy Family."

When Carpenter was finished, engravings of the painting were made and widely distributed. However, many of Lincoln's friends and admirers disliked the picture, in which the focus of attention seemed to be Seward rather than Lincoln. Eventually Carpenter revised it. He changed the president's face so he no longer seemed to be listening with a deferential regard to his secretary of state, transferred to Lincoln's right hand a quill pen that previously had rested close to Seward's fingers, and put into his left hand a mass of papers that had been on the table. This is the version of the painting that was presented to Congress in 1878 and that now hangs in the Senate wing of the Capitol.

However, Ned Seidler based his design for the indicium of the aerogramme on the engravings that were made from the earlier version of the painting — which is why his Lincoln looks slightly different from the Lincoln in the painting as it now exists. Blair and the other cabinet members are the same in both versions.

For the large portrait of Blair on the reverse side of the aerogramme, Seidler worked from a photograph by Matthew Brady, whose camera recorded hundreds of faces and scenes from the Civil War period. The photograph had been made into a *carte de visite* of the kind frequently used in place of a calling card.

In developing the final design of the aerogramme, Seidler modified some of his early concept sketches. His original cachet design showed a mailbag catcher arm beside the tracks, but James Bruns, a curator at the Smithsonian Institution's National Philatelic Collection and expert on the history of postal equipment, pointed out that these devices didn't come into use until after Blair's term, so the design was changed to remove the anachronism. Seidler also made the plumes of smoke from the stacks of the two locomotives more similar in appearance, removed lines of longitude that he had sketched on the globe, and, in the indicium, added a dark-colored tapestry background and placed some books on the table beside Lincoln and Blair.

Seidler had earlier designed the Civilian Conservation Corps commemorative of 1983 and the Express Mail stamp of 1988, but this was

Francis B. Carpenter's revised painting of Lincoln reading the Emancipation Proclamation to his cabinet, from which the figures in the aerogramme indicium were extracted. From left, Secretary of War Edwin Stanton; Secretary of the Treasury Salmon P. Chase; Lincoln; Secretary of the Navy Gideon Welles; Secretary of the Interior Caleb B. Smith; Secretary of State William Seward; Postmaster General Montgomery Blair, and Attorney General Edward Bates.

his first aerogramme. USPS officials gave him a copy of the Mark Twain aerogramme of 1985 to use as a guide in placing the design elements on the various sections.

First-Day Facts

USPS had originally set November 19 as the date of issue for the Blair aerogramme and November 20 for the sheet version of the Classic Mail Transportation stamps. Later it switched the two dates.

November 20, when the aerogramme appeared, was UPU Day at World Stamp Expo. Other countries holding first-day-of-issue ceremonies that day were Grenada (a Walt Disney set), Palau (stamps depicting plant and animal life) and Israel (a miniature sheet variation of its recent issue "Ducks of the Holy Land").

The principal speaker at the Blair aerogramme dedication was Adwaldo Cardoso Botto de Barros of Brazil, director general, International Bureau of the UPU. His remarks were translated by an inter-

The large portrait on the aerogramme was based on this Matthew Brady photograph of Montgomery Blair, which was used as a carte-de-visite. Photo courtesy of the Historical Society of Washington, D.C.

preter. The aerogramme was dedicated by Edward E. Horgan Jr., associate postmaster general.

Attendees at the Blair aerogramme ceremony received a program consisting of a booklet that included the aerogramme, canceled "First Day of Issue," and a card insert giving the program agenda. The same booklet, but with different inserts, was later used for the first-day ceremonies held for the four other U.S. postal stationery items issued at World Stamp Expo.

At 7 p.m. the same day a second dedication ceremony was held at the Montgomery Blair High School in Silver Spring, Maryland. A ceremony program was prepared and a pictorial cancellation showing a facsimile of Blair's signature was applied to covers.

25¢ WORLD STAMP EXPO '89 ENVELOPE

Date of Issue: December 3, 1989

Catalog Numbers: Scott U617   Minkus EN917   USPS 2156

Colors: blue; hologram

First-Day Cancel: Washington, D.C. (World Stamp Expo '89 stamp show)

FDCs Canceled: unavailable

Size: 9

Watermark: none

Markings: ©USPS 1989 under flap

Stamp Art: Ken Hodges of Los Alamitos, California

Designer: Richard Sheaff (CSAC)

Project Manager: Joe Brockert (USPS)

Printing: Holograms in rolls on foil by American Bank Note Holographics; Westvaco-USEnvelope Division printed in 1-color flexography, affixed hologram and formed envelopes on a VH machine.

Quantity Ordered: 7,609,000 (plain)
  46,500 (corner card, commercial)
Quantity Distributed: 7,609,000 (plain)
  46,500 (corner card, commercial)

Tagging: bracket to right of hologram

The Envelope

USPS saved its most interesting and unusual postal issue of 1989 for last. In fact, the item, which made its debut December 3 at World Stamp Expo '89, represented the most radical innovation in manufacturing technology for U.S. stamps and stationery since the first stamps were printed in 1847.

The product was an envelope with a window opening in the "stamp corner" containing a type of hologram — a three-dimensional picture with elements that shifted their relative position depending on the horizontal angle at which it was held and colors that changed depending on the vertical angle.

Other stamp printing methods were long established when the United States adopted them. The last major method to be introduced for U.S. stamps — gravure, in 1967 — had been used by other postal administrations around the world for decades.

But holography was, and is, a new medium. Related to photography, it makes pictures without lens and using only the light of a laser — a device that wasn't invented until 1960.

Not until the 1980s were holograms mass-produced for such things as credit cards, book and magazine covers and advertising, and studied as a possible anti-counterfeiting element for U.S. currency. Not until 1988 did Austria pioneer their use on postage stamps. The USPS envelope, depicting a space scene, was the first postal stationery in the world to use a holographic picture in its indicium.

The space picture itself was on a piece of metallic foil attached to the inside of a die-cut window, which was 1¼ inches square with rounded corners. No typography appeared on the foil. The inscription "USA 25" was printed by conventional flexography on the envelope to the left of the image area, in the style introduced on U.S. stamped envelopes in 1988.

The first announcement of the new envelope was made October 11, 1989. "We started looking at the application of holograms to postage in December 1987," said Joe Brockert of USPS, project manager for the envelope.

"In 1988 we undertook to learn as much as we could about the process. We sat down with three hologram manufacturers, told them what we were interested in and exchanged information and ideas.

"We looked at all the pluses and minuses, and realized that one of the minuses of putting a hologram on a postage stamp was the fact that it would have to be very tiny. And a hologram, to be effective, needs to be big and visible and immediately obvious.

"If you have to hold the stamp at a certain angle to read the denomination, that's another disadvantage. Still another problem is that if the hologram covers all or most of the stamp surface, it becomes virtually impossible to cancel. Having it take a cancellation was our main concern at that point.

"That's when we hit on the idea of putting a foil hologram on a stamped envelope, either as an adhesive label or patched into a window. It wouldn't matter whether it held a cancellation. It's the envelope — the entire piece — that's canceled.

"Foil tends not to hold a cancellation, but on the other hand it doesn't repel ink, either. We ran some tests with the help of our Engineering and Development Center, and they said that foil was acceptable. The canceling ink wasn't flying off and ruining other things. We weren't getting offset onto other mail."

USPS brought its envelope maker, Westvaco-USEnvelope, into the talks. The production requirements of USEnvelope and the hologram manufacturers had to be compared and reconciled. An optimum size, shape and placement of the window in the envelope corner had to be found. Many other seemingly routine details had to be worked out.

To make the hologram itself, USEnvelope ultimately chose American Bank Note Holographics Inc. of Elmsford, New York. This corporate associate of the long-established American Bank Note Company made the three-dimensional dove for VISA's credit cards and the logo for MasterCard's cards and produced the eagle that was shown on the

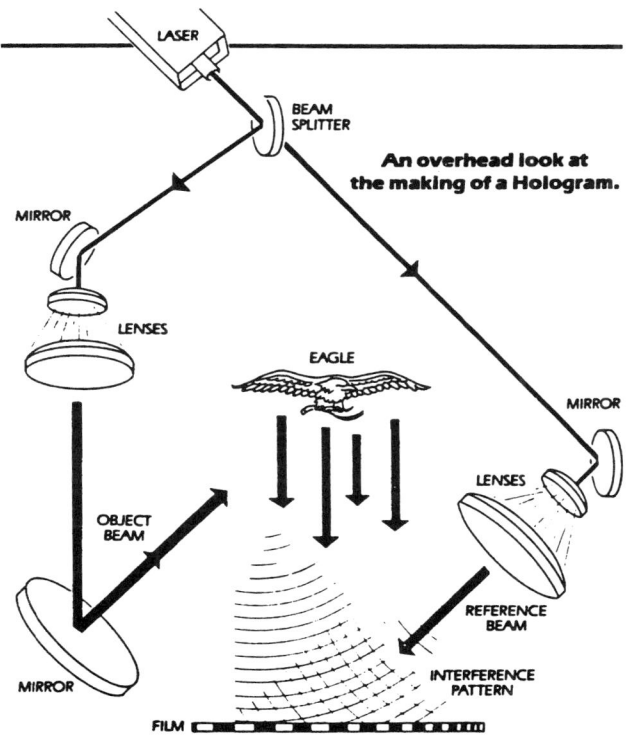

Diagram for a hologram, courtesy of American Bank Note Holographics, Inc.

National Geographic's pioneering hologram magazine cover of March 1984.

ABN Holographics contracted to supply the holograms in large rolls to USEnvelope. For the envelope maker, the job of patching the foil into openings in the envelope corners was much more complicated than applying a conventional glassine window in the address portion. The holograms had to be uniformly cut and registered so the same image always showed through to the outside. To accomplish this, USEnvelope retro-fitted an electric-eye registration device to its VH envelope-forming machine.

Because the large webs of hologram foil contained splices at intervals, the company's inspectors had to cull out any envelopes that emerged from the production line with spliced images. As of this writing there have been no reports of hologram envelopes with splices reaching the public.

USPS officials believe that in the long run the simple process adopted for integrating the hologram with the envelope may prove to be even more significant to their product line than the hologram itself.

As Don McDowell, general manager of the Stamps Division, explained it, USEnvelope have never been able to do four-color process work in close registration for USPS because they have to use paper of a certain roughness — what the trade calls "tooth" — to activate the friction-feed system in the envelope-forming machinery. The smooth paper needed for high-quality printing won't work.

"Now we know we can put into a window on a stamped envelope just about anything we want to," McDowell said.

"Plastic, for instance, is a wonderful printing substratum. You can do very high-quality gravure printing on plastic or film. Gravure loves surface smoothness, and plastic can be smoother than the smoothest triple-coated paper.

"If we print the denomination, USA 25, beside the window as we did with the hologram, and we have an inventory of pre-printed plastic webs with images on them, we can put very high-quality printing into the stamp position on the envelope by taking the mountain to Mahomet. We can change in production from envelope design A to design B in about 10 minutes. That's truly revolutionary.

"So we think that one of the really important new frontiers is going to be stationery. Materials and manufacturing technology may open up avenues for new and better kinds of postal stationery products, even more so than with postage stamps."

The word "holography" comes from Greek roots: *holos,* meaning whole or complete, and *graphos,* meaning to sign or write. It was invented in 1947 by a Hungarian-born scientist, Dennis Gabor, who was seeking a tool that would improve the quality of photographs from the electron microscope. Gabor won the Nobel Prize in physics in 1971 for his invention. Holograms as we know them today were first produced in the 1960s, after the laser was invented, by two University of Michigan researchers, Emmett Leith and Juris Upatnieks.

A brief explanation of the process of making a hologram was supplied by ABN Holographics (see accompanying diagram):

"Holograms are possible because of a property of laser light known as coherence, which is best understood as light that is only one wavelength of the visible spectrum and possesses a high degree of organization.

"When you make a hologram you split the laser light into two beams. One beam, the object beam, illuminates the object or scene being imaged. The other beam, the reference beam, illuminates the film plate onto which the hologram will be recorded. Some of the light shining on the object will be reflected toward the film where it will interfere with light shining directly on the film. This interference pattern is recorded in the light-sensitive emulsion of the film."

A hologram can be made to appear as a three-dimensional image floating in space by illuminating the developed film with a laser from the same angle as the original reference beam, ABN Holographics said.

"The interference pattern recorded on the film bends some of the light, striking it into a re-creation of the pattern of light which origi-

Richard Sheaff's original concept sketch for the hologram envelope, with instructions to the artist. At this point the denomination was still inside the indicium.

nally came from the object beam, because of a property of light known as diffraction. The reconstructed object beam contains all the original information it once carried, so the viewer sees the object in full three-dimensionality, just as if it were actually there."

To create a "reflection hologram" on foil, viewable in ordinary, or white, light, the manufacturer makes a second hologram from the first, masking out some of the information — specifically, the angles that provide different vertical views of the object.

The resulting picture has only "horizontal parallax," meaning the 3-D views change only when seen from side to side. But it offers a spectrum of colors as the viewer's eye moves up and down and catches the varying wavelengths that make up white light reflecting at a variety of angles.

To mass-produce reflection holograms, the emulsion is developed, rendering the interference pattern as a series of ultra-fine ridges. A nickel mold is made, it impresses the interference pattern onto plastic, and a thin aluminum coating is applied. The coating acts like a mirror to reflect white-light waves through the interference pattern and create the changing images in the viewer's eye.

Austria's pioneering use of a hologram on a stamp came in 1988 to mark the Austria Export Congress. It consisted of a foil that was bonded onto a portion of a conventional stamp. The holographic message on the foil read "Made in Austria" or showed the letter "A," depending on the angle of vision.

If USPS ever uses a hologram in this way, Joe Brockert said, it will probably be on an extra-large stamp — for Express Mail or Priority Mail — so that a relatively large holographic image could be employed and ample room left to display the denomination and receive the canceling ink.

The Design

For its first hologram-type issue, the Postal Service wanted a design subject that was "as high-tech as the process," Joe Brockert said. It also wanted a non-realistic subject that wouldn't seem incongruous when viewed in changing colors.

To USPS officials, that meant something either mythical or futuristic. Futuristic was deemed most appropriate, specifically a futuristic space scene, similar in concept to those on the Future Mail Transportation block of airmail stamps that was also scheduled to be issued at World Stamp Expo.

The same design team that created the Future Mail Transportation block was assigned to the envelope project: Richard Sheaff, art director, and Ken Hodges, designer. Sheaff took part with Joe Brockert in the meetings with the hologram manufacturers.

Out of these talks came the decision to make the holographic image from layers of flat artwork rather than a three-dimensional plaster model, although the model option was seriously considered and had its advocates among the industry representatives.

"The whole thing was done in a short period," recalled Sheaff. "The Postal Service was a little afraid they might use up most of their time with the plaster model approach and not like what they were seeing and then be out of time."

The design they worked out shows a space station orbiting a cratered planetary body, with another planet visible over the horizon. A space shuttle is about to dock in one of the eight berths radiating out from the domed control area; seven other shuttles are already docked. Two astronauts free-float nearby, and planets and stars fill the black void in the background.

On Sheaff's instruction, Hodges provided three layers of black-and-white art. The base layer, with sky, heavenly bodies and the more distant astronaut, was done in continuous tone. The foreground astronaut — who appears somewhat blurred in the finished product — was on a layer of his own, also in continuous tone. In the middle was the space station with the shuttles, rendered in line art with pen and ink.

In converting the base layer to a 3-D hologram, Sheaff said, the ABN Holographics technicians actually further subdivided it into two layers, then tilted the corner of the foreground layer — the nearer of the two large planets — toward the viewer, to enhance the illusion of curvature. "They bent the artwork," Sheaff said. "They had a feeling that it might turn out nicely that way, and it did."

This was the original Sheaff concept sketch for the bottom layer of the three-layer hologram art.

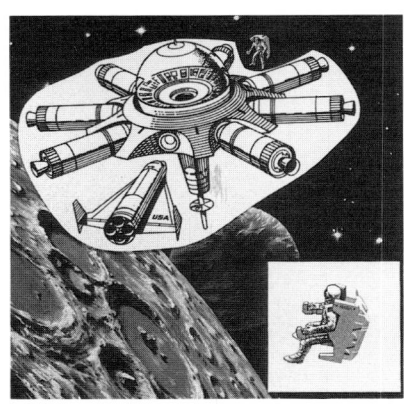

The final artwork for the hologram consisted of three layers: a continuous-tone rendering of an astronaut, planets and stars in the background; a line drawing of a space station and a docking space shuttle in the center, and another tonal rendering of an astronaut in the foreground.

Early in the process, to give the Citizens' Stamp Advisory Committee and Postal Service officials an idea of what the final visual effect might be, Hodges made a framed display containing the three layers of artwork on acetate, with Styrofoam to hold them apart and provide an appearance of depth.

In keeping with the futuristic theme, the typography was made to resemble the letters and numbers on a digital clock or VCR. For a model, Brockert programmed his wristwatch to read "USA 25." Sheaff sketched the readout and then modified the characters somewhat to make them more legible on the envelope.

Originally, bright orange was considered for the typography. The envelope manufacturer discouraged this idea on grounds that fluorescent colors, flickering past workers' eyes on a production line, tend to have a "strobe effect" that is hypnotic. Proofs in green were made, but in the end blue was chosen because it seemed to best complement the holographic image.

First-Day Facts

Howard Paine, art director of the *National Geographic* and a design coordinator for CSAC, was the speaker at the first-day ceremony. The envelope was dedicated by Gordon Morison, assistant postmaster general.

December 3, the last day of World Stamp Expo, was designated Stamp Designers Day at the show. Eight artists and art directors involved in the design of U.S. stamps and postal stationery were on hand to meet showgoers and provide autographs: Chris Calle, Paul Calle, Ken Hodges, Jay Haiden, Howard Paine, Chuck Ripper, Richard Schlecht and Richard Sheaff.

POSTAL CARDS

1989 was a bumper year for postal cards. USPS issued 18 varieties, an all-time high total for that once-neglected subdivision of philately. In the process, it continued to explore the potential of the five-color Roland Man 800 offset press that was installed by the Government Printing Office in 1987 to enhance postal card quality.

Putting the Roland Man to new uses, USPS launched a pair of experimental marketing efforts. It produced two glossy picture postal cards to test the reaction of tourists and other buyers to the availability of such cards with the postage prepaid. And it responded to requests for postal cards that could be easily imprinted with addresses and messages by photocopiers or computer printers by issuing four different cards on one perforated sheet of appropriate size.

The America the Beautiful series that was launched with a single card in 1988 blossomed with five additions in 1989. All of these would remain available as long as current rates were in force, USPS said. An offshoot of the series was the "cityscape" set, saluting four cities that delegates to the 20th Universal Postal Congress in Washington could easily visit during their stay in the United States; these were sold only in the specific cities and for a limited time.

The Citizens' Stamp Advisory Committee continued to pursue its policy of using postal cards to commemorate anniversaries of institutions and events in categories it had ruled inappropriate for postage stamps. Thus, there were cards for Georgetown University's 200th anniversary and the centennials of the Oklahoma land rush and Hull House in Chicago.

15¢ DESERT POSTAL CARD
AMERICA THE BEAUTIFUL SERIES

Date of Issue: January 13, 1989

Catalog Numbers: Scott UX127   USPS 0267
Minkus PC123   UPSS S144

Colors: magenta, yellow, cyan, black

First-Day Cancel: Tucson, Arizona (Aripex '89 stamp show)

FDCs Canceled: 51,891

Size: 5½ by 3½ inches

Format: Printed in 80-card sheets, but available to collectors only in single cards. Printing plates of 80 subjects (8 across, 10 around).

Markings: ©USPS 1988

Designer: Bart Forbes of Dallas, Texas

Art Director: Derry Noyes (CSAC)

Typographer: Bradbury Thompson (CSAC)

Project Manager: Joe Brockert (USPS)

Printing: U.S. Government Printing Office (GPO) on a 5-color Roland Man 800 sheetfed offset press

Quantity Ordered: 25,000,000
Quantity Distributed: 48,574,000

Tagging: vertical bar to right of stamp

The Postal Card

In 1988 the Postal Service initiated a series of four-color postal cards called America the Beautiful with a card celebrating the nation's prairie scenery.

On November 10, 1988, the Postal Service announced that four more cards in the series would be issued in 1989 — for the Desert, the Seashore, the Marshlands (Wetlands) and the Woodlands. Later, additions were made to the list.

The 15¢ Desert card turned out to be the first postal item issued by USPS in 1989. It made its debut January 13 in Tucson, Arizona, in conjunction with the opening of the Aripex '89 stamp show.

USPS emphasized that as new America the Beautiful cards were issued, the others would continue to be available. Postmasters were invited to order the cards most appropriate to their areas.

The Design

The indicium of the Desert card, like that of the 1988 America the Beautiful card, was based on an original watercolor painting by Bart Forbes of Dallas, Texas.

USPS described the scene as "the Sonora Desert, captured in the golden glow of sunset ... a composite of several elements which dot the southwestern landscape, including the saguaro cactus and the ocotillo, a thorny plant with whiplike branches. A swooping hawk is prominent in the foreground and a rugged line of buttes and mountain peaks shape the horizon."

Though the plants were identifiable to USPS, it turned out that the hawk wasn't. A reader wrote *Linn's Stamp News* complaining that the bird was a white-tailed hawk, a species that doesn't inhabit the Sonora Desert. But Joe Brockert, project manager for the card, said the hawk was meant to be generic, not a particular species. By the same token, he said, the landscape shown in the painting didn't really represent any specific desert location.

An earlier version of Forbes' design included prairie dogs, but no bird. "The committee saw a problem there," Brockert said. "You had

This is the first of a series of special pictorial first-day cancellations prepared by USPS for the America the Beautiful series.

these straight-up-and-down cacti, and you had these straight up-and-down silhouettes of prairie dogs, and it was hard to distinguish one from the other. The committee said, 'the prairie dogs aren't reading too well in this, so let's take them out and put a bird or something else in,' and that's what Bart did."

Like the first card in the series, this one carried only the words "America the Beautiful," letting the picture alone convey the fact that its specific theme was desert regions.

Forbes previously designed the Abigail Adams stamp of 1985, and the Winter and Summer Olympics stamps of 1988.

First-Day Facts

Gordon C. Morison, assistant postmaster general, gave the principal address at the dedication ceremony at the Tucson Convention Center. Other speakers included Dr. Donald J. Pinkava, professor of botany at Arizona State University, and Betsy G. Towle, chairperson for the Tucson Stamp Club-sponsored Aripex '89.

With this card, USPS introduced a series of pictorial first-day cancellations for its America the Beautiful series, each featuring an illustration appropriate to the subject. The Desert cancellation depicted a stylized saguaro cactus. Aripex '89 also provided a pictorial show cancel, based on the show's theme, "Fly High With Philately."

The USPS pictorial cancel was also used on the cards inserted into the first-day ceremony programs. With the programs, two different types of cancellation were reported.

For programs distributed at the ceremony, the canceling device employed was a rubber composition imprinter, which made a crisp, clear image. These cancels were applied at the U.S. Postal Service facility in Merrifield, Virginia.

Some 5,000 programs were also prepared for subscribers to USPS' new program service, but for these the cards were canceled by Minnesota Diversified Inc. of Minneapolis, a private contractor, using a rubber handstamp. The image was thicker and blurrier, and a comma was missing after "Jan. 13." According to information received by *Linn's Stamp News*, the cancellation ink used by Minnesota Diversified apparently reacted with the rubber of the handstamp, causing it to deteriorate as it was used.

After *Linn's* published reports of the existence of cancellation varieties on this postal card and two other items issued in early 1989, the Healy Hall postal card and Montana Statehood stamp, USPS halted the use of an independent contractor to apply cancellations. Minnesota Diversified, under its contract, would still affix stamps to subscription-service programs, USPS said, but all canceling would be done using the rubber composition imprinter at Merrifield.

USPS also agreed to a request from Scott Pelcyger, vice president of the American Ceremony Program Society, that it make available to

Handstamp markings look more heavily inked and blurry than the imprints. The Merrifield mechanical imprint cancels have a crisp, clear appearance.

subscribers copies of the Desert and Healy Hall postal cards canceled with the Merrifield device, so they would have both varieties of cancellation for each card. John Spiehs, philatelic programs manager of the Philatelic Marketing Division, told Pelcyger that the two Merrifield cards would be included free in a future shipment to subscribers. They would also be offered for sale to dealer subscribers, who obtain the programs at a heavily discounted price.

Pelcyger acknowledged that it would be impractical to ask that subscribers be provided with Merrifield cancellations on the Montana stamp. Stamps are affixed directly to first-day programs and canceled. Thus to correct the problem with Montana the entire program would have had to be reprinted, which could easily have created still more collectible varieties, Pelcyger said.

15¢ HEALY HALL POSTAL CARD
HISTORIC PRESERVATION SERIES

Date of Issue: January 23, 1989

Catalog Numbers: Scott UX128 USPS 0218
Minkus PC124 UPSS S145

Colors: magenta, yellow, cyan, black

First-Day Cancel: Washington, D.C. (Georgetown University)

FDCs Canceled: 54,897

Size: 5½ by 3½ inches

Format: Printed in 80-card sheets, but available to collectors only in single cards. Printing plates of 80 subjects (8 across, 10 around).

Markings: ©USPS 1988

Designer: John Morrell of Arlington, Virginia

Art Director: Derry Noyes (CSAC)

Typographer: Bradbury Thompson (CSAC)

Project Manager: Joe Brockert (USPS)

Printing: U.S. Government Printing Office (GPO) on a 5-color Roland Man 800 sheetfed offset press

Quantity Ordered: 15,000,000
Quantity Distributed: 15,000,000

Tagging: vertical bar to right of stamp

The Postal Card

A 15¢ postal card picturing Healy Hall at Georgetown University was issued January 23 in conjunction with the celebration of the 200th anniversary of the Washington, D.C., institution's founding.

The card was another in USPS' continuing Historic Preservation series, which began in 1977 with a 9¢ card depicting the Federal Courthouse at Galveston, Texas. It was the second card in the series in eight months to show a Washington landmark; the first was the Blair House card of May 4, 1988.

For USPS, the Healy Hall card represented a new solution to its old problem of too many requests for commemorative stamps from institutions of higher learning. The solution was put into policy form when stamp criteria were revised by the Citizens' Stamp Advisory Committee in April 1987.

A new Section 11 said that requests for commemoration of significant anniversaries of universities and other institutions of higher education should be considered only in regard to Historic Preservation series postal cards featuring an appropriate building on the campus.

The Healy Hall card was the first issued under this section. Officially, it didn't honor Georgetown, but rather commemorated the university's historic administration building.

In recent years, USPS has found other ways of indirectly marking the anniversaries of colleges and universities. Later in 1989, it issued a $1 stamp in the Great Americans series depicting the philanthropist Johns Hopkins in connection with the 100th anniversary of the university, hospital and medical school bearing his name. (See Johns Hopkins chapter.)

Georgetown is the country's oldest Catholic institution of higher learning. The school, like the U.S. Government, began its existence in 1789.

On January 23 of that year, Archbishop John Carroll of Baltimore, an intimate of both George Washington and Benjamin Franklin, accepted the deed to a hilltop parcel overlooking the Potomac River. Carroll was a cousin of Charles Carroll, famed for his fearless signature on the Declaration of Independence. (Charles Carroll was depicted on two 1985 postal cards, a non-denominated and a 14¢ value.) A prospectus issued before any students were enrolled attested that "The School will be open to Students of every Religious Profession," and that has always been its policy.

The site chosen was in the town of Georgetown, Maryland. One location that was considered and dismissed because it was too remote was an undeveloped rise called Jenkins Hall, 3½ miles away. Later, when the federal capital was moved to the shores of the Potomac and Georgetown was incorporated into the District of Columbia, city planner Pierre L'Enfant chose Jenkins Hill for another purpose — as the site for the U.S. Capitol.

In 1797 President George Washington rode up from Mount Vernon to Old North, the second college building erected, and addressed the student body. Many of his successors as chief executive have paid similar visits to the institution.

Nearly 100 years after the university's founding, Father Patrick Healy became the first black president of a major American college and the "second founder" of Georgetown. Healy dreamt of molding the college's destiny, of creating an international university. He believed that expanding the academic program and improving studies in the sciences was critical.

Essential to that dream was the construction of a new building with laboratories, classrooms, dormitory rooms and meeting space for alumni. The new building would be the gateway to establishing Georgetown's role as an academic leader. In 1877, John L. Smithmeyer and Paul J. Pelz, architects of the Library of Congress building, were enlisted to transform Healy's aspiration into bricks and mortar.

Recovery from the Civil War was slow and, as the building began to take shape, Healy was forced to spend a good portion of this time raising funds to finance the $300,000 construction cost. Two million bricks and 3,000 cubic yards of stone were used to fashion the Flemish Romanesque architecture of Healy Hall. Opened in 1881, it doubled Georgetown's total square footage, and its space served all the requirements in Healy's plan.

Healy Hall contained a reading room, classrooms, science laboratories, lecture and debating halls plus living space, offices for administrators and a large Memorial Hall for commencement and alumni meetings. Its new library held four times the number of books of the existing library. It was a building worthy of a great university.

The Design

John Morrell, 36, of Arlington, Virginia, a fine-arts professor at Georgetown and a university alumnus, made his debut as a postal designer with a painting of Healy Hall based on early drawings and photographs.

The view of the building featured in the predominantly pastel-colored image showed the 312-foot-long stone face and one side of the building, with the 209-foot lookout tower at the center. Shrubbery complemented the structure shown under a blue, pink and yellow sky.

USPS followed a precedent it set with the 28¢ Yorkshire postal card of 1988 by placing only USA and the denomination in the design portion of the card. The other relevant information — Healy Hall/Georgetown/Washington, DC/HISTORIC PRESERVATION — was placed in four lines of black type at the lower left.

First-Day Facts

Postmaster General Anthony M. Frank made the crosstown trip

from L'Enfant Plaza to Georgetown to deliver the principal address at the dedication ceremony, which was held in Gaston Hall, the auditorium in the Healy building.

The university itself was well-represented, with remarks by the Reverend Timothy S. Healy, president (who is no relation to the builder of Healy Hall); Dr. Dorothy M. Brown, president of the Faculty Senate, and Eileen D. Roberts, a member of the Class of 1989. (Later in the year, Reverend Healy resigned his university post to become president of the New York City Public Library.)

As happened with the America the Beautiful (The Desert) postal card, two different types of first-day cancellations were reported on cards inserted into first-day ceremony programs.

The canceling device used with the programs distributed at the ceremony was a rubber composition imprinter used by USPS' facility at Merrifield, Virginia. Its image was crisp and clear.

Subscribers to the Postal Service's first-day program subscription service received cards hand-canceled by Minnesota Diversified Inc., an independent contractor. These cancellations had a different ZIP code. They also had a fuzzier appearance with larger lettering and numerals.

As reported in the Desert Postal Card chapter, USPS announced that it would henceforth do all canceling for first-day ceremony programs at Merrifield. USPS also promised to provide subscription customers with free specimens of the Desert and Healy Hall cards canceled with the Merrifield device so they would have both available varieties of each card.

Both cancellations appeared on Healy Hall first-day ceremony programs. The upper one was applied by a rubber composition imprinter; the lower was applied by hand.

15¢ WETLANDS POSTAL CARD
AMERICA THE BEAUTIFUL SERIES

Date of Issue: March 17, 1989

Catalog Numbers: Scott UX129	USPS 2268
Minkus PC125	UPSS S146

Colors: magenta, yellow, cyan, black

First-Day Cancel: Waycross, Georgia (Okefenokee Swamp Park)

FDCs Canceled: 58,208

Size: 5½ by 3½ inches

Format: Printed in 80-card sheets, but available to collectors only in single cards. Printing plates of 80 subjects (8 across, 10 around).

Markings: ©USPS 1989

Designer: Bart Forbes of Dallas, Texas

Art Director: Derry Noyes (CSAC)

Typographer: Bradbury Thompson (CSAC)

Project Manager: Joe Brockert (USPS)

Printing: U.S. Government Printing Office (GPO) on a 5-color Roland Man 800 sheetfed offset press

Quantity Ordered: 20,000,000
Quantity Distributed: 30,042,000

Tagging: vertical bar to right of stamp

The Postal Card

The third in the America the Beautiful series of postal cards had as its theme the nation's wetlands. In the original announcement of the card, USPS had described it as commemorating the "marshlands." "The name has been changed to reflect the card's design more accurately," USPS said in a December 20, 1988 news release.

Actually, "wetlands" as a generic term for marshes, swamps and flood plains is a term that has come into vogue only in recent years. It is unlisted in several dictionaries, including the Second Edition of Webster's New International Dictionary (although it did make it into the Third).

The card was first placed on sale March 17 in Okefenokee Swamp Park, near Waycross, Georgia. Okefenokee is an Indian word meaning "Land of Trembling Earth," a reference to the centuries-old layers of swamp vegetation that shake underfoot. The swamp is in reality a watershed, covering more than 650 square miles and serving as the headwaters for the Suwannee and St. Mary's Rivers. Set aside in 1937 as a national wildlife refuge by President Franklin D. Roosevelt, Okefenokee is home to more than 200 species of birds, 50 species of reptiles, 40 species of mammals and 32 species of amphibians. Among the endangered species that live there are the American alligator, the Florida panther and the bald eagle.

In 1986 the Okefenokee National Wildlife Refuge was cited as a "Wetland of International Importance," the fourth of this description in the United States. It is one of 400 refuges administered by the Department of the Interior's U.S. Fish and Wildlife Service, and has its base in Folkston, Georgia, at the Suwannee Canal Recreation Area, the eastern entrance to the swamp. The Stephen C. Foster State Park near Fargo provides facilities and access from the west.

Okefenokee Swamp Park, where the first-day ceremony was held, is a private, non-profit development leasing land from the refuge. The facility includes a serpentarium, a swamp creation center and a wildlife observatory.

Until the environmental movement became prominent in the 1960s, engineers and developers routinely drained, filled and reclaimed marshes, bogs and swamps. However, once it became widely understood that wetlands were vital to the quality of human life and in fact were the point of origin of the food chain for much of nature,

The great white heron on this 1947 commemorative stamp (Scott 952) is less animated than the bird depicted on the 1989 Wetlands postal card.

USPS offered this special pictorial first-day cancellation for the Wetlands postal card.

government agencies began taking steps to preserve what was left.

The Design

A watery green is the prominent color in Bart Forbes' design, which shows a heron about to fly from its rock in a flooded forest. The USPS news release identified the bird as a great blue heron, but its light plumage bears more of a resemblance to that of an egret or the great white heron depicted on the Everglades National Park commemorative stamp of 1947 (Scott 952).

Forbes himself is uncertain about the bird's species. "These (America the Beautiful) designs aren't necessarily bird studies," he said. "In doing them, I go with a lot of photo references. That particular shot was from a photo that I took myself, and to me it was immaterial what the bird was. It fit with that section of the country, and it designed well in the horizontal format."

First-Day Facts

"Pogo Possum" was among the honored guests at the first-day ceremony, and so was Mrs. Walt Kelly, widow of the creator of Pogo, Albert Alligator and the other famous comic-strip residents of Okefenokee Swamp. William A. Campbell Jr., regional postmaster general, gave the address and presented the souvenir albums. Among the other speakers were Gwen McKee, co-chairman of the Georgia Conservancy's Fresh Water Wetlands Task Force, and Floyd Turk, president of Okefenokee Swamp Park Inc.

The first-day cancellation featured a circular pictorial design and bore the name "Okefenokee, Georgia," the name recognized by USPS for its contract post office in the Swamp Park.

15¢ SETTLING OF OKLAHOMA POSTAL CARD

Date of Issue: April 22, 1989	
Catalog Numbers: Scott UX130	USPS 2219
Minkus PC126	UPSS S147

Colors: magenta, yellow, cyan, black

First-Day Cancel: Guthrie, Oklahoma (Carnegie Library)

FDCs Canceled: 68,689

Size: 5½ by 3½ inches

Format: Printed in 80-card sheets, but available to collectors only in single cards. Printing plates of 80 subjects (8 across, 10 around).

Markings: ©USPS 1989

Designer and Typographer: Bradbury Thompson (CSAC)

Art Director and Project Manager: Joe Brockert (USPS)

Printing: U.S. Government Printing Office (GPO) on a 5-color Roland Man 800 sheetfed offset press

Quantity Ordered: 15,000,000
Quantity Distributed: 15,000,000

Tagging: vertical bar to right of stamp

The Postal Card

A postal card celebrating the Land Run of 1889 that opened Oklahoma to settlement was dedicated at high noon April 22, 1989 — 100 years to the minute from the beginning of the famous horse race for homesteads.

The card also marked two other milestones in the history of the state, and the three-way commemoration was noted in the inscriptions in the cachet area: First Land Run, 1889/Territory Established, 1890/Cherokee Strip Run, 1893.

For the Cherokee Strip Run, the card was the second postal commemorative. In 1968 a 6¢ stamp (Scott 1360) had noted this event's 75th anniversary.

The United States acquired Oklahoma as part of the Louisiana Purchase of 1803. Various Indian tribes — Cherokees, Choctaws, Chickasaws, Seminoles and Creeks (or Muskogees) — were relocated here from the East and given sovereignty by treaty. These Indians, who had lived and worked fairly closely with whites and had adopted many of their habits and customs, were known as the Five Civilized Tribes. Among their legacies to the territory is its name: "Okla homa" is Choctaw for "red people."

Most of the Indians were relocated between 1820 and 1842, and many died along the way — a fact reflected in the poignant name the Cherokee and Choctaw Indians have given to the movement, the "Trail of Tears."

After the Civil War, the United States exacted concessions from all the tribes, using the excuse that some of them had been Southern sympathizers. Treaties in 1866 ceded central and southwest portions of Indian land back to the government and granted railroads access to Indian territory. Apache, Cheyenne, Comanche and other Plains Indians were eventually moved into the southwest portion.

This left the central section as "Unassigned Lands," barred to settlement by anyone other than Indians, but not deeded to a particular tribe. But by the late 1870s, pressure was mounting to open these lands to white settlement. Organized bands of whites known as "Boomers" were moving in despite federal law, and the Eastern press encouraged their efforts.

This 1968 commemorative (Scott 1360), designed by Norman Todhunter, showed a side view of the 1893 land rush into the Cherokee Strip.

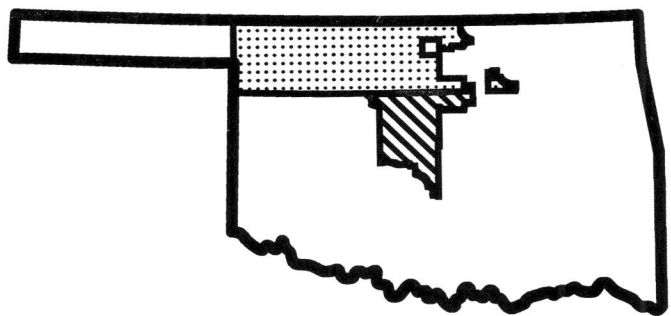

This map of Oklahoma, showing the area opened up to settlement with the Land Run of 1889 (striped section) and the Cherokee Strip that was opened in 1893 (dotted section), was at one time intended for use in the cachet area of the postal card.

Despite the pleas of delegations to Washington from the Five Tribes, missionary societies and others, the Indians were overwhelmed. In 1889 Congress gave in. The U.S. government paid the Creeks and Seminoles for clear titles to the Unassigned Lands. Homesteaders could claim 60 acres by staking claims first, recording the claims and living on and working the claims for five years.

Newly elected President Benjamin Harrison decided that distribution would be handled by a run for the land on April 22 — first come, first served. Thousands of land-hungry people prepared to take part in "Harrison's hoss race." On the north side, homeseekers crossed the Cherokee Strip from Kansas to reach the starting line at the Oklahoma border; on the south side they crossed the Chickasaw Nation.

As noon approached on a brilliant, sunny April 22, the waiting crowds became quiet, poised for flight. Horsemen strained forward in their saddles, checking and rechecking cinches. Men in wagons daubed a last extra bit of grease on their axles. In the Santa Fe trains — which were prohibited on that day from traveling any faster than a horse could run — engineers gripped their throttles and passengers clung to every available handhold. At 12 o'clock, the starting flags dropped, bugles sounded, and cavalry guns along the line repeated the signal. The race was on.

One problem was an unprincipled minority known as "Sooners" who had managed to sneak in and settle claims before the run officially started. The term remained one of disapproval — that is, until the University of Oklahoma football teams in the 20th century converted it to a nickname of honor. Historians H. Wayne Morgan and Anne Hodges Morgan told how two men on fast horses arrived in central Oklahoma before anyone else on April 22. "They were startled to find an elderly farmer peacefully plowing with a team of oxen," the Morgans wrote. "Onions stood four inches high in his new garden. When queried, the man swore that the soil was so rich that the onions had grown that much in the 15 minutes since he planted them!"

Guthrie and Okahoma City, two whistlestops along the railroad, became boom towns overnight. On April 21, Guthrie had two buildings. By nightfall on the 22nd, 15,000 people had taken up residence. Wooden dwellings sprang up, and within six months Victorian buildings of brick and sandstone replaced them. Soon this thriving railroad, banking and cultural center became the territorial capital, and in 1907 it became the first capital of the state of Oklahoma.

Three other land runs into newly opened territory followed the charge of the "Eighty-Niners." The most famous of these was the September 16, 1893, run into the Cherokee Outlet, or Cherokee Strip, a 58- by 100-mile piece of land across the northern third of the present-day state of Oklahoma. Unlike the previous races, this one spawned confusion, lawlessness and violence as more than 100,000 people stampeded into the Strip on a day when the mercury hit 100 degrees and emotions ran even hotter.

Previous stamps relating to Oklahoma included the Louisiana Purchase centennial series of 1904 (the 10¢ value, Scott 327, depicts a map of the Purchase) and a single 3¢ commemorative (Scott 1020) issued in 1953 for the sesquicentennial. A 3¢ stamp (Scott 972) in 1948 marked the centennial of the arrival of the Five Civilized Tribes, and another 3¢ commemorative in 1957 (Scott 1092) noted the 50th anniversary of statehood.

Oklahoman Will Rogers has appeared on stamps of 1948 and 1979.

The Design

Bradbury Thompson, design coordinator and typographer of the Citizens' Stamp Advisory Committee, adapted the dramatic picture in the card's stamp from a portion of the painting *Opening of the Cherokee Strip* by Olaf Wieghorst. Through a deep carpet of dust, horses charge toward the viewer as riders and wagon drivers furiously lash them to top speed. Thompson offered CSAC an alternative cropping of the painting that showed more riders, sky and prairie, but the members preferred the more exciting, tightly cropped close-up.

As its title indicates, this painting depicted the land rush of 1893, not the original run of 1889. Wieghorst painted the 48-inch by 28-inch oil on canvas in 1982 in fulfillment of a commission he had received some 25 years earlier from Dr. Otey G. Johnson, a medical instructor, oil millionaire and philanthropist. Dr. Johnson purchased the work for the Ardmore Institute of Health in Ardmore, Oklahoma, a health maintenance facility that he had helped establish. At the time, the Institute had no facilities for displaying art, so the painting hung in the Thomas Gilcrease Museum in Tulsa, Oklahoma, until March 1989, when it was finally moved to Ardmore.

Wieghorst was born in Denmark and came to the United States as a

Olaf Wieghorst's dramatic painting showed dozens of land-seekers and their horses — and even a dog — charging into the Cherokee Strip.

merchant seaman in 1919. He jumped ship and became, in order, a U.S. cavalryman, a cowboy and a New York City mounted policeman — and, along the way, a U.S. citizen. He began sketching horses in his free time and discovered that there was a market for his works.

In 1944 he retired from the police force and moved to El Cajon, California, to devote full time to art. That career brought him fame and wealth. He produced some 3,000 paintings and sculptures; Presidents Eisenhower, Ford and Reagan all owned Wieghorst paintings, and two of his pieces, *The Navajo Madonna* and *Navajo Man*, sold for $1 million in 1985. Wieghorst died at age 88 April 28, 1988, less than a year before his Cherokee Strip painting was featured on a U.S. postal card.

The painting came to the attention of CSAC after a committee member, Jack Rosenthal of Casper, Wyoming, called a friend at the

One proposed version of the postal card would have used more of Wieghorst's painting in the image area and listed only two events instead of three in the cachet.

Gilcrease museum for some suggestions. The friend mentioned the Wieghorst work, then on display at the Gilcrease museum. A color reproduction was sent to CSAC, which approved the work as the basis for the postal card design.

"There have been some good lateral pictures of the Oklahoma land rushes," Rosenthal said, "but this was the only one I have ever seen from the head-on perspective."

It was a side view, in fact, of the Cherokee Strip land rush that was shown on the 1968 stamp that marked the event's 75th anniversary. That one bore stamp designer Norman Todhunter's original painting of racing homesteaders, showing a man in a buggy in the foreground leaning forward as his horse strained at the reins, while two mounted horsemen sped along in the rear.

CSAC originally intended that the postal card's cachet portion should refer only to the initial land run of 1889 and the territorial anniversary. Later it decided to add the 1893 run to the list — which was appropriate, because that was the event that was actually illustrated in the stamp.

In this original plan for the cachet, a small map of Oklahoma was also incorporated, with the sites of the two major land runs marked and connected by lines to the appropriate wording. Such a map had been used successfully with the Northwest Territory/Settlement of Ohio postal card of 1988. But the committee dropped the map idea after the members learned that in the 1889-1893 period, several other, smaller areas of Oklahoma had been separately opened to settlement, and that to omit them from the map would be arbitrary.

First-Day Facts

The first-day ceremony for the postal card was held in front of the Carnegie Library in Guthrie. Among those speaking were Oklahoma Governor Henry Bellmon; Bert Mackie, a member of the USPS Board of Governors, and William A. Campbell Jr., regional postmaster general, who dedicated the postal card. The ceremony kicked off Guthrie's Centennial Parade.

USPS produced no official program for the ceremony.

21¢ MOUNTAINS POSTAL CARD
AMERICA THE BEAUTIFUL SERIES

Date of Issue: May 5, 1989

Catalog Numbers: Scott UX131   USPS 2258
Minkus PC127   UPSS S148

Colors: magenta, yellow, cyan, black

First-Day Cancel: Denver, Colorado (Rompex '89 stamp show)

FDCs Canceled: 59,303

Size: 5½ by 3½ inches

Format: Printed in 80-card sheets, but available to collectors only in single cards. Printing plates of 80 subjects (8 across, 10 around).

Markings: ©USPS 1989

Designer: Bart Forbes of Dallas, Texas

Art Director: Derry Noyes (CSAC)

Typographer: Bradbury Thompson (CSAC)

Project Manager: Joe Brockert (USPS)

Printing: U.S. Government Printing Office (GPO) on a 5-color Roland Man 800 sheetfed offset press

Quantity Ordered: 5,000,000
Quantity Distributed: 3,387,000

Tagging: vertical bar to right of stamp

The Postal Card

A postal card featuring mountain scenery was a belated addition to USPS' 1989 program.

Originally only four cards in the America the Beautiful series were listed for 1989. On February 10, USPS announced that a fifth, The Mountains, would be issued May 5 in Denver, Colorado, and that it would carry the 21¢ denomination, which is the rate for mailing postcards to Canada. All other cards in the series had been of the 15¢ first-class rate.

Bart Forbes adapted this design, prepared for the 22¢ Winter Olympics stamp of 1988 but not used, for the 21¢ The Mountains postal card.

The Design

Bart Forbes' design — jagged, snowcapped mountain peaks, with four Canada geese flying in the foreground — was an adaptation of one he had earlier proposed for a stamp honoring the 1988 Winter Olympics in Calgary, Alberta, Canada.

The Citizens' Stamp Advisory Committee had originally suggested that the designs for the Winter and Summer Olympics stamps of 1988 be travel poster-type scenes from the host countries rather than the traditional pictures of athletes. After seeing some sketches, however, the committee decided it preferred the traditional approach, and Forbes provided a downhill skier for the Winter Olympics commemorative. Set aside, as a result, was his vertical-format watercolor of a scene evocative of the Canadian Rockies.

Mountains are mountains, CSAC decided, and the Olympics leftover would do nicely as a representation of a U.S. mountain landscape. And because the card was issued primarily for mailing to Canada, the design might even be viewed as a symbol of the two countries' unity (although USPS didn't suggest that interpretation).

"We thought at first maybe we could get by with Bart's original painting, just masking out the Olympic rings," said Joe Brockert, project manager. But the format that was developed for the America the Beautiful series called for a long, relatively shallow horizontal picture. "So we had him redo it, rearranging the four geese to spread them out farther and lengthening the mountain range.

"Basically, we turned a vertical image into a horizontal image. It worked very nicely. I think it's one of the best of the America the Beautiful series."

Canada geese — big, handsome birds immediately recognizable by the white patches on the front of their throats — had previously appeared on the Capex souvenir sheet of 1978 (Scott 1757c), the Louisiana World Exposition commemorative stamp of 1984 (Scott 2086) and one of the 50 American Wildlife stamps of 1987 (Scott 2334). They also were shown on the Migratory Bird Hunting (duck) stamps of 1936 and 1976.

First-Day Facts

The first-day ceremony was held in the Denver Holiday Inn shortly after Kenneth J. Hunter, associate postmaster general, cut a ribbon of Mountains postal cards to open the 40th annual Rocky Mountain Philatelic Exhibition (Rompex). Hunter was principal speaker at the dedication of the card, and others who took part included Victoria Allen Fair, president of Rompex; Michael Milam, Rompex vice president; John Willard of the Colorado Postal History Society, and designer Bart Forbes. A featured "guest" was a large golden eagle accompanied by Peter Reshetniak, president of the Raptor Education Foundation.

USPS furnished a special pictorial first-day cancellation showing mountains, with a lake and evergreen trees in the foreground.

USPS offered this special pictorial first-day cancellation for the Mountains postal card.

15¢ SEASHORE POSTAL CARD
AMERICA THE BEAUTIFUL SERIES

Date of Issue: June 17, 1989

Catalog Numbers: Scott UX132 USPS 2265
Minkus PC128 UPSS S149

Colors: magenta, yellow, cyan, black

First-Day Cancel: Cape Hatteras, North Carolina (Visitors Center)

FDCs Canceled: 67,073

Size: 5½ by 3½ inches

Format: Printed in 80-card sheets, but available to collectors only in single cards. Printing plates of 80 subjects (8 across, 10 around).

Markings: ©USPS 1989

Designer: Bart Forbes of Dallas, Texas

Art Director: Derry Noyes (CSAC)

Typographer: Bradbury Thompson (CSAC)

Project Manager: Joe Brockert (USPS)

Printing: U.S. Government Printing Office (GPO) on a 5-color Roland Man 800 sheetfed offset press

Quantity Ordered: 25,000,000
Quantity Distributed: 30,706,000

Tagging: vertical bar to right of stamp

The Cape Hatteras seashore, including the distinctive lighthouse, was depicted on this block of four confluent stamps in 1972.

The Postal Card

The fifth postal card in the America the Beautiful series, and the fourth of 1989, focused on America's seashore areas. It was issued June 17 at Cape Hatteras, North Carolina, the nation's first designated national seashore.

Situated on an angular bend of North Carolina's Outer Banks, the Cape Hatteras shore, like all beaches, is in constant transition. Its lighthouse — the tallest in the country — was more than 1,500 feet from the shoreline when it was built in 1870, but so great have been the eroding and reshaping effects of wind, waves, tides and storms that now the water has advanced to within 200 feet of the tower's base. On June 21, 1989, four days after the postal card was issued by the Postal Service, the National Park Service unveiled an $8.7 million proposal to save the lighthouse by jacking it up and moving it on rails about a half mile inland.

The Cape Hatteras National Seashore was the subject of a se-tenant block of four 2¢ stamps issued in 1972. The lighthouse, with its distinctive diagonal candy-stripes, is depicted on the upper right-hand stamp of the block (Scott 1449). USPS announced August 4, 1989, that the Hatteras lighthouse would also be pictured on a five-stamp booklet pane featuring lighthouses to be issued in 1990.

The Design

Collectors got their first glimpse of the Seashore postal card design in the May-June issue of USPS' *Philatelic Sales Catalog*. USPS formally released the design and related information on June 5.

Bart Forbes' painting depicted three horizontal bands representing sea, sand and sky. Behind a dune at the left rises a red and white lighthouse, reminiscent of but not identical to the Cape Hatteras tower (the stripes on this one are horizontal rather than diagonal). Typically, Forbes' America the Beautiful designs include some form of wildlife: This one showed three seagulls in flight.

The scene, like other America the Beautiful images, wasn't intended to represent a specific place. In making the painting, Forbes said he drew on his own picture files and memories of frequent visits to various seashores, including Cape Cod.

First-Day Facts

The first-day ceremony was held at the Hatteras Island Visitors Center near Buxton, North Carolina. In a typical display of Outer Banks weather, the event began in sunshine, but ended prematurely when a rainstorm began during Assistant Postmaster William T. Johnstone's remarks. Johnstone invited all those present onto the covered porch that served as the stage and finished his dedication speech there. Also participating in the ceremony were David Stick, a historian, and Thomas Hartman, superintendent of Cape Hatteras National Seashore.

USPS provided this special pictorial first-day cancellation for the Seashore postal card.

15¢ WOODLANDS POSTAL CARD
AMERICA THE BEAUTIFUL SERIES

Date of Issue: August 26, 1989

Catalog Numbers: Scott UX133   USPS 2269
                         Minkus PC129   UPSS S150

Colors: magenta, yellow, cyan, black

First-Day Cancel: Cherokee, North Carolina (Mountainside Theater)

FDCs Canceled: 67,878

Size: 5½ by 3½ inches

Format: Printed in 80-card sheets, but available to collectors only in single cards. Printing plates of 80 subjects (8 across, 10 around).

Markings: ©USPS 1989

Designer: Bart Forbes of Dallas, Texas

Art Director: Derry Noyes (CSAC)

Typographer: Bradbury Thompson (CSAC)

Project Manager: Joe Brockert (USPS)

Printing: U.S. Government Printing Office (GPO) on a 5-color Roland Man 800 sheetfed offset press

Quantity Ordered: 25,000,000
Quantity Distributed: 27,697,000

Tagging: vertical bar to right of stamp

The Postal Card

The sixth in the America the Beautiful series of postal cards celebrated America's woodlands and was dedicated August 26 in Cherokee, North Carolina. Like all others in the series except for The Mountains card, it bore the 15¢ domestic rate.

Cherokee is in the heavily wooded foothills of the Great Smoky Mountains, the home of a national park that consistently ranks as the country's most popular. It was a wooded Great Smokies vista that provided the design subject for the 10¢ value of the 1934 National Parks series of commemorative stamps (Scott 749).

The Woodlands postal card was the third postal item of the year to make its debut in North Carolina. Four days earlier the 25¢ North Carolina Statehood stamp had been issued in Fayetteville, and on June 17 the America the Beautiful postal card for The Seashore was dedicated at Cape Hatteras.

The Design

Bart Forbes used autumnal earth tones to create a tranquil woodland scene. A lone buck deer stands alert beside a waterfall. A dozen or so golden maple leaves stretch across the lower left foreground, as if on an invisible branch. "I needed some color in that corner," Forbes explained. Pine trees line the horizon.

Like all Forbes' paintings in the series, this one is generic, and intentionally represents no actual woodland scene. "It could be North Carolina, or it could be Wisconsin, or a wide variety of places," the artist said. In making the painting, he worked from a packet of photographs, which were unlabeled as to locale, provided by the U.S. Department of Interior.

The Postal Service made available this pictorial cancellation for The Woodlands postal card.

First-Day Facts

The dedication ceremony was held at the Unto These Hills Mountainside Theater in the foothills of the Great Smoky Mountains. The outdoor theater is named for a drama that has been performed there for 40 seasons. "Unto These Hills" re-enacts the tragic story of the Cherokee Indians, uprooted from their ancestral woodland home in the 19th century and driven halfway across the continent to the plains of Oklahoma.

The card was dedicated by Stanley W. Smith, assistant postmaster general. Speakers included Jonathan L. Taylor, principal chief, Eastern Band of Cherokee Indians; Randall R. Pope, superintendent, Great Smoky Mountains National Park; Edith C. Crutcher, commissioner, Indian Arts and Crafts Board, U.S. Department of Interior, and Wilbur Paul, superintendent, Cherokee Indian Agency, Bureau of Indian Affairs.

As with the America the Beautiful cards issued earlier in the year, USPS provided a special pictorial first-day cancellation. This one depicted a buck leaping over a log.

15¢ HULL HOUSE POSTAL CARD
HISTORIC PRESERVATION SERIES

Date of Issue: September 16, 1989

Catalog Numbers: Scott UX134   USPS 2220
　　　　　　　　　　Minkus PC130   UPSS S151

Colors: magenta, yellow, cyan, black

First-Day Cancel: Chicago, Illinois (University of Illinois, Chicago)

FDCs Canceled: 53,773

Size: 5½ by 3½ inches

Format: Printed in 80-card sheets, but available to collectors only in single cards. Printing plates of 80 subjects (8 across, 10 around).

Markings: ©USPS 1989

Designer: Michael Hagel of Arlington Heights, Illinois

Art Director and Project Manager: Joe Brockert (USPS)

Typographer: Bradbury Thompson (CSAC)

Printing: U.S. Government Printing Office (GPO) on a 5-color Roland Man 800 sheetfed offset press

Quantity Ordered: 10,000,000
Quantity Distributed: 10,000,000

Tagging: vertical bar to right of stamp

The Postal Card

Hull House, the pioneering settlement house in Chicago founded by Jane Addams, was honored on its centennial by issuance of a 15¢ postal card in the Historic Preservation series.

The card was dedicated Saturday, September 16. Originally USPS had announced the issue date as September 18, the actual 100th anniversary of the day Hull House began serving the physical, cultural and emotional needs of poor immigrants on Chicago's near west side. Later the event was moved up two days.

The card was the result of a campaign begun in September 1986 by Patricia L. Sharpe, executive director of the Hull House Association, the agency that carries on Miss Addams' legacy of service.

"In our business we're constantly having to raise money, and my husband and I started talking about the centennial and what we would do for a special fund-raiser," Sharpe said. "We're both philatelists, and he said, 'You should apply to the Postal Service for a postage stamp.'"

She agreed, and began rallying support for the request. Among other things, she had postcards printed with the message "I support the Hull House Centennial Commemorative Stamp" and the address of the Citizens' Stamp Advisory Committee on one side and a pen-and-ink drawing of the original building on the other.

These were mailed to the institution's friends and supporters with a cover letter urging them to sign and send them to CSAC and to urge others to do the same. "If you are looking for something a little more challenging," the letter added, "you can write a letter of support to any member" of the committee.

This pen-and-ink sketch of Hull House by a University of Illinois student was used on the postcards prepared by Patricia L. Sharpe as part of her campaign to persuade USPS to issue a Hull House stamp.

Jane Addams, founder of Hull House, was shown on the 10¢ value of the Famous Scientists issue of 1940.

"The Stamp Advisory Committee is very close-mouthed about what they're considering," Sharpe recalled. "Periodically over the months that followed we would call to find out the status of our request and their response always was, 'Well, it has not been turned down.' We talked to our senators and representatives and they all sent back very cordial letters wishing us the best but saying, 'Of course, it's not a political decision. ...' "

The campaign focused on Hull House rather than Jane Addams herself, Sharpe said, because Miss Addams had been depicted on a 10¢ stamp of the Famous Americans series of 1940 (the Post Office Department, for want of a better category, placed her in the Scientists subdivision of the series) and it seemed unlikely USPS would issue another stamp with her picture. Of the 35 Famous Americans, only two have been postally portrayed again: John James Audubon on a Great Americans definitive and Mark Twain on an aerogramme.

"Eventually we heard that we would get a postal card," Sharpe said. "It would be nice if it had been a 25¢ stamp, but the card is very appropriate. I didn't know at the time there was such a thing as a Historic Preservation series."

Hull House had been the object of a successful preservation effort in 1961, when the complex was sold to the University of Illinois. The original building and the nearby dining hall were saved and restored, using donations totaling $350,000 from many individuals. The structures were designated a national historic landmark in 1967, and today constitute a museum. All the other buildings were demolished to make way for the university's new Chicago Circle campus; its large modern structures now surround the quaint, columned-and-cupolaed red-brick Hull House.

Jane Addams, a businessman's daughter from Cedarville, Illinois, was 29 when she and her friend Ellen Gates Starr opened Hull House. In England the two women had seen Toynbee Hall, which was founded on the principle that privileged and educated people who sought to cure evils in the slums must settle there themselves (hence, "settlement work"), and they came home determined to transplant the idea to Chicago.

Addams found her site in the empty mansion that the late Charles J. Hull, a real estate speculator, had built on South Halsted Street in

1856. A suburban villa when it was new, it had survived the great fire of 1871 but was now surrounded by squalid tenements, smoking factories and streets that were quagmires of black mud.

The women rented it from Hull's sole beneficiary, his cousin and secretary Helen Culver, and moved in September 14, 1889. For one year Culver observed her tenants. Then she came to Addams and put in her hand the deed to the house and lot, and other Chicago property. "It is what Mr. Hull would have done," she explained.

Following the Toynbee formula, Addams created a situation in which rich people and poor, intellectuals and illiterates, citizens and newcomers could meet and interact. Hull House was a place, as she put it, "where many primitive and actual needs are found, in which young women, who had been given over too exclusively to study, might learn of life from life itself." Young people, she discovered, "felt a fatal want of harmony between their theory and their lives."

Many such young people enlisted. By 1910 Hull House had become a "campus" of 13 buildings, including a women's residence, a coffee shop, a gymnasium, an art gallery, an auditorium, a labor museum, a nursery — and a post office, of which Jane Addams was postmistress. In its theater, John Galsworthy's play *Justice* had its American premiere; in its music school, the 12-year-old Benny Goodman learned to play the clarinet. (When Goodman died in 1986, he left a bequest to Hull House.)

As a result of Addams' leadership in the peace movement during World War I and her work at Hull House, she was awarded the Nobel Peace Prize in 1931, becoming the first American woman to receive the honor. She died in 1935.

Today her legacy continues in the work of the Hull House Association, its six neighborhood centers and their 21 outposts. The centers serve more than 30,000 persons each year through more than 100 programs, ranging from early childhood education and day care to counseling for the elderly, from recreation to neighborhood organization and economic development.

The Design

The image area of the postal card shows a painting of the original Hull House in bucolic surroundings, as it might have looked when Charles Hull lived there in the middle 19th century.

The painting was done in acrylic by Michael Hagel of Arlington Heights, Illinois, a Chicago suburb. Hagel based his depiction of the building on photographs he took himself, so that it looks very much as it does today. He altered the setting, however, eliminating a present-day street and an iron fence in front of the building and adding trees and flowers.

To help him "restore" the 19th-century landscaping, the artist used a pencil sketch furnished by the Hull House Museum that in turn was based on an old painting made from memory by one of Jane Addams' early Hull House clients. Hagel's angle of view, like that of the early painting, is from the right, but is somewhat more to the center, he said.

Between his original color "composition" of the accepted design and the final painting, Hagel added some additional color at the suggestion of Joe Brockert, project manager and art director, by changing the summer foliage on the trees to fall foliage.

Earlier, Hagel had also prepared an essay showing the large complex of buildings into which Hull House ultimately developed, basing his painting on photographs and other material from the Hull House Museum. In this picture, the original Hull House was concealed behind the additions. CSAC concluded that this was an inappropriate image for a Historic Preservation postal card because it showed only structures that no longer existed.

Hagel had to deal with a complication of a kind that only Postal Service artists encounter. They are instructed by USPS not to prematurely disclose that a stamp or postal card has been approved. "You start asking questions and searching for references," said Hagel, "and people ask you, 'What's this for?' So you have to make up some story. It would be easy to go to a source and explain what you're up to, but they don't want you to do that."

As with many recent commemorative postal cards, this one contained textual information in the cachet location. In an early version, the cachet read: "Hull House, 1889/Established by Jane Addams/Chicago, Ill./Historic Preservation." The wording finally chosen was: "Jane Addams'/Hull House/Chicago, 1889/Settlement House."

"The committee decided that the 'Historic Preservation' series label wasn't that important," said Joe Brockert. "They thought it was more important to provide a little explanation. They decided that the term

This essay by artist Michael Hagel showed the Hull House complex at its fullest development. Unfortunately, the buildings that are visible have all been demolished, and in the picture, they conceal from sight the original Hull mansion, which still survives.

'Settlement House' was widely recognized, so they asked that that line be added, and they wanted 'Jane Addams' made more prominent, which we did by calling it 'Jane Addams' Hull House,' which is how it is currently referred to. They didn't think 'Illinois' was necessary with 'Chicago.' So we made some adjustments, and I think that with fewer words we managed to convey more information."

CSAC has learned through experience, Brockert added, not to end an informational inscription with a city and state name (such as "Chicago, Ill."). That's because some automated equipment — or postal clerks — might mistake the line for part of a return address and route the card "back" to that city if it should be undeliverable as addressed. This had happened with the Blair House postal card of 1988, whose cachet inscription read: "President's Guest House, Washington, D.C."

First-Day Facts

Some 300 people attended the dedication ceremony in the Illinois Room of the Chicago Circle Center, University of Illinois. The site on South Halsted Street is a short distance from the Hull House Museum, which was deemed too small to host the event.

A long list of participants from USPS, Hull House and the university included Patricia Sharpe, who led the campaign that resulted in issuance of the postal card; Mary Ann Johnson, director of the museum; Ann McK. Robinson, USPS consumer advocate; Prudence Beidler, president of the Hull House board of trustees, and Ann E. Smith, associate chancellor of the Chicago Circle Center. Artist Michael Hagel was also on hand to sign cards and programs. For Hagel, it was almost a double first-day-of-issue ceremony; less than 48 hours later, his wife delivered their third child, William Patrick Hagel.

Back in 1940, the Jane Addams stamp had had its first-day sale in the Benedict Art Galleries located in the Hull House complex itself. Its issuance on April 26 came only a few months after Hull House had celebrated its 50th anniversary.

15¢ PHILADELPHIA POSTAL CARD
AMERICA THE BEAUTIFUL SERIES

Date of Issue: September 25, 1989

Catalog Numbers: Scott UX135   USPS 2226
                     Minkus PC131   UPSS S152

Colors: magenta, yellow, cyan, black

First-Day Cancel: Philadelphia, Pennsylvania (Independence Hall)

FDCs Canceled: 61,659

Size: 5½ by 3½ inches

Format: Printed in 80-card sheets, 16 each of two cards (Baltimore, Washington) and 24 each of two cards (Philadelphia, New York), but available to collectors only in single cards. Printing plates of 80 subjects (8 across, 10 around).

Markings: ©USPS 1989

Designer: Bart Forbes of Dallas, Texas

Art Director: Derry Noyes (CSAC)

Typographer: Bradbury Thompson (CSAC)

Project Manager: Joe Brockert (USPS)

Printing: U.S. Government Printing Office (GPO) on a 5-color Roland Man 800 sheetfed offset press

Quantity Ordered: 7,000,000
Quantity Distributed: 7,000,000

Tagging: vertical bar to right of stamp

The Postal Card

To help commemorate the 20th Congress of the Universal Postal Union meeting in Washington in November 1989, USPS issued four special postal cards in its America the Beautiful series.

These bore scenes from Philadelphia, Baltimore, New York and Washington — four Eastern Seaboard cities that UPU delegates could easily visit during their stay in Washington. USPS selected the cities from a larger list of potential delegate destinations that also included Williamsburg, Virginia.

The six previous cards in the series had all shown generic scenes representative of the type of landscape they featured: prairie, desert, wetlands, seashore, mountains and woodlands. None of the images on these cards represent any particular place.

However, the four "cityscape" cards were site-specific. Each showed a recognizable landmark in the city being honored.

In announcing the first of the cards, for Philadelphia, USPS also disclosed that the quartet would later be issued in an unprecedented se-tenant sheet of four, perforated for easy separation.

The four cards had another unusual aspect, as well. Each was sold only in the city featured in the design, although they were also available at philatelic centers and by mail order from the Philatelic Sales Division. Such sales restrictions have been applied in the past to souvenir sheets and other special material, but very rarely to stamps or postal stationery created for general use.

The card for Philadelphia, the nation's fifth largest city, carried an aerial view of Independence Hall and was dedicated at that building September 25 in a joint ceremony with the 25¢ Bill of Rights commemorative stamp.

Independence Hall, where the Continental Congress adopted the Declaration of Independence in 1776 and the Constitutional Convention wrote the Constitution in 1887, has frequently appeared on stamps and postal cards.

Its exterior was depicted on the 10¢ stamp of the 1954-61 Liberty series (Scott 1044); a 10¢ 1974 stamp commemorating the First Continental Congress (Scott 1546); a 13¢ Flag definitive in 1975 (Scott 1622), and the 14¢ Constitutional Convention postal card (Scott UX116) and 22¢ Pennsylvania Bicentennial stamp (Scott 2337) of

This 1974 stamp commemorating the First Continental Congress (Scott 1546) is one of many U.S. stamps picturing Independence Hall in Philadelphia.

A more conventional view of Independence Hall was shown on the Pennsylvania Statehood bicentennial commemorative of 1987 (Scott 2337).

1987. The interior has been shown on several stamps that depicted the signing of the Declaration of Independence or the Constitution.

The four cityscape cards, like other U.S. postal cards, were printed by the Government Printing Office in Washington on its five-color offset Roland Man machine. The Roland Man produces sheets of 80 subjects, arranged eight across by 10 down.

In this case, however, the plate layout varied from the norm. All four cityscape cards were printed on the same sheet and were later guillotined and processed into individual cards, using a combination of the cut-and-pack system used for all other cards and some hand packing.

An earlier postal card showing a cityscape was this airmail card of 1986 (Scott UXC23) depicting the skyline of Chicago, site of Ameripex.

The first and third horizontal rows on the sheet were Baltimore cards and the second and fourth rows were Washington cards. The fifth, seventh and ninth rows featured the New York card and the sixth, eighth and tenth rows were the Philadelphia card.

This meant that the 80-subject plate contained 16 Baltimore, 16 Washington, 24 New York and 24 Philadelphia cityscape postal cards. Total production figures for the New York and Philadelphia cards, then, were 1½ times larger than the figures for the Baltimore and Washington cards.

According to Joe Brockert, project manager for the cards, this type of layout was more efficient than making individual plates for each design. Preparing individual plates and setting up the press for each design is a time-consuming project, and the combination system thus required less plate-production and press-setup time.

The Design

Bart Forbes, whose watercolor paintings had provided the images for all previous America the Beautiful cards, designed the four cityscape cards as well. USPS gave Forbes the list of four cities it wanted to honor with the cards, but left it to him to suggest the specific landmarks to be depicted.

The Philadelphia card was somewhat of a problem, Forbes said, because "most of the recognizable buildings and monuments that say 'Philadelphia' tend to be vertical rather than horizontal."

The layout of an 80-subject printing sheet of Cityscape postal cards, shown in this mockup using the stamped images, shows that all four designs are printed on the same sheet and that there are more New York and Philadelphia cards than Baltimore and Washington cards.

"I wanted to do something with the Liberty Bell, but it just didn't work out in that long horizontal design format used with postal card," the artist continued. "So the Postal Service agreed I should try something else.

"To me, Independence Hall more than anything else represents Philadelphia, but it is a very vertical building. But I was able to find an overhead shot of Independence Hall which enabled me, by adding a shadow effect, to work in that horizontal format."

In Forbes' painting, the building is canted at a slight angle, as if seen from a helicopter that was banking, and the top of the cupola is cropped off — making it a far different image of the "Birthplace of Liberty" than any previously shown on stamps or postal cards.

A flock of white doves or pigeons, fluttering upward, is seen outlined against green trees at the right of the building. Forbes admitted he "had to fudge a little bit" when he included those trees in his painting.

"The grounds aren't exactly like that," he said. "I decided to simplify it rather than get into detailed sidewalks and the other things that exist over at the right, and the people from the Postal Service seemed to agree with that approach. That whole right side I just made up. I drew it and I let the shadow carry the pattern over to that side. I didn't want a lot of detail that would detract from the building itself."

The words "Philadelphia:" and "Independence Hall" are printed in two lines of black type at the lower left.

First-Day Facts

Information on the first-day ceremony is given in the chapter on the 25¢ Bill of Rights commemorative stamp.

15¢ BALTIMORE POSTAL CARD
AMERICA THE BEAUTIFUL SERIES

Date of Issue: October 7, 1989

Catalog Numbers: Scott UX136   USPS 2227
Minkus PC132   UPSS S153

Colors: magenta, yellow, cyan, black

First-Day Cancel: Baltimore, Maryland (Fells Point, no ceremony)

FDCs Canceled: 58,746

Size: 5½ by 3½ inches

Format: Printed in 80-card sheets, 16 each of two cards (Baltimore, Washington) and 24 each of two cards (Philadelphia, New York), but available to collectors only in single cards. Printing plates of 80 subjects (8 across, 10 around).

Markings: ©USPS 1989

Designer: Bart Forbes of Dallas, Texas

Art Director: Derry Noyes (CSAC)

Typographer: Bradbury Thompson (CSAC)

Project Manager: Joe Brockert (USPS)

Printing: U.S. Government Printing Office (GPO) on a 5-color Roland Man 800 sheetfed offset press

Quantity Ordered: 5,000,000
Quantity Distributed: 5,000,000

Tagging: vertical bar to right of stamp

The Postal Card

Baltimore, the largest city in Maryland and the 11th largest in the United States, was the subject of the second "cityscape" postal card in the America the Beautiful series. The card was issued October 7 and was available to the general public only in Baltimore.

Baltimore's Inner Harbor is featured in the design, with the angled architecture of the National Aquarium shown against the sky and the U.S. Navy frigate *Constellation* in the foreground.

Inner Harbor, overlooking the Patapsco River, is downtown Baltimore's focal point and the proudest achievement of an urban renewal program that has made the city a major tourist destination on the East Coast. It consists of 95 acres along the water's edge that a few years ago boasted little except decayed docks and shabby warehouses.

Its center is Harborplace at Pratt and Light streets, an award-winning project by James Rouse that has served as a model for many other inner-city sites. The shopping and dining complex houses more than 140 restaurants, boutiques, bistros, cafes, specialty stores and gourmet markets in two glass-enclosed pavilions. Among its attractions is a variety of food ranging from Baltimore's famous crabcakes and Maryland cheese bread to exotic ethnic fare.

Nearby are The Gallery, a multilevel complex of upscale stores; the World Trade Center; and, at the end of Pier 3, the futuristic National Aquarium, the biggest and most technically advanced aquarium in the United States. There, some 8,000 specimens of 600 varieties of fish, mammals, plants, birds, reptiles and amphibians live in re-creations of their natural environments.

The *Constellation*, launched at Fell's Point in Baltimore in 1797, was the first commissioned ship in the U.S. Navy. It fought in the undeclared war with France in 1799-1800, the battle with the Barbary pirates in Algeria, the War of 1812 and the Civil War. The ship was designated a national historic landmark in 1964, and was repaired and restored in 1979 at a cost of $1.5 million.

A 6¢ Tourism Year postal card in 1972 depicted the *Constellation*, as did an 8.4¢ non-profit stamped envelope in 1988.

The **Constellation** *was most recently depicted on this non-profit envelope of 1988.*

The Design

Choosing a scene for the Baltimore card was the most difficult of the four "cityscape" assignments, said artist Bart Forbes, "simply because Baltimore is hard to recognize to the average person, someone

Two unused essays by Bart Forbes for the Baltimore cityscape postal card. One shows the U.S.S. Constellation with the skyline of downtown Baltimore in the background; the other shows a close-up view of the National Aquarium with sailboats in the foreground.

who is not from Baltimore and familiar with that area. It's hard to symbolize it in a skyline or buildings as we did the other three cities and have people know what it is."

To help find a satisfactory image, Joe Brockert, USPS project manager for the four postal cards, went to Baltimore and circled the Inner Harbor, taking photographs from a variety of angles.

Working from these photos, Forbes did a series of sketches, some featuring the Aquarium more prominently than others, some with sailboats in the foreground rather than the *Constellation*. In the scene that was finally chosen, the artist took a major liberty: The *Constellation* appears to be at anchor offshore, whereas it actually is tied up to a dock so tourists can easily go aboard.

"The dock would have just absolutely destroyed a nice clean image, so we eliminated it," Brockert explained.

The words "Baltimore: Inner Harbor" appear in the lower left corner of the card.

First-Day Facts

The card was issued during the annual Fell's Point Festival, but without a first-day ceremony. It was the second postal item to make its debut in Baltimore in 1989, following a $1 Great Americans stamp depicting Johns Hopkins, which had been dedicated in the city June 7.

15¢ NEW YORK CITY POSTAL CARD
AMERICA THE BEAUTIFUL SERIES

Date of Issue: November 8, 1989

Catalog Numbers: Scott UX137 USPS 2228
Minkus PC133 UPSS S154

Colors: magenta, yellow, cyan, black

First-Day Cancel: New York City (ASDA stamp show, no ceremony)

FDCs Canceled: 48,044

Size: 5½ by 3½ inches

Format: Printed in 80-card sheets, 16 each of two cards (Baltimore, Washington) and 24 each of two cards (Philadelphia, New York), but available to collectors only in single cards. Printing plates of 80 subjects (8 across, 10 around).

Markings: ©USPS 1989

Designer: Bart Forbes of Dallas, Texas

Art Director: Derry Noyes (CSAC)

Typographer: Bradbury Thompson (CSAC)

Project Manager: Joe Brockert (USPS)

Printing: U.S. Government Printing Office (GPO) on a 5-color Roland Man 800 sheetfed offset press

Quantity Ordered: 7,000,000
Quantity Distributed: 7,000,000

Tagging: vertical bar to right of stamp

The Postal Card

The third of the four "cityscape" postal cards in the America the Beautiful series was issued November 8 by the Postal Service and featured a scene in New York City. Like the others in the series, it was sold only in the city it honored.

The indicium showed the Queensborough Bridge (called the "59th Street Bridge" in the USPS press release), which crosses the East River between Manhattan and Queens, with the Manhattan skyline in the background.

The Queensborough Bridge was 80 years old in 1989, but it is the newest of the bridges that span the East River. Designed by architects Palmer & Hornbostel and built by the Municipal Department of Bridges, it is of cantilever construction. Its angular appearance contrasts with the graceful continuity and flow of the older suspension bridges — the Brooklyn, the Manhattan and the Williamsburg.

For years the Queensborough Bridge provided the only road access to the city hospitals on Welfare Island, which is now called Roosevelt Island. Trucks, ambulances and even trolley cars reached the island by boarding large elevator cars at roadway level and descending through a 10-story tower to the ground below. The elevators stopped running in 1955 after a bridge was built to the island from Queens, and the tower was demolished.

New York City, the nation's largest metropolis, has provided the subject matter for many U.S. postal issues. Stamps that have featured its dramatic skyline include the 15¢ international airmail stamp of 1947 (Scott C35) and the 14¢ Fiorello LaGuardia definitive of 1972 (Scott 1397). New York City bridges previously shown on stamps were the Verrazano Narrows Bridge between Brooklyn and Staten Island, shown on a 1964 5¢ stamp commemorating its completion (Scott 1258), and the Brooklyn Bridge, depicted on a 1983 20¢ commemorative marking its centennial (Scott 2041).

The Design

Designer Bart Forbes looked over a large number of slides he had shot of New York scenes, and made some preliminary sketches of New York harbor and the Statue of Liberty.

"They probably would have worked," he said, "but they were a little more complex. The key to doing these things, I've found, is simplification, because of the small size of a stamp or postal card. I've found I'm better off if I can distill the information I've got or the scene that I'm working with into a very simplified shape.

"It's going to 'read' a lot better than if I get into complicated stuff, with too many buildings or people or too much going on."

Eventually Forbes settled on a Queensborough Bridge view with a

Manhattan skyline, which he could interpret effectively with his watercolors in simple shapes and silhouettes. The artist set his scene in the afterglow of sunset, with the city's buildings outlined against a yellow and orange sky.

First-Day Facts

The card had its first-day sale in conjunction with the opening of the American Stamp Dealers Association show in Madison Square Garden. As with the Baltimore card, there was no ceremony.

15¢ WASHINGTON, D.C., POSTAL CARD
AMERICA THE BEAUTIFUL SERIES

Date of Issue: November 26, 1989

Catalog Numbers: Scott UX138   USPS 2229
Minkus PC134   UPSS S155

Colors: magenta, yellow, cyan, black

First-Day Cancel: Washington, D.C. (World Stamp Expo '89 stamp show)

FDCs Canceled: unavailable

Size: 5½ by 3½ inches

Format: Printed in 80-card sheets, 16 each of two cards (Baltimore, Washington) and 24 each of two cards (Philadelphia, New York), but available to collectors only in single cards. Printing plates of 80 subjects (8 across, 10 around).

Markings: ©USPS 1989

Designer: Bart Forbes of Dallas, Texas

Art Director: Derry Noyes (CSAC)

Typographer: Bradbury Thompson (CSAC)

Project Manager: Joe Brockert (USPS)

Printing: U.S. Government Printing Office (GPO) on a 5-color Roland Man 800 sheetfed offset press

Quantity Ordered: 5,000,000
Quantity Distributed: 5,000,000

Tagging: vertical bar to right of stamp

The Postal Card

The last of the four "cityscape" postal cards in the America the Beautiful series featured Washington, D.C., the nation's capital and site of the two events — World Stamp Expo '89 and the 20th Universal Postal Union Congress — that inspired the set. It was placed on sale November 26 at the stamp show, and was available to the general public only in the Washington area, although it could be purchased at philatelic centers. The design featured the building at the city's hub — the U.S. Capitol.

Washington, the nation's 16th largest city, and its landmarks have been featured on dozens of U.S. stamps and postal stationery items. In 1989 alone, two stamps depicted well-known artifacts inside the Capitol, and four postal cards, including this one, showed familiar Washington buildings.

The Capitol's exterior had previously been the subject of nearly a score of stamps, beginning with the 4¢ value of the 1901 Pan-American Exposition issue, which showed an electric automobile driving past the building (Scott 296).

The Design

Designer Bart Forbes knew from the beginning, he said, that he wanted to paint the Capitol for this postal card, but to paint it in a way it hadn't been postally shown before: at night.

Working from a photograph he had made himself, he prepared a watercolor of the West Front, bathed in floodlights, as seen from a point at the center of the Mall. His photo had been taken in the evening, so he darkened the sky, sprinkled stars and hung a larger-than-life full moon to the left of the dome.

First-Day Facts

The card was dedicated by Senior Assistant Postmaster General Comer S. Coppie. The principal speaker was Thomas Ward, supervising engineer, U.S. Capitol. The day, November 26, was designated Dinosaurs Day at World Stamp Expo.

15¢ THE WHITE HOUSE PICTURE POSTAL CARD

Date of Issue: November 30, 1989

Catalog Numbers: Scott UX139   USPS 2244
  Minkus PC135   UPSS S156

Colors: magenta, yellow, cyan, black

First-Day Cancel: Washington, D.C. (World Stamp Expo '89 stamp show)

FDCs Canceled: unavailable

Size: 5½ by 3½ inches

Format: Printed on Krome Coat paper in 72-card sheets, 36 each of two different designs (White House, Jefferson Memorial), but available to collectors only in single cards. Printing plates of 72 subjects (8 across, 9 around).

Markings: ©USPS 1989

Designer: Pierre Mion of Lovettsville, Virginia

Art Director and Project Manager: Joe Brockert (USPS)

Typographer: Bradbury Thompson (CSAC)

Printing: U.S. Government Printing Office (GPO) on a 5-color Roland Man 800 sheetfed offset press

Quantity Ordered: 5,000,000
Quantity Distributed: 2,458,000

Tagging: vertical bar to right of stamp

The Postal Card

For nearly a century, Americans have been sending picture postcards — cards with illustrations on one side and the message, address and a place for the stamp on the other. Such cards got a tremendous boost from the World's Columbian Exposition of 1893 and have been popular ever since.

But not until 1989 had the public been able to buy "picture postal cards," issued by the government, with the postage prepaid and an indicium in the spot where the stamp would normally go.

Two such hybrid cards made their debut at World Stamp Expo '89 in Washington, D.C. Both featured scenes in Washington. One, issued November 30, depicted the White House on the picture side and in the indicium; the other, which followed two days later, showed the Jefferson Memorial.

The cards were sold only in the Washington area and through philatelic centers and were billed as experimental. If they proved popular with tourists in the capital, USPS indicated, they would be the forerunners of other cards using matching pictures and indicia from other American cities and tourist centers.

At least two factors went into the decision to issue the two cards. One was that USPS had built up enough confidence in the capability of the Government Printing Office's five-color Roland Mann offset press, which began printing postal cards in 1987, to take the radical step of adding a picture side on glossy stock. Another was World Stamp Expo, which provided both a reason and a forum for unveiling innovative postal items.

USPS sold the cards to the public at 50¢ each, which included 15¢ postage (the first-class postal card rate). At that price, they were cheaper than maximum cards, which they resembled; USPS sells these at 50¢ each, too, but they have no built-in postage.

However, the cards were also offered in quantity at large discounts. They could be purchased in packs of 250 for $62.50, or 25¢ a card, and in quantities of 10,000 or more for 20¢ a card.

"They are intended primarily as a wholesale product," explained Joe Brockert, the USPS project manager and art director for the cards. "We would prefer that post offices not be the main sales points. We don't think the average tourist goes to a post office to buy a picture

This 1950 National Capital Sesquicentennial stamp showed the same south front of the White House that is depicted on the 1989 picture postal card and makes an interesting comparison with the later issue.

postcard. We would much rather sell these at the Smithsonian, at the White House gift shop, at the Capitol gift shop, through street vendors, and so on. The same principle will apply if we expand the concept to other cities."

Unlike commercially produced envelopes — with which the Postal Service also "competes" after a fashion — most picture postcards sold in the United States are manufactured in the Far East. Consequently, USPS heard little complaint of unfair competition from the industry. Even so, the Postal Service, in pricing the cards, sought to avoid underselling retailers.

"We checked to see what the going price was for picture postcards," Brockert said. "It tended to be anywhere from 25¢ to 50¢, even $1 in some places, but averaging 35¢ to 40¢. So we picked 35¢, added the 15¢ for the postage and came up with 50¢.

"Could a vendor who bought a pack of our cards at a wholesale price set his own retail price? Absolutely. In fact, we hope they will decide to be competitive and sell them for 49¢ each, or 45¢, or whatever they like. If a stamp dealer wants to offer these to his customers at 25¢, that's fine. The markup is strictly up to them.

"We're more interested in finding wholesalers who will provide the sales force and sales location for these cards than we are in trying to sell them in post offices. That just isn't efficient."

The wholesale pricing policy took effect January 1, 1990, and was scheduled to remain in place at least six months. During that time, USPS would gauge the response. The announcement that quantity discounts would be available wasn't made in the initial press release announcing the cards because USPS was still working out the details.

If the cards proved popular, Brockert said, others would be printed. He estimated that initially, because of production costs, a city or tourist area would have to be able to sell at least a million cards before USPS would design and print a card for that location.

Eventually, however, commercial card makers might contract with USPS to produce their own postage-imprinted picture postcards and pass along to USPS the postage value of each card sold. If that happens, Brockert said, "the sky could be the limit" on the number of varieties that might be made.

"There are lots of options down the road," he said. "It will be interesting to see which ones work out the best or which ones we'll find cost-effective."

Because the cards represented such a departure from GPO's previous work for USPS, and because of uncertainty as to whether the so-called one-side cover stock (with glossy finish on one side) would be available, the final decision to go ahead with the project wasn't made until the spring of 1989. This provided an unusually short lead time for a stamp or stationery item. Public announcement that the cards were coming wasn't made until October 24.

As it turned out, two different suppliers had the paper, and GPO awarded the contract to the James River Mills. Neither supplier, however, could furnish sheets in the size normally used for postal cards. The James River Mills sheets were 1½ inches narrower than normal, and as a result, the picture postal cards had to be made from 72-subject plates rather than the customary 80s. Given enough advance notice on future projects, GPO officials said, they could get the one-side cover stock in the exact dimensions wanted.

If the glossy-sided paper had been unavailable, Brockert said, USPS would have had to decide whether to print the cards on regular stock or drop the project. Color proofs made on normal postal card paper "didn't look bad," he said, but weren't up to the quality that was eventually achieved with the special stock.

GPO's Roland Man press prints on one side only, so two separate passes of each sheet were necessary to produce the new cards. If USPS decides it wants to obtain even more "archival quality" with any future picture cards, Brockert said, it may ask GPO to use the tagging station of the press — which wasn't employed on the picture side of the two Washington cards — to provide an overcoating for the four-color pictures.

In selecting Washington scenes for the subject matter of the cards, the Citizens' Stamp Advisory Committee and USPS officials ruled out the Capitol, which had been pre-empted for the Washington cityscape postal card that was already scheduled for release during World Stamp Expo. That left four buildings and monuments in the running: the White House, the Jefferson Memorial, the Washington Monument and the Lincoln Memorial.

The White House was quickly chosen because of its recognizability and its connection with Abraham Lincoln, who was a kind of "theme personality" for World Stamp Expo because the seeds of the Universal Postal Union were planted in his administration. By the same token, the Lincoln Memorial would have been appropriate, but its setting didn't seem to offer the possibilities for design color inherent in the Jefferson Memorial, with its springtime backdrop of cherry blossoms. Besides, officials realized, the Jefferson Memorial could be shown from an angle that would also allow the Washington Monument to be depicted in the background.

The White House was designed by Irish-born James Hoban, begun in 1792, first occupied by John and Abigail Adams in 1800, and rebuilt after it was burned by the British in the War of 1812. It made its first appearance on a U.S. stamp relatively late, in 1938, on the 4½¢ value of the Presidential series (Scott 809). Since then, it has been featured on several definitive and commemorative stamp designs, including two stamps in 1981 honoring Hoban (Scott 1935-1936).

The Design

USPS officials considered using color photographs as the basis for the artwork on the two picture postal cards, but decided against it. They wanted something better than the conventional picture-postcard look that photos would have given. They also wanted to be able to take artistic license — to remove extraneous people and automobiles, for instance, and even to adjust some of the picture elements and perspectives for better effect.

For the artwork, USPS hired Pierre Mion of Lovettsville, Virginia, an artist and magazine illustrator who the year before had executed two design assignments involving buildings: the 15¢ Blair House postal card and the 25¢ Virginia Statehood stamp that featured the Capitol building in old Williamsburg.

For the White House card, Mion prepared a single painting in gouache, an opaque watercolor, which was used for both the picture side and the indicium. It showed the south front of the executive mansion on a sunny summer day, with a broad expanse of lawn, fountains, flowers and trees in the foreground, a blue sky overhead and the American flag fluttering high above the portico.

"Because it was a painting, we were able to trim some of the trees so that more of the windows showed," said Joe Brockert. "The trees in front of the White House have grown so large in the last few years that most of the windows are obscured. The fountain in the painting has actually been enlarged a little from a sort of false perspective, but not to the point where it looks at all unusual. The flag on the flagpole — in a photograph you wouldn't be able to pick out any detail on it, so we enlarged it just a little bit in the painting so that it 'reads' as a flag, and it still looks perfectly normal."

To prepare for the project Mion visited both sites and took numerous photographs.

First-Day Facts

Postmaster General Anthony M. Frank dedicated the White House card. Also taking part in the ceremony were John Sununu, White House chief of staff, and William Seale, a historian. The day, November 30, was designated Sports Day at World Stamp Expo.

60¢ CITYSCAPES SHEET OF FOUR POSTAL CARDS
AMERICA THE BEAUTIFUL SERIES

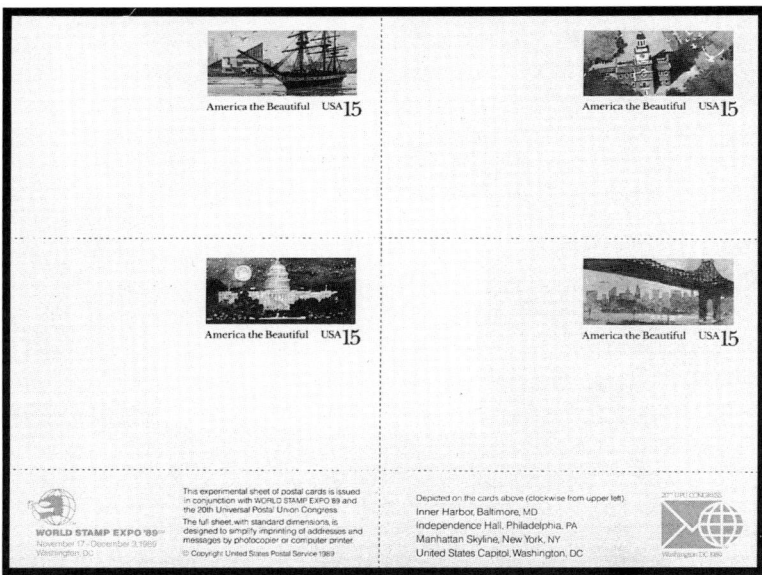

Date of Issue: December 1, 1989

Catalog Numbers:	Scott UX140	USPS 2230
	Minkus PC136	UPSS S157-1-4

Colors: magenta, yellow, cyan, black

First-Day Cancel: Washington, D.C. (World Stamp Expo '89 stamp show)

FDCs Canceled: unavailable

Size: 11 by 8½ inches

Format: Printed from 64-subject plates (8 across, 8 around) to produce 16 sheets containing four cityscape cards (Baltimore, Philadelphia, Washington, New York). Available to collectors in hyphen-hole perforated sheets of four cards.

Markings: None on cards; ©United States Postal Service 1989 and other information in sheet margin.

Designer: Bart Forbes of Dallas, Texas

Art Director: Derry Noyes (CSAC)

Typographer: Bradbury Thompson (CSAC)

Project Manager: Joe Brockert (USPS)

Printing: U.S. Government Printing Office (GPO) on a 5-color Roland Man 800 sheetfed offset press

Quantity Ordered: 2,500,000
Quantity Distributed: 1,947,000

Tagging: vertical bar to right of stamps

The Sheet

As one of a series of philatelic innovations linked to World Stamp Expo '89 and the 20th Congress of the Universal Postal Union, USPS produced its first-ever se-tenant sheet of postal cards.

The four cards on the hyphen-hole perforated sheet were the four "cityscape" cards of the America the Beautiful series, which reproduced Bart Forbes' paintings of scenes in Philadelphia, Baltimore, New York and Washington, D.C. Each had been issued earlier as a separate card.

The cards on the sheet differed from their individually issued counterparts in two ways. They had perforated rather than smooth edges, of course. And they lacked the descriptive printing that the separate cards bore in their lower left corners.

However, printed information was contained in selvage at the bottom of the sheet. The inscriptions there read:

"This experimental sheet of postal cards is issued in conjunction with WORLD STAMP EXPO '89 and the 20th Universal Postal Union Congress. The full sheet, with standard dimensions, is designed to simplify imprinting of addresses and messages by photocopier or computer printer. Depicted on the cards above (clockwise from upper left):/Inner Harbor, Baltimore, MD/Independence Hall, Philadelphia, PA/Manhattan Skyline, New York, NY/United States Capitol, Washington, DC."

The selvage also contained the World Stamp Expo logo, the 20th UPU Congress logo and the USPS copyright line.

The dimensions of the sheet were 8½ by 11 inches, the size of a standard piece of typing paper.

"This sheet of four cards is an important milestone in the quest for philatelic products that are responsive to today's computer-based technology," said Assistant Postmaster General Gordon Morison in a USPS news release.

The sheet, like the individual cards, was printed on the Government Printing Office's five-color offset Roland Man machine. Its printing plate contained 64 subjects, arranged eight rows across by eight down. The entire area of the printing plate was the same size as the standard 80-subject plate used for individual cards, but contained fewer subjects because of the inclusion of the marginal inscription at the bottom of each sheet of four cards. Each margin was the size of a half row of cards, and so the margins occupied two rows of otherwise-usable card printing space of every sheet.

The inclusion of the margins was dictated by the requirement that the sheets measure 8½ by 11 inches and contain four cards each. In devising the plate layout, Joe Brockert of USPS, project manager for the item, was pleased to find that the dimensions of the plate nicely accommodated an even number of sheets.

"The big question was whether and how well the sheets could be perforated," Brockert said. That also turned out to pose no real problem. GPO had an ancient line perforator that it used for such jobs as perforating tearout-coupon inserts in publications. The device made narrow dash-shaped perforations — almost a roulette — in one direction only. Consequently, the sheets of postal cards had to be put through twice, with the spacing between the rows of perfs reset between passes.

"The quality of the perfs was a little bit variable," Brockert said. "Certainly it wasn't as clean or as uniform as stamp perforations. But there weren't any large hunks of card sticking out which would present a problem for anybody feeding the sheets through a photocopy machine. The uniformity of the perfs was within acceptable ranges.

"There were two things we were concerned about. We wanted people to be able to separate the cards fairly easily, without tearing them, but we didn't want the perfs to be so wimpy that the sheets would start binding or bunching up in copying machines or folding in people's hands.

"Out of pure luck, we seemed to get a nice compromise. If we hadn't, we would have had to consider modifying the existing equipment or getting new equipment or subcontracting the perforating job.

"But we approved every stage of the process. We tested tearing them, and I even ran them through a photocopy machine, and sure enough, it photocopied messages on the back of the cards. When that worked we knew we had what we wanted."

Brockert acknowledged that the public's reaction to the sheet would be unpredictable.

"There was a demand and a market for a postal card format that was compatible with photocopiers or computer printers," he said. "We don't know whether this is going to meet that demand.

"We don't know if people are going to want to tear off the tabs, or whether they wanted the sheets die-cut rather than perforated, or whether they wanted no cuts or perfs at all but intended to put them through their own cut-and-trim process.

"We may find that so-called desk-top publishing is so widespread that these small sheets will replace part of the market that's now using full uncut sheets of postal cards and having them privately printed. Or we may find that as people use these, and then learn that full sheets exist, they'll convert to full sheets."

The Design

In designing the four individual cityscape cards, artist Forbes deliberately set each scene at a different time of day — Baltimore in the morning, Philadelphia in the afternoon, New York at sunset and Washington by moonlight. This artistic device is most obvious on the sheet, which brings the four pictures together in one place.

First-Day Facts

The sheet of cards was issued December 1, which was designated America the Beautiful Day at World Stamp Expo.

Miss America Debbye Turner, a student of veterinary medicine at the University of Missouri, joined Assistant Postmaster General Gordon C. Morison in dedicating the sheet. James M. Ridenour, director of the National Parks Service, also spoke.

In line with standard policy, customers were given the option of supplying their own sheets of cards for first-day cancellations or sending 60¢ per sheet and having USPS furnish them. In either case, collectors were instructed to provide an addressed, stamped envelope for return mailing. The initial announcement neglected to make clear that if the collector wanted the sheet returned unfolded, as most would, the envelope would have to be large enough to accommodate it.

15¢ JEFFERSON MEMORIAL PICTURE POSTAL CARD

Date of Issue: December 2, 1989

Catalog Numbers: Scott UX140   USPS 2245
Minkus PC137   UPSS S158

Colors: magenta, yellow, cyan, black

First-Day Cancel: Washington, D.C. (World Stamp Expo '89 stamp show)

FDCs Canceled: unavailable

Size: 5½ by 3½ inches

Format: Printed on Krome Coat paper in 72-card sheets, 36 each of two different designs (White House, Jefferson Memorial), but available to collectors only in single cards. Printing plates of 72 subjects (8 across, 9 around).

Markings: ©USPS 1989

Designer: Pierre Mion of Lovettsville, Virginia

Art Director and Project Manager: Joe Brockert (USPS)

Typographer: Bradbury Thompson (CSAC)

Printing: U.S. Government Printing Office (GPO) on a 5-color Roland Man 800 sheetfed offset press

Quantity Ordered: 5,000,000
Quantity Distributed: 2,472,000

Tagging: vertical bar to right of stamp

The Postal Card

The second of the two experimental picture postal cards of Washington scenes featured the Jefferson Memorial and was issued at World Stamp Expo December 2, the next to last day of the show.

Like the first card, its companion had a face value of 15¢ and sold for 50¢, or in bulk at $62.50 for 250 or $2,000 for 10,000.

Unlike the first card, which depicted the White House, the Jefferson Memorial card employed two different views of its subject — one in the indicium and the other on the picture side. The latter showed the Memorial from an angle that placed the Washington Monument prominently in the background.

"Will the buyers of these picture postal cards want to get two different pictures for their money, as with this card, or will they expect the front and back to be the same?" Joe Brockert, project manager and art director for the cards, asked rhetorically.

"It's totally experimental in that way, too. We may find out that one style is preferred over the other," he said.

The Washington Monument and Jefferson Memorial, honoring the first and third presidents, are among the national capital's most popular tourist attractions.

The Jefferson Memorial, on the edge of the Tidal Basin, is a colonnaded marble structure designed by John Russell Pope in the classic Greco-Roman style that Thomas Jefferson admired. It was completed in 1942. It has been shown on a 1966 commemorative publicizing President Lyndon B. Johnson's "Plant for a More Beautiful America" campaign (Scott 1318) and a 10¢ definitive of 1973 (Scott 1510).

The Washington Monument, which stands at the west end of the Mall on a line with the Capitol and the Lincoln Memorial, was begun in 1848. Because of political quarrels and lack of funds, it wasn't completed until 1884. At a height of 555 feet, it is the tallest all-stone structure (without steel) in the world. It has been pictured on the International Civil Aeronautics Conference commemorative stamps of 1928 (Scott 649-650), the Sixth International Philatelic Exhibition souvenir sheet of 1966 (Scott 1311) and an 18¢ George Washington definitive of 1985 (Scott 2149).

Cherry blossoms and the Jefferson Memorial were also combined in the design of the 5¢ stamp issued in 1966 to publicize President Lyndon B. Johnson's "Plant for a more beautiful America" campaign (Scott 1318).

The Design

For the indicium, designer Pierre Mion painted a view of the Jefferson Memorial in springtime as seen across the Tidal Basin from the west, with its columns reflecting in the water. The Memorial's north portico is visible, Japanese cherry trees line the Tidal Basin and the blossom-laden branches of another cherry tree extend out from the upper left corner of the picture.

His painting for the picture side of the card was made from a point farther south and closer to the Memorial. The portico doesn't show, but the statue of Jefferson that stands at the center of the structure can be seen through the columns. In the background, across the Tidal Basin, is the Washington Monument. Serendipitously, the White House can also be seen in the distance from this angle, and close inspection of the card shows it there, between the two monuments.

To get the view he wanted for the picture side, Mion took photographs from the busy Fourteenth Street Bridge that links Washington with Arlington, Virginia, across the Potomac. Because the cherry trees weren't in bloom at the time, the artist based that element in his paintings on other photos.

First-Day Facts

Gary Scott, regional historian for the National Capital Region of the National Parks Service, was the featured speaker at the first-day ceremony, which was held on Olympics Day at World Stamp Expo. The card was dedicated by Samuel Green Jr., Eastern regional postmaster general.

The statue of Thomas Jefferson can be seen through the columns of the Jefferson Memorial on the picture side of the postal card.

PHILEXFRANCE 89 SOUVENIR CARD (USPS)

On July 14, 1989, the French Ministry of Posts, Telecommunications and Space and the United States Postal Service issued stamps commemorating the anniversary of the French Revolution. First day of issue ceremonies were held in Washington, D.C. and Paris.

In 1789, King Louis XVI lost most of his power to a new governing body in France, the National Assembly, which published a document entitled, "The Rights of Man and the Citizen." This declaration described the basic freedoms to which all people are entitled. The French Revolution was under way. Inspired in part by the American Revolution, this movement in France brought remarkable changes not only to that country, but to all of Europe, and eventually much of the world.

The U.S. Postal Service is pleased to issue this souvenir card to honor the PHILEXFRANCE 89 International Philatelic Exhibition.

Le 14 juillet 1989, le Ministère français des Postes, des Télécommunications et de l'Espace et le Service postal des Etats-Unis ont émis des timbres commémorant l'anniversaire de la Révolution française. Les manifestations de premier jour eurent lieu à Washington, D.C. et à Paris.

En 1789, le roi Louis XVI perdit la plus grande partie de son pouvoir au profit du nouveau gouvernement de France : l'Assemblée nationale qui publia un document intitulé "Les Droits de l'homme et du citoyen". Cette déclaration définit les libertés individuelles de chacun. La Révolution française était en route. S'inspirant en partie de la Révolution américaine, ce mouvement a apporté des changements considérables non seulement en France, mais dans toute l'Europe et finalement dans une grande partie du monde.

Le Service postal des Etats-Unis a le plaisir de publier cette carte-souvenir en l'honneur de l'Exposition philatélique mondiale PHILEXFRANCE 89.

© 1989 U.S. Postal Service

Date of Issue: July 7, 1989

Catalog Numbers: USPS 2509 (mint)
USPS 509C (canceled with 45¢ U.S. stamp)
USPS C509 (canceled with 25¢ U.S. stamp)

Colors: yellow, red, cyan, black, blue, silver (offset); black (intaglio)

Size: 8 by 6 inches

Designer: Joe Brockert (USPS)

Modeler: Frank Waslick (BEP)

Paper Stock: Super White Rising Tempo Bristol 120 lb. card stock

Printing: 6-color Miller offset sheetfed press (4-subject plates); intaglio die stamper

Quantity: 65,000

The Card

USPS issued the first of its two souvenir cards of 1989 for Philexfrance 89, the international stamp show held at the Parc des Expositions in Paris from July 7 to July 17 as part of France's celebration of the bicentennial of its revolution.

The card was the 81st to be issued by USPS and its predecessor, the Post Office Department, in a series that began in 1960 when a special card was created to recognize the First International Philatelic Congress in Barcelona, Spain.

With the Philexfrance 89 card, USPS returned to its practice of using the Bureau of Engraving and Printing as its souvenir card printer. Its sole souvenir card in 1988, for Finlandia 88 in Helsinki, Finland, had been made by a private printer, Presstar Inc. of Silver Spring, Maryland.

Presstar had produced the Finlandia 88 card by the offset process, leading to speculation that USPS was downgrading souvenir cards from their status as security-printed items. However, there was no downgrading with the Philexfrance 89 card.

It was printed by an offset-intaglio combination, and featured a die imprint of a U.S. stamp, made from an unaltered intaglio die that had been used in the production of the stamp itself. This made it the first USPS-sponsored souvenir card to bear a die imprint, although recent souvenir cards issued by BEP as part of the Bureau's own card program had been of that type.

The card actually carried the images of two stamps — one U.S., one French — that were issued July 14 to commemorate the French revolution bicentennial. The U.S. stamp was a 45¢ airmail bearing the engraved allegorical figures of Liberty, Equality and Fraternity. The French stamp was one of three that France issued as a se-tenant triptych, showing the symbolic figures individually; the one used on the card was "Equality." Both were defaced, or "canceled," by a diagonal black line across the lower right corner.

The intaglio, or engraved, portion of the U.S. stamp image was die-stamped, thus qualifying it as a proof under accepted terminology. However, the offset portion of the stamp design wasn't printed from an offset plate that had been prepared for a stamp, but rather was

The Philexfrance '89 logo was featured on the USPS show cancel that was offered with the souvenir card.

produced along with the rest of the offset material on the card — the French stamp image, text and logos. For this reason, the die imprint was actually a unique hybrid.

The text, which briefly referred to the stamps and gave a thumbnail history of the French revolution, was in two blocks, one English, one French. At the top, in red and blue, was the Philexfrance 89 logo, consisting of a stylized liberty cap — the cap of the revolutionists — and a postage stamp bearing the outline of Paris' Eiffel Tower. The logo of USPS, in blue, completed the design.

The card's designer was Terrence McCaffrey of USPS' Communications Support Division. McCaffrey had previously designed the 13¢ Energy Conservation and Development se-tenant stamps and stamped envelope of 1977.

USPS sold the souvenir card in three varieties. On July 7, the opening day of Philexfrance, it was offered with the show cancel and a 25¢ Flag With Clouds stamp of 1988 for $2.25. On July 14, it could be obtained with a show cancel of that date applied to a U.S. French Revolution stamp to mark the stamp's first day of issue (price $2.45). Mint cards could be obtained for $2.

Philexfrance 89 was one of the best attended stamp shows of all time. Paid attendance for the 11-day event exceeded 260,000, as compared to the 160,000 drawn by the highly successful Ameripex 86 in Chicago. Much of its success was due to widespread publicity, which included signs and posters throughout Paris, including subway stations and on the sides of buses, bearing the show's logo. "Even for non-speakers of French," wrote *Linn's Stamp News* editor Michael Laurence, "it was not possible to visit Paris in early July without quickly learning that there was a stamp show going on."

WORLD STAMP EXPO 89 SOUVENIR CARD (USPS)

Date of Issue: November 17, 1989

Catalog Numbers: USPS 2502 (mint)
USPS 502C (canceled)

Colors: magenta, yellow, cyan, black (offset); blind embossing

Size: 8 by 6 inches

Designer: Terrence McCaffrey (USPS)

Paper Stock: White Linen Champion 80 lb. card stock

Printing: Offset lithography by Art Litho Co. (Baltimore, Maryland); embossing by Raff Embossing and Foilcraft (Washington, D.C.)

Quantity: 65,000

The Card

USPS issued its second and final souvenir card of 1989 to honor World Stamp Expo '89. The card was placed on sale on opening day, November 17, at the Washington Convention Center.

The card featured offset reproductions of the same four versions of the 1869 90¢ Lincoln stamp — the stamp itself and three trial color proofs — that were shown on the $3.60 World Stamp Expo '89 miniature sheet that made its debut the same day. The stamp images on the card, which were slightly smaller than those on the miniature sheet, were "canceled" with black diagonal lines across the lower right corners. Because the paper of the card had a linen finish, there was a slightly blurry appearance to the stamp impressions.

The most striking and unusual feature of the card was its prominent embossed montage of four major tourist attractions in Washington: the Supreme Court, Washington Monument, Capitol and Jefferson Memorial. Also unusual was the fact that the card's textual material, describing World Stamp Expo '89, was printed on the reverse.

Terrence McCaffrey of USPS designed the card, which was printed by the offset process by Art Litho Company of Baltimore, Maryland, and embossed by Raff Embossing and Foilcraft of Washington, D.C. A total of 65,000 copies were produced.

Until 1988, all USPS souvenir cards had been printed by the Bureau of Engraving and Printing. BEP also manufactured the card that was issued earlier in 1989, honoring Philexfrance '89. The World Stamp Expo card was the second to be made for the Postal Service by a private printer.

The card was available mint for $2 and canceled for $2.25. The canceled version bore the 25¢ World Stamp Expo '89 commemorative stamp issued March 16, 1989, and the stamp show's November 17 Lincoln Day theme cancellation.

STAMPSHOW '89 SOUVENIR CARD (BEP)

Date of Issue: August 24, 1989

Catalog Numbers: BEP 976 (mint)
BEP 977 (canceled)

First-Day Release: Anaheim, California (Stampshow '89) and Washington, D.C. (BEP Visitor's Center)

Colors: magenta, yellow, cyan, black (offset); brown, green (intaglio); gold foil (letterpress); black (offset back plate)

Size: 10 by 8 inches

Conceptual Design: Steve Mansett (BEP)

Designer: Ronald Sharpe (BEP)

Modeler: Peter Cocci (BEP)

Paper Stock: Crane artificial parchment card stock

Printing: 6-color Miller offset sheetfed press; foil stamping on Kluge letterpress; intaglio die stamper

Quantity: 9,000

The Card

The Bureau of Engraving and Printing produces its souvenir cards on a fiscal year schedule. To honor Stampshow, the annual meeting of the American Philatelic Society held in Anaheim, California, August 24-27, BEP issued the second of two philatelic cards for fiscal 1989. It was the only philatelic card issued by BEP during calendar 1989.

In keeping with the year's theme for souvenir cards and prints, "American Heritage," the card featured a die imprint of the 14¢ stamp of the 1922-1926 definitive series depicting Chief Hollow Horn Bear of the Brule Sioux tribe.

An additional, larger engraving of Hollow Horn Bear also appears on the card, and a third likeness, printed by offset and greatly enlarged, serves as the background for the engravings.

The original flat-plate version of the 14¢ stamp was issued May 1, 1923. The portrait used was based on a negative by Delancy Gill, provided by the Bureau of American Ethnology, which is now the Department of Anthropology, at the Smithsonian Institution. Gill was employed by the BAE as an illustrator and photographer.

C.A. Huston, a long-time designer with the BEP, was credited with modeling the stamp. The stamp portrait was engraved by L.S. Schofield; the ornamental engraving by J.C. Benzing; the frame by E.M. Hall, and the numerals by Hall and F. Lamasure. The larger engraving on the card was created by Schofield.

BEP dies used to produce the card were numbers PO697 and 10644.

The item was the fifth BEP philatelic or numismatic card to bear a stamp die imprint, that is, a reproduction of the complete stamp engraving, with lettering and numerals, made from the original die. Until the Sescal '87 card of 1987, new dies were made, without the denomination. These didn't qualify as die imprints.

Like the four previous cards in this category, the Stampshow '89 card had the die imprint "canceled" with a single diagonal black line across the lower right corner.

The cards were available at Stampshow for $4 mint and $4.25 canceled, and by mail from BEP, at a cost of $5.50 mint and $5.75 canceled.

1989-90 DUCK STAMP SOUVENIR CARD (FISH AND WILDLIFE SERVICE)

Date of Issue: June 30, 1989 (mint only, Washington, D.C.)

Catalog Number: BEP 4017 ($19.50, by mail, with Duck stamp)

First-Day Release: June 30, 1989 (Washington, D.C., Smithsonian Institution)
July 1, 1989 (Lincoln, Nebraska, State Capitol)

Colors: magenta, yellow, cyan, black, brown, purple (offset); gold foil (letterpress); gray (offset) text on back of card

Size: 10 by 8 inches

Designer, Typographer and Modeler: Ronald Sharpe (BEP)

Paper Stock: uncoated card stock

Printing: 6-color Miller offset sheetfed press (4-subject plates); Kluge letterpress for gold foiling

Quantity: 10,000

The Card

For the third consecutive year, the National Fish and Wildlife Foundation, a non-profit organization chartered by Congress to support wildlife conservation projects, sponsored a duck stamp souvenir card to help fund its programs.

The card, printed by the Bureau of Engraving and Printing, bore an enlarged replica of the 1989 duck stamp. A specimen of the $12.50 stamp itself was affixed to each card.

A total of 10,000 cards were printed, with cancel and serial number differences. There were 8,250 mint, unnumbered cards with no cancels for $18 each.

There were 1,000 unnumbered cards with the two "first-day" cancellations that were used for the stamp — June 30, at Washington's Duck Stamp Station, and July 1 at Lincoln, Nebraska, the home city of the stamp's designer, Neal R. Anderson. These sold for $25 each.

There were 750 numbered cards with cancels. Cards numbered 1 to 10 cost $150 each. Cards numbered 11 to 100 cost $75, and cards numbered 101 to 750 sold for $50.

According to Norma Opgrand, coordinator of the federal duck stamp program, everyone who purchased a 1988 card bearing a number was given a period of time to buy the 1989 card with the same number.

The $12.50 cost of the stamp was deducted from the proceeds of each card and the Washington-based Foundation retained the balance. After paying the Bureau of Engraving and Printing for the printing costs, the Foundation used the funds to promote duck stamp sales. One example of its projects, Opgrand said, was the implementation of a "junior duck stamp program" in the schools.

THE YEAR IN REVIEW

World Stamp Expo '89

For stamp collectors, the biggest event in the United States in 1989 was World Stamp Expo '89, the first international stamp show sponsored by the U.S. Postal Service. It was held in conjunction with the 20th Universal Postal Congress in Washington, D.C.

During the 14 days between November 17 and December 3 that the show was open, 125,300 persons passed through Expo's gates at the Washington Convention Center.

They bought stamps and accessories at booths rented by 126 postal administrations and 137 stamp dealers, or bid at 13 auctions held during the show at the Sheraton Washington Hotel. They viewed 33 exhibits at the Court of Honor, many of which were winners of international Grand Prix or American Philatelic Society Champion of Champions awards, and saw displays provided by 104 stamp clubs.

They attended a wide range of seminars, including a series of discussions led by members of the Citizens' Stamp Advisory Committee. They saw and heard high-tech audiovisual displays by USPS. They visited 11 U.S. and 17 foreign first-day ceremonies in which sports, aerospace and show-business celebrities took part. And they brought their children to a colorful, dinosaur-theme youth area.

At the end, Postmaster General Anthony M. Frank reported that World Stamp Expo '89 and the U.S. postal items issued there had

The American Journey video wall was one of the most popular attractions at World Stamp Expo '89, the USPS show held in Washington.

For each day of World Stamp Expo '89, USPS set a theme and created an appropriate pictorial cancellation.

brought in all the revenue needed to finance the UPU Congress. The cost was estimated before the show at $20 million.

World Stamp Expo '89 drew generally enthusiastic reviews. Bernard A. (Bud) Henning Sr., a Chicago lawyer who served as president of Ameripex '86, said: "This was one of the greatest philatelic events of the 20th century in the United States. It will be remembered by all participants, and some day they will look back and say, 'I was there.' "

20th Universal Postal Union Congress

For the first time since 1897, the Universal Postal Union held its quinquennial Congress in the United States. From November 13 to December 14, delegates from 170 UPU member countries met at the Washington Convention Center to transact UPU business.

The theme of the 20th Congress was "Caring for the Customer." Modernization of the international postal system was another major concern of the delegates. These concerns were reflected in the Washington Action Plan, which was adopted by the Congress.

The plan called for postal administrations to create market-led cultures in which the customer would command top priority. It called on all member countries to "give the highest consideration to providing service excellence in all postal services and products, both nationally and internationally."

Among other things, the Congress introduced optional classification systems based on speed of service or on envelope sizes, and an optional international business reply service by which respondents could send reply cards or envelopes back to the business of origin in another country without paying additional postage.

Seoul, Korea, was chosen as the site for the 1994 Congress.

Carousel Animals Top Linn's Stamp Poll

The se-tenant block of four stamps depicting carousel animals, issued October 1, 1988, to launch USPS' National Stamp Collecting Month, was an easy winner in the 1988 *Linn's Stamp News* stamp popularity poll. More than 4,300 votes were cast in the biggest response in the poll's 40-year history.

The Carousel Animals block won the "favorite stamp" category, topping the runner-up, the Classic Cars booklet, 789 to 480. It also won in the "best design — commemoratives" classification, with 1,212 votes to 688 for the runner-up, which again was Classic Cars.

The Carousel Animals stamps also received an award of excellence from the Government Postage Stamp Printers' Conference, held July 3-7, 1989, in Perigueux, France. A panel of stamp designers and engravers from 18 countries determined the block to be the best multiple issue of the year. Multiples include pairs, blocks, panes and sheets.

Paul Calle created the original art for the stamps. Clarence Holbert of the Bureau of Engraving and Printing was the modeler, Thomas Hipschen engraved the vignettes and Dennis Brown engraved the inscriptions. The stamps were printed by a combination of offset and intaglio on BEP's D press.

Other *Linn's* poll winners were: best design — definitives, 25¢ Flag Over Yosemite; best design — postal stationery, 15¢ America the Beautiful postal card; worst stamp, Special Occasions booklet; least necessary — commemorative, Special Occasions booklet; least necessary — definitives, 23¢ Mary Cassatt; least necessary — postal stationery, 25¢ Snowflake envelope.

Jenny Plate Block Sells For $1.1 Million

The unique plate number block of four of U.S. C3a, the inverted Jenny airmail stamp of 1918, was sold for $1 million at auction in New York City October 12, 1989, the highest amount ever paid for a philatelic item at a public auction. With the 10-percent buyer's fee added, the total cost to the anonymous purchaser was $1.1 million.

The block had been part of the stock of New Orleans stamp dealers Raymond and Roger Weill, and was auctioned by Christie's of New York. At the same sale, a guideline block of four of the inverted Jenny fetched $480,000 plus the buyer's fee.

On the same day, Christie's auctioned off the Weills' postmasters' provisionals, described as the most complete and important collection of these postage-stamp forerunners ever assembled. The 5¢ Annapolis stamped envelope (Scott 2XU1) sold for $286,000. A cover bearing the finest known 1846 5¢ Alexandria, Virginia, type II on buff (Scott 1X1a) went for $221,000. Another cover, bearing 12 specimens of the 1845 New York provisionals (Scott 9X1), brought $187,000. The unique Boscawen, New Hampshire, provisional (Scott 4X1) on cover brought $176,000, and the unique Lockport, New York, provisional (Scott 6X1) on cover fetched $164,000. The only known unused copy of the 5¢ provisional of Millbury, Massachusetts (Scott 7X1) sold for $121,000.

USPS accelerates marketing efforts

Faced with a growing deficit, USPS in 1989 increased its efforts to make money through the development and sale of philatelic products other than stamps.

Joining USPS headquarters in these efforts were regional and local postal managers who were given freedom to create and market their own special material. ·

The result was an unprecedented flood of merchandise, a large part of it calculated to appeal as much to the general public as to stamp collectors.

Among the product lines the Office of Stamps and Philatelic Marketing offered for the first time in 1989 were:

- A board game. Called "Stampin', the Lively Game of Stamp Acquisition," it included dice, play money and 15 sets of four playing cards featuring full-color reproductions of stamps. "Not quite like playing post office," *USA Today* headlined its story. Price: $13.95.
- Two different Christmas tree ornaments (obviously launching an annual tradition). Each ornament contained one of the two 1989 Christmas stamps, traditional and contemporary, mounted on crimson aluminum and sealed in clear epoxy. Price: $12.95 each.
- Dinosaur T-shirts, produced as part of a large-scale multimedia promotion of the Prehistoric Animals block of four. Price: $6.95.

USPS also continued to mine veins it had first tapped in previous years, with three new stamp posters ($10 each), a cacheted first-day cover ($3.50), and a large assortment of catalogs, booklets and brochures, some with stamps, some without.

Meanwhile, beyond the Potomac River, regional and city postmasters were offering collectors such instant collectibles as a set of 45 special-event covers celebrating the U.S. Olympic Festival in Oklahoma ($199 per set from the Oklahoma City post office) and a "limited edition print" of the 25¢ Hemingway stamp, matted with a first-day canceled copy of the stamp itself ($25 from the postmaster at Key West, Florida).

For the buyer of more modest means, the Cooperstown, New York, post office made available at the Lou Gehrig stamp first-day ceremony chocolate reproductions of the Gehrig and Babe Ruth stamps ($5 each), a Gehrig stamp key chain ($4) and pin replicas of various U.S. baseball stamps ($3 each). Pin reproductions of Love stamps, Christmas stamps and other colorful issues were offered for sale in many post offices around the country.

USPS contended that such merchandise helped build interest in stamps among non-collectors, but some in the philatelic world took a dim view of the intensity of the Postal Service's marketing efforts.

Michael Laurence, editor-publisher of *Linn's Stamp News*, expressed in his column the fear that by draining dollars from the "collector marketplace," USPS might help put stamp dealers out of business, to the long-range detriment of stamp collecting.

"USPS has the potential to contribute mightily to the future of our hobby," Laurence wrote. "It also has the potential to do great harm. The collector community generally, and the hobby press in particular, must do everything possible to keep USPS on the right road."

USPS Explores Stamp Printing Options

In June 1989, USPS contracted with the firm of Deloitte Haskins and Sells to evaluate stamp-production options that could encompass a larger role for the private sector.

The study's objectives were to identify additional private-sector sources capable of producing stamps and to address the advantages and disadvantages of contracting out all, or part of, stamp production to private firms. Among other things, the study would explore the feasibility of dividing stamp production evenly between competing private sector firms and a government-owned facility.

Postal Service officials told the General Accounting Office (GAO) that a government-owned facility that could share stamp production with the private sector might be (1) the current Bureau of Engraving and Printing plant at 14th and C Streets, S.W., in Washington, which was built in 1914 and expanded in 1938; (2) a new Bureau facility, or (3) a USPS-acquired and owned facility operated by BEP or by a private sector contractor.

A GAO report released December 12, 1989, disclosed that USPS' interest in the subject arose from several factors.

One was a concern that BEP, which now produces around 36 billion stamps a year and could go to 45 billion without increasing capacity, might be unable to keep up with a Postal Service demand for stamps that USPS said could reach between 63 billion and 84 billion annually by the year 2000.

Another was a dissatisfaction with stamp quality and costs at BEP and the belief that the Bureau "was slow in making requested stamp production changes and did not provide the Postal Service adequate customer service."

This problem was exacerbated by a difference in the way the two agencies perceived their relationship: USPS officials saw it as strictly customer-and-supplier and saw no reason why they should negotiate over their requirements, while BEP considered it to be more of a partnership. Matters were made even worse by an inability on the part of the agencies' officials to communicate effectively.

In fact, GAO revealed, relations between USPS and BEP deteriorated in the 1980s to the point where in late 1988 "oral communications virtually stopped and stamp requirements were transmitted in writing only." The proximate cause of the breakdown was, apparently, a major misunderstanding.

BEP officials told GAO they had thought USPS was primarily concerned with the need to improve the quality of the approximately 1 percent of stamp production that is selected for philatelic purposes. USPS, however, had much more than that on its mind — specifically, the additional costs it was incurring because of poor gum that caused stamps to fall off mail and "other technical problems that prevented proper stamp cancellation and allowed stamps to be fraudulently reused." If the Bureau didn't address these concerns, USPS officials told GAO, "they were prepared — whether or not there was a significant increase in stamp demand — to turn increasingly to the private sector for their stamp needs, possibly removing stamp production from the Bureau altogether."

Near the end of 1988, following appointment of a new director and deputy director at BEP, USPS and BEP officials "began a concerted effort to improve their relationship," GAO said. "They created several joint committees to develop solutions to ... production problems and instituted regular management meetings. Postal Service officials said they are pleased with the strides the agencies have made in resolving their disputes."

However, GAO added, the relationship between the agencies "remains tenuous." For one thing, BEP had declined to furnish some of the information requested by Deloitte Haskins and Sells for the USPS study out of concern that it would be used "to enhance the position of private sector competitors at the expense of the Bureau." "Because the interagency agreement under which stamps are produced is not specific about production standards and requirements, disagreements could arise and relations could quickly deteriorate again," GAO said.

Frank Sees Rate Increase In 1991

USPS will propose raising the cost of a first-class stamp in 1991 from the current 25¢ to between 28¢ and 32¢, Postmaster General Anthony M. Frank predicted in an interview on NBC's *Today* show.

He estimated that the overall rate increase would be 20 to 25 percent for all categories of mail.

Frank told a *Los Angeles Times* reporter that USPS would suffer its worst deficit ever in fiscal 1990 — more than $1.5 billion — because labor cost increases and inflation were exceeding the revenue produced by the April 3, 1988, rate hikes.

However, Frank said he planned no cutbacks in post office operating hours or delivery schedules. He said he was confident that an ambitious cost-reduction program, heavily dependent on automation, could keep finances under control until the next rate hike.

The postmaster general said a vital element in automation was the use of bar codes, which help reduce the number of people handling each piece of mail. About 40 percent of all letters carried bar codes in 1989, up from 7 percent at the start of 1988. Frank said he hoped to encourage businesses to increase the figure to 60 percent by the end of 1990, and to raise the discount given to businesses that use bar codes.

USPS Phases Out Merrifield, Virginia, Facility

In the fall of 1989 USPS began phasing out its Philatelic Sales Division operation at Merrifield, Virginia, and consolidating it with its facility in the limestone caves near Kansas City, Missouri. It hoped to save $1 million a year in operating costs by the merger, which was recommended by a 1987 study.

Since 1982, Merrifield had handled most first-day cancellations and processed most stamp orders, which were then sent for filling to Kansas City, where stamps are stored in optimum temperature and humidity conditions. Merrifield also prepared and marketed souvenir pages, commemorative panels and first-day ceremony programs; worked with the eight international dealers who serve as USPS agents; prepared V.I.P. albums, and serviced souvenirs for the postmaster general, such as Christmas cards and other items.

All current employees of the Merrifield facility were given the option of moving to Kansas City or transferring into another Washington area position. Job reductions would come from early retirements or normal attrition, USPS said.

The merger was described as only a small part of the overall USPS effort to cut employment, which is responsible for 83 percent of its costs. As of September 23, the opening day of fiscal 1990, a total of 37 management sectional centers and two field divisions were consolidated into other MSCs and divisions in a move to eliminate 1,000 managerial and administrative positions at an estimated saving of $30 million to $35 million.

USPS Will Sponsor 1992 Olympic Games

Postmaster General Frank announced at a press conference in November 1989 that the U.S. Postal Service had become an official sponsor of the 1992 Olympic Games, to be held in Albertville, France (Winter Games) and Barcelona, Spain (Summer Games).

A typical worldwide sponsorship costs $10 million to $15 million. Frank said the purpose of USPS' involvement was to improve its image, raise additional revenue and show support of the Olympics.

The envisioned increase in revenue (several hundred million dollars by 1992) would come, in large part, from philatelic products.

In an internal USPS publication, Frank said: "We have many opportunities to increase the contribution our key products are making, and we must capitalize on them. ...With a moderate investment in sponsorship, we will gain an enormous push in the area of stamp collecting, Express Mail, Priority Mail and international mail products." Express Mail, according to USPS, would be featured as the official expedited mail service of the Olympics.

USPS also acquired licensing rights for the Olympics for resale to companies and individuals marketing Olympic-related products. In addition, the Postal Service planned to sell a number of Olympic-related philatelic products of its own. The first of these, a folder resembling a first-day ceremony program, was used as a program for the Frank press conference.

Inside, the program contained copies of the 1988 Summer and Winter Olympic Games stamps, tied by a pictorial postmark showing the USPS Olympic logo. The folder was sold through the Philatelic Sales Division for $4.95.

One of the sponsors of the 1988 Olympics, Federal Express, a USPS competitor, didn't renew its option. According to USPS, Federal Express didn't know "how to exploit its opportunities."

USPS Revises Policy on Precancels

USPS made a change, long sought by collectors, in its policies governing the use and sale of precanceled stamps. It legalized the sale of unused precancels by permit holders by striking from the *Domestic Mail Manual* the antiquated provision forbidding such sales, calling it "unnecessary and impossible to administer."

This provision had been widely ignored in the past, particularly with the advent of plate number coils, many of which are available only in service-inscribed (what the Postal Service calls precanceled) form. In many cases, permit holders who are stamp dealers were unaware that by freely buying and selling precanceled coil stamps they were violating USPS policy.

AUTOPOST

In 1989 USPS began testing a new self-service mailing system called Autopost, which weighed letters and packages and dispensed pressure-sensitive postage strips in the correct denomination.

As of this writing, the Scott Publishing Company was still considering whether to give catalog listing to these strips. A Scott spokesman indicated that the key consideration would be whether the strips were significantly different from meter imprints.

Two designs were used by USPS in 1989. One prominently featured a "USA" and stars, the other a Universal Pricing Code type of marking representing the destination ZIP code.

The strips included the amount of postage paid. Unlike the typical machine-dispensed Frama strips of Europe, however, they also bore the date, the machine number and the number of the transaction produced by that machine, the weight of the item, and the post office and ZIP code of origin. The strips were printed on a coated strip stock affixed to a release liner, with an orange stripe along the left side containing the tagging material.

Autopost made its debut August 23 with two machines at the Martin Luther King Jr. station at 1400 L St. N.W. in Washington, D.C. A second set of machines was put in use September 1 at the White Flint Mall station in Kensington, Maryland.

A third set of two machines, not available to the general public, was set up in the Washington Convention Center from November 13 through December 14 for use by delegates to the 20th Universal Postal Congress.

Autopost is essentially a mechanical vending machine with a computerized operating system. It can generate postage strips for first-class, Priority Mail, Express Mail, parcel post and third-class mail.

The customer accesses the machine through a series of "menus" on a video screen. He touches the menu selection desired, and the screen, through sensors, detects which selection is being made.

The customer then inserts coins or bills in the appropriate slots, and the strip is dispensed to a tray at the bottom of the machine. At least some of the machines used Susan B. Anthony dollars in making change for $5 bills.

An example of a first-class strip Autopost sold on the first day in Washington, August 23, 1989.

In addition to first-class postage strips, third-class, Priority Mail, Express Mail and parcel post strips were vended by Autopost machines.

Autopost also produces receipts, giving all relevant information on the transaction and ending with a cheery "Thank You!" Also accompanying each postage strip is an "advertising" strip bearing one of two messages: "Developed by Technology Resource Department" or "We Deliver . . . United States Postal Service."

There were some operational problems with the program. For example, customers reported that the machines at the Martin Luther King Jr. station were frequently out of service.

First-class (25¢) Autopost strips were available by mail order through the Philatelic Sales Division in sets of two — one each from Washington and Kensington — for 50¢. The strips weren't listed in the division's *Philatelic Catalog*, and a few months after they first went on sale, they were being advertised for sale by one stamp dealer for $5.25 per set of two first-class singles.

Richard Stambaugh and David Clark, editor and co-editor of the Meter Stamp Society's *Bulletin*, wrote in *Linn's Stamp News* that the strips could be collected at various levels of specialization. A basic collection would include one strip from each participating post office. A more complete collection would contain a strip from each machine at each post office, and a very detailed collection would include strips of all five categories of mail service from each machine. Collateral material, such as first-day covers, receipts and advertising strips, would complement such a collection, they wrote.

VARIETIES

15¢ America the Beautiful card: Myrtle Beach overprint

After Hurricane Hugo had swept across South Carolina in September 1989, causing widespread destruction, the Myrtle Beach Golf Holiday organization contracted with USPS to produce a number of 15¢ America the Beautiful postal cards (Scott UX120) with a promotional overprinted message declaring that the Myrtle Beach golf courses were still in good condition.

The overprinted postal cards were the first that USPS had ever produced for a postal customer. The overprinting was done at the Government Printing Office, where the cards themselves were manufactured.

Myrtle Beach Golf Holiday, a non-profit group, serves as a kind of chamber of commerce for 52 Myrtle Beach courses. It handles all national advertising for its members, which also include three airlines and two car rental organizations.

USPS delivered 760,000 cards to Myrtle Beach Golf Holiday and also offered 140,000 cards for sale through the Philatelic Sales Division, although the item wasn't listed in the division's catalog.

Myrtle Beach Golf Holiday sent the cards out at a rate of about 100,000 a day beginning October 12, Doug Hart, general manager, told *Linn's Stamp News*. They were mailed to golf enthusiasts across the country, and bore advertising copy, including reservation information, printed on the reverse.

This is the imprint added to the 15¢ America the Beautiful postal card of 1988 for the Myrtle Beach Golf Holiday organization. Note that the word "shone" is misspelled "shown" in the imprint.

On the front of the card, the association's return address appeared in three lines in the upper left portion, along with a request for forwarding and address correction.

A logo appeared at lower right, featuring a white silhouette of a golfer against a black background. "From the Myrtle Beach, South Carolina Area" appeared above the logo, and beneath it were the words: "Where the Sun has never shown (sic) brighter or the golf courses been in better condition, even after Hugo."

25¢ Circle of Stars envelope: Virginia Lottery

At the request of the Virginia state lottery commission, USPS custom-manufactured a special kind of 25¢ Circle of Stars envelope (Scott U611) for the agency. The number 10-size envelopes were put in use around October 20, 1989.

The envelopes bore the address of the Virginia Lottery's Second Chance Drawing, its bar code and facing identification marks (FIMs). These weren't overprints, but were applied during production at Westvaco-USEnvelope Division plant.

The additional material was printed in black by flexography while the stamped envelope paper was still part of the original web. Flexography is the same process by which the red denomination is applied. After the embossed indicium containing the stars was added, the paper was cut and folded into finished envelopes.

A USEnvelope Division spokesman told *Linn's Stamp News* that three million Stars envelopes with the printed address were produced initially, with another three million to be printed when necessary.

The envelopes for the Second Chance drawing were needed because of the inability of USPS to verify lottery mail before delivery, according to Jim Packard, stamp editor for the *Richmond Times Dispatch*.

Packard told *Linn's* that many pieces of non-lottery mail had become mixed with the 6,000-per-week random entries that the Virginia Lottery used for its weekly drawing. Because of the volume of entries, all pieces of mail couldn't be opened to verify that they were, in fact, lottery mail. As a result, there was a possibility that other mail might be destroyed along with the losing envelopes.

The new imprints weren't expected to completely solve the mail identification problem because there was no way to require all contestants to use the envelopes. But it was anticipated that they would alleviate it.

The preprinted bar code at the bottom of the envelope encoded the nine-digit ZIP code of the Lottery so that optical character readers (OCRs) could read it. The vertical FIM markings at the top of the envelope identified pre-bar-coded mail to postal equipment early in the processing cycle. This allowed this kind of mail to be faced and separated from the normal mailstream, thus speeding delivery.

USPS considered the envelopes to be analagous to those that any

This is a photographically cropped picture of the 25¢ Circle of Stars stamped envelope pre-printed with address, bar code and facing identification marks for the Virginia state lottery commission.

customer may obtain, in quantities of 50 or more, with his return address imprinted in the corner. For this reason, the Philatelic Sales Agency didn't stock the variety. However, the envelopes were obtainable from post offices and other outlets in Virginia. In November 1989, one stamp dealer was advertising mint copies at $2.50 each.

25¢ Circle of Stars envelope: color omission error

More than 160 number 10 and also number 6¾ 25¢ Circle of Stars envelopes (Scott U611) were found minus the red flexographic print-

This is one of the red-omitted 25¢ Circle of Stars legal envelopes found in a quantity of envelopes purchased by an Ohio private school.

ing. This included the 25¢ denomination and the copyright notice on the back flap.

The error was first spotted as such by a *Linn's Stamp News* reader who received one of the number 10 envelopes in the mail from the Magnificat High School in Rocky River, Ohio. *Linn's* then contacted the school and was told that the error envelopes were bought in mid-June 1989 for a large all-school mailing. The school buys envelopes in quantities of 10,000, then has its return address applied by a local printer.

One of the women who worked on the mailing noticed that some of the envelopes had no denomination. The school then asked its local post office if the envelopes were valid for use. After some hesitation, the postal clerk said it would be all right to use them.

After the call from *Linn's*, school officials were able to find 163 unused errors and three that had been used as return envelopes. One of the latter even had a 25¢ stamp placed over the non-denominated indicium.

Joan Franz, business manager of Magnificat High School, told *Linn's* the school would sell the error envelopes.

22¢ Flag Over Capitol coil: color error

A California stamp collector who wished to remain anonymous reported finding a coil of 100 of the 22¢ intaglio Flag Over Capitol stamps of 1985 (Scott 2115) on which black ink instead of blue was used to print the field of the flag.

A pair of stamps from the coil was examined spectrophotometrically by the Bureau of Engraving and Printing. BEP confirmed in April 1989 that the stamps were printed with the wrong ink — specifically, with black ink in the press fountain that should have contained blue. This may have occurred during a job change on the press, BEP said. The coil was printed from sleeve 8 on either the C or D press at BEP.

The owner noticed the black field on the stamps when he first bought the roll at a post office in Los Angeles. He sent a pair to the Jacques C. Schiff auction house in May 1988. Schiff believed the black field was simply the result of ink contamination from the black ink used to print the Capitol, but suggested that the owner send a pair to BEP for its opinion, which he did.

22¢ Constitution booklet: color omission error

A single used copy on cover of a stamp from the 1987 Drafting of the Constitution booklet (Scott 2358) was found with the light blue background color missing, according to Suburban Stamp Company of Springfield, Massachusetts, which offered it for sale at auction in June 1989.

The stamp was on an insurance payment envelope postmarked in St. Louis, Missouri, November 27, 1987.

The Constitution booklet consisted of five varieties on each pane, and was printed in four colors on BEP's seven-color Andreotti gravure press. The ink colors used were light blue, red, yellow and black.

The error stamp was certified genuine by the American Philatelic Society (Certificate number 64483, dated March 16, 1988).

The top stamp has the light blue patterned background color omitted. It has been photographically cropped from a cover. At bottom is a normal stamp for comparison.

25¢ Honeybee coil: color omission error

Numerous copies of the 25¢ Honeybee coil stamp of 1988 (Scott 2281) were found with the black color missing in one of two ways. Some lacked the intaglio black and the sleeve number that normally appeared on every 48th stamp in a roll. The bee is outlined, or highlighted, in intaglio black. The bee's body is offset yellow. Others were minus the offset black, consisting of the "25 USA" inscription and the frameline.

Stamps lacking intaglio black were first reported in California. Missing-offset stamps were located in Tennessee and the Fort Worth, Texas, area.

A New York dealer advertised both types of error for sale in singles and pairs. For the missing-intaglio variety, he asked $425 per stamp; for the missing offset, $750 per stamp.

The Honeybee coils were printed by two different press configurations at BEP. Originally the printing was done in two separate press runs, with offset colors applied on the Goebel Optiforma press and intaglio impressions on the C press. Later the bulk of the printing was

These are examples of the two types of color-missing error on the 1988 Honeybee stamp. The stamp on the left is missing the offset black ink (frameline and inscription). The stamp on the right is missing the intaglio black outline of the honeybee.

done in one operation on the D press.

$8.75 Express Mail stamp: marginal marking omission

A printing of the $8.75 Express Mail stamp of 1988 (Scott 2394) was made in 1989 without the copyright symbol and inscription that had appeared in the pane margins on the original printing.

The stamps were printed on BEP's combination offset-intaglio D press. When they were first released October 4, 1988, each stamp in the top and bottom rows on each pane of 20 had a marginal marking of some kind in the adjacent top or bottom selvage. These included an intaglio sleeve number (number 1), five offset plate numbers (1 1 1 1 1) and, opposite the middle stamp of the row of five, the copyright symbol and inscription.

When additional stamps were needed in 1989, BEP prepared five new offset printing plates, each numbered "2," and used the same

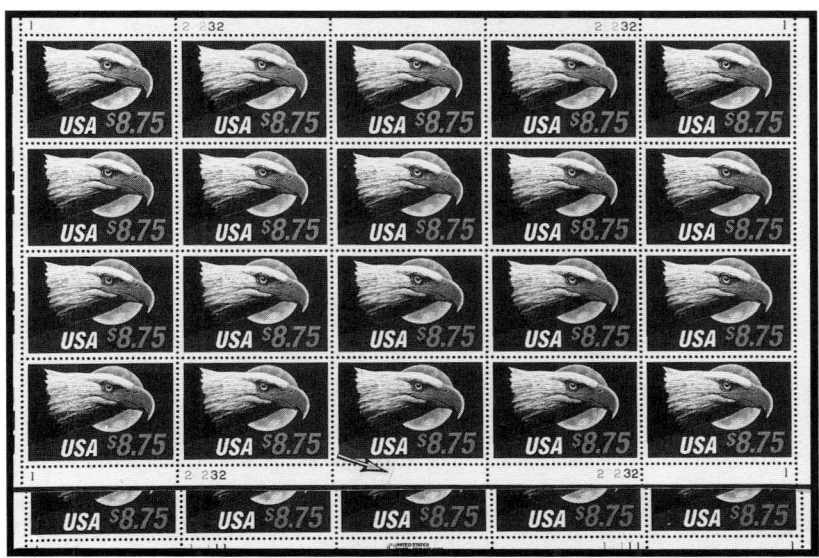

This picture shows Express Mail panes from the original printing (beneath) and the 1989 printing bearing the offset plate numbers 22232, without the USPS copyright symbol and inscription in the selvage.

number 1 intaglio printing sleeve it had used originally. The new offset plate made for the black part of the stamps and the marginal markings was defective, so a third plate, numbered "3," was hastily manufactured.

But in making the film for this plate, the copyright notice was inadvertently blocked out. Thus the panes from the new printing, bearing intaglio sleeve number 1 and offset plate numbers 22232, had only blank selvage opposite the third stamps in the top and bottom rows of each pane.

Coil stamps: new roll sizes

At the request of *Reader's Digest*, the Postal Service produced two old Transportation coil stamps in new, larger rolls. Neither received any publicity from USPS, and it was left to collectors to discover that they had been issued.

One was the tagged, non-precanceled 12.5¢ Pushcart stamp of 1985. In 1988, USPS had it reprinted from intaglio sleeve number 2 and issued in coils of 3,000. The original stamps, from sleeve number 1, had been produced in rolls of 500.

The existence of unprecanceled stamps from sleeve number 2 wasn't reported until April 1989, shortly before the basic stamp and its precanceled counterpart were scheduled to be removed from sale by the Philatelic Sales Division. A sleeve number 2 pair — its face value totaling the 25¢ first-class rate — had turned up on a letter

A 10,000-stamp coil of 2¢ Locomotive stamps prepared in May 1989 for Reader's Digest *is shown here, together with 500- and 3,000-stamp coils of 25¢ Flag stamps for comparison.*

mailed in southern California by a man who had retrieved the stamps from a *Reader's Digest* sweepstakes mailing. The stamps had been supplied as an incentive to return the entry.

Not long afterward, the unprecanceled 12.5¢ Pushcart stamp was quietly returned to the Philatelic Sales Division's catalog, in rolls of 3,000 from sleeve number 2.

The other new printing was of the 2¢ Locomotive stamp of 1987, in coils of 10,000. The supply of these was exhausted before collectors learned of their existence. Fortunately for collectors of plate number coils (PNCs), all these *Reader's Digest* stamps were printed from sleeve number 1, so no desirable new varieties were lost.

Reader's Digest had hoped the entire stamp order would be produced in the large coils, to be broken down into strips of three and attached to seven million *Reader's Digest Books* sweepstakes coupons. But USPS was still testing the large rolls at that time, and so almost two-thirds of the order had to be shipped in coils of 3,000.

USPS polled large mailers to determine which stamps they wanted available in the 10,000-stamp rolls. The four top vote-getters were approved, and this time USPS formally announced their issuance. They were the 10.1¢ Oil Wagon, 13.2¢ Coal Car, 16.7¢ Popcorn Wagon and 25¢ Flag Over Yosemite stamps.

These larger rolls were printed on BEP's B press and bore the same plate numbers and positions that appeared on the corresponding rolls of 500 and 3,000. Random splicing was required to produce the rolls.

Earlier in 1989, the 20¢ Cable Car stamp of 1988 became available in rolls of 100. Previously it had been sold only in rolls of 500 and 3,000. Supplies of the 1981 Flag Over Supreme Court coil stamps were exhausted, USPS explained, and 20¢ coils were used to cover the first-class rate for the second ounce and each additional ounce.

PLATE NUMBERS

All reported plate numbers for Transportation coil and Great Americans sheet stamps.

Prior Transportation Coils (not precanceled)

1¢ Omnibus (1983) 1,2,3,4,5,6
1¢ Omnibus (1986) 1,2
2¢ Locomotive (1982) 2,3,4,6,8,10
2¢ Locomotive (1987) 1
3¢ Handcar (1983) 1,2,3,4
3¢ Conestoga Wagon (1988) 1
3.4¢ School Bus (1985) 1,2
4¢ Stagecoach (1982) 1,2,3,4,5,6
4¢ Stagecoach (1986) 1
4.9¢ Buckboard (1985) 3,4
5¢ Motorcycle (1983) 1,2,3,4
5¢ Milk Wagon (1987) 1
5.2¢ Sleigh (1983) 1,2,3,5
5.5¢ Star Route Truck (1986) 1
5.9¢ Bicycle (1982) 3,4
6¢ Tricycle (1985) 1
7.1¢ Tractor (1987) 1
7.4¢ Baby Buggy (1984) 2
8.3¢ Ambulance (1985) 1,2
8.5¢ Tow Truck (1987) 1
9.3¢ Mail Wagon (1981) 1,2,3,4,5,6
10¢ Canal Boat (1987) 1
10.1¢ Oil Wagon (1985) 1
10.9¢ Hansom Cab (1982) 1,2
11¢ Caboose (1984) 1
11¢ Stutz Bearcat (1985) 1,2,3,4
12¢ Stanley Steamer (1985) 1,2
12.5¢ Pushcart (1985) 1,2
14¢ Iceboat (1985) 1,2,3,4
14¢ Iceboat (1986) 2
15¢ Tugboat (1988) 1,2
17¢ Electric Auto (1981) 1,2,3,4,5,6,7
17¢ Dog Sled (1986) 2
17.5¢ Racing Car (1987) 1
18¢ Surrey (1981) 1 through 18 complete
20¢ Fire Pumper (1981) 1 through 16 complete
20¢ Cable Car (1988) 1,2
25¢ Bread Wagon (1986) 1 through 5 complete

Prior Transportation Coils (precanceled)

3.4¢ School Bus (1985) 1,2
4¢ Stagecoach (1982) 3,4,5,6
4.9¢ Buckboard (1985) 1,2,3,4,5,6
5.2¢ Sleigh (1983) 1,2,3,4,5,6
5.3¢ Elevator (1988) 1
5.5¢ Star Route Truck (1986) 1,2
5.9¢ Bicycle (1982) 3,4,5,6
6¢ Tricycle (1985) 1,2
7.1¢ Tractor (1987) 1
7.4¢ Baby Buggy (1984) 2
7.6¢ Carreta (1988) 1,2
8.3¢ Ambulance (1985) 1,2,3,4
8.3¢ Ambulance (1986) 1,2
8.4¢ Wheel Chair (1988) 1,2
8.5¢ Tow Truck (1987) 1,2
9.3¢ Mail Wagon (1981) 1,2,3,4,5,6,8
10.1¢ Oil Wagon (1985) 1,2
10.1¢ Oil Wagon (1988) 2,3
10.9¢ Hansom Cab (1982) 1,2,3,4
11¢ Caboose (1984) 1
12¢ Stanley Steamer (1985) 1,2
12¢ Stanley Steamer (1987) 1
12.5¢ Pushcart (1985) 1,2
13¢ Patrol Wagon (1988) 1
13.2¢ Coal Car (1988) 1,2
16.7¢ Popcorn Wagon (1988) 1
17¢ Electric Auto (1981) 1,2,3,4,5,6,7
17.5¢ Racing Car (1987) 1
20.5¢ Fire Engine (1988) 1
21¢ Railroad Mail Car (1988) 1,2
24.1¢ Tandem Bicycle (1988) 1

1989 Transportation Coils (precanceled)

7.1¢ Tractor (1989) 1

Prior Great Americans Sheet Stamps

1¢ Dix (1983) 1 (in-line perf), 1-2 (L perf)
1¢ Mitchell (1986) 1
2¢ Stravinsky (1982) 1,2,3,4,5,6
2¢ Mary Lyon (1987) 1,2
3¢ Clay (1983) 1,2
3¢ White (1986) 1,2,3
4¢ Schurz (1983) 1,2,3,4
4¢ Flanagan (1986) 1

5¢ Buck (1983) 1,2,3,4	
5¢ Black (1986) 1,2	
6¢ Lippmann (1985) 1	
7¢ Baldwin (1985) 1	
8¢ Knox (1985) 3,4,5,6	
9¢ Thayer (1985) 1	
10¢ Russell (1984) 1	
10¢ Red Cloud (1987) 1	
11¢ Partridge (1985) 2,3,4,5	
13¢ Crazy Horse (1982) 1,2,3,4	
14¢ Lewis (1985) 1	
14¢ Julie Ward Howe (1987) 1,2	
15¢ Buffalo Bill Cody (1988) 1,2	
17¢ Carson (1981) 1,2,3,4,13,14,15,16	
17¢ Lockwood (1986) 1,2	
18¢ Mason (1981) 1,2,3,4,5,6	
19¢ Sequoyah (1980) 39529, 39530 (BEP numbers)	
20¢ Bunche (1982) 1,2,3,4,5,6,7,8,10,11,13	
20¢ Gallaudet (1983) 1,2,5,6,8,9	
20¢ Truman (1984) 1 (L perf), 2 (revised format Eureka perf)	
21¢ Chester Carlson (1988) 1	
22¢ Audubon (1985) 1 (L perf), 3 (revised format Eureka perf)	
23¢ Mary Cassatt (1988) 1	
25¢ London (1986) 1,2	
30¢ Laubach (1984) 1 (L perf), 2 (revised format Eureka perf)	
35¢ Charles Drew (1981) 1,2,3,4	
37¢ Millikan (1982) 1,2,3,4	
39¢ Clark (1985) 1 (L perf), 2 (revised format Eureka perf)	
40¢ Gilbreth (1984) 1 (L perf), 2 (revised format Eureka perf)	
45¢ Harvey Cushing (1988) 1	
50¢ Nimitz (1985) 1,2,3,4 (L perf), 1, 2 (Eureka perf)	
56¢ Harvard (1986) 1	
65¢ H.H. "Hap" Arnold (1988) 1	
$1 Revel (1986) 1	
$2 Bryan (1986) 2	
$5 Bret Harte (1987) 1	

1989 Great Americans Sheet Stamps

28¢ Sitting Bull (1989) 1	
$1 Johns Hopkins (1989) 1	

ITEMS WITHDRAWN FROM SALE IN 1989

Commemoratives: 1986 22¢ U.S. Presidents (36 designs in four miniature sheets), 2/28
1987 22¢ American Wildlife (50 designs), 4/30
1988 22¢ Georgia Statehood, 4/30
1988 22¢ Connecticut Statehood, 4/30
1988 22¢ Winter Olympics, 4/30
1988 22¢ Australia Bicentennial, 4/30
1988 22¢ Cats, 4/30
1988 22¢ Knute Rockne, 4/30
1988 22¢ James Weldon Johnson, 6/30
1988 22¢ Massachusetts Statehood, 6/30
1988 22¢ Maryland Statehood, 6/30
1988 25¢ South Carolina Statehood, 12/31
1988 25¢ Francis Ouimet, 12/31
1988 25¢ New Hampshire Statehood, 12/31
1988 25¢ Virginia Statehood, 12/31
1988 25¢ New York Statehood, 12/31
1988 25¢ Antarctic Explorers (4 designs), 12/31
1988 25¢ Summer Olympics, 12/31
1988 25¢ Carousel Animals (4 designs), 12/31

Special Stamps: 1988 25¢ Christmas Traditional, 12/31
1988 25¢ Christmas Contemporary, 12/31

Definitives: 1982 4¢ Stagecoach, Cottrell press, 2/28
1983 5¢ Motorcycle, 2/28
1984 30¢ Frank Laubach, L perforator (floating plate numbers), 2/28
1985 22¢ Flag Over Capitol, B and C press, 2/28
1985 12¢ Stanley Steamer, 2/28
1985 12¢ Stanley Steamer (precancel), 2/28
1985 14¢ Iceboat, Cottrell press, 2/28
1986 14¢ Iceboat, B press, 6/30
1985 8.3¢ Ambulance, 2/28
1985 8.3¢ Ambulance (precancel), 2/28
1985 6¢ Tricycle, 2/28
1985 12.5¢ Pushcart (coils of 500), 4/30
1985 12.5¢ Pushcart (precancel), 4/30
1985 21.1¢ Letters, 6/30
1985 21.1¢ Letters (precancel), 6/30
1985 11¢ Alden Partridge, 8/31
1986 5.5¢ Star Route Truck, 2/28
1986 5.5¢ Star Route Truck (precancel), 2/28
1986 25¢ Bread Wagon, 4/30
1986 $1 Bernard Revel, 8/31
1987 7.1¢ Tractor, 2/28
1987 7.1¢ Tractor (precancel), 2/28
1987 22¢ Flag With Fireworks, 2/28
1988 E (25¢) sheet stamp, 6/30
1988 E (25¢) coil stamp, 6/30
1988 E (25¢) booklet stamp, 6/30

Airmails: 1985 33¢ Alfred Verville, 4/30
1985 39¢ Lawrence & Elmer Sperry, 4/30

Express Mail: 1985 $10.75 Eagle booklet and single, 2/28

Penalty Mail: 1988 E (25¢), 6/30

Stamped Envelopes: 1985 22¢ Penalty Mail with window, 2/28

Aerogrammes: 1985 36¢ Travel, 2/28

Postal Cards: 1985 33¢ China Clipper, 2/28
1985 25¢ Flying Cloud, 2/28
1986 33¢ Ameripex '86, 2/28

Duck Stamps: 1986 $7.50 Fulvous Whistling Duck, 6/30

Souvenir Cards: 1987 Capex, 2/28
1988 Finlandia, 2/28
1989 Philexfrance

Exhibition Cards: 1988 36¢ Sydpex, 2/28

Maximum Cards: 1986 Stamp Collecting (set of 4), 2/28
1986 Franklin D. Roosevelt, 2/28
1986 Swedes and Finns, 2/28
1986 Philatelic Truck, 2/28
1986 APS Convention, 2/28
1988 U.S.-Australia, 8/31

1988 FIRST-DAY CANCELLATION TOTALS

The following are first-day cancellations for 1988 issues unreported in the 1988 *Yearbook*. All totals, except for postal cards, include 40,000 to 50,000 souvenir page cancellations.

Commemoratives
25¢ Antarctic Explorers (Block of Four) 720,537
25¢ Carousel Animals (Block of Four).....................856,380

Special Issues
25¢ Christmas Greetings...............................412,213
25¢ Christmas Madonna and Child......................247,491
25¢ Special Occasions Booklet 246,767

Definitives
5.3¢ Elevator (Precanceled)...............................142,705
20.5¢ Fire Engine (Precanceled) 123,043
21¢ Chester Carlson 288,073
24.1¢ Tandem Bicycle (Precanceled) 138,593
20¢ Cable Car 150,068
13¢ Patrol Wagon (Precanceled)..........................132,928
23¢ Mary Cassatt 322,537
65¢ General Henry ("Hap") Arnold......................129,829

Airmails
$8.75 Express Mail......................................66,558

Postal Cards
15¢ Hearst Castle Postal Card............................84,786
15¢ Federalist Papers Postal Card 37,661

ERRATA

In *Linn's U.S. Stamp Yearbook* for 1988, the picture that appears with the chapter headed "25¢ Official Mail Saving Bond Envelope" on page 318 is not of that item. It is a picture of a similar envelope, the 25¢ Official Mail envelope, which was issued on the same day, April 11, 1988, in Washington, D.C. (Another picture of the Official Mail Envelope appears in its correct place on page 316.)

A picture of the 25¢ Official Mail Savings Bond envelope can be found on page 329 of the 1988 *Yearbook*, illustrating a chapter on a second version of this envelope. The later version, issued November 28, 1988, differs from the earlier one by having a message printed on the back flap. The front is identical for both envelopes.

Some of the data given for the second version of the envelope on page 329 actually applies to the first version. This includes the number of first-day covers canceled, quantity of envelopes ordered and quantity distributed.

Under "Markings," the following information should be added: "On back flap, 'Buy and Hold U.S. Savings Bonds/The Great American Investment/Call 1-800-US-BONDS.'"